Eisenhower and the Art of Warfare

To the memory of J. H.

Eisenhower and the Art of Warfare

A Critical Appraisal

D. J. Haycock

McFarland & Company, Inc., Publishers
Jefferson, North Carolina, and London

LIBRARY OF CONGRESS CATALOGUING-IN-PUBLICATION DATA

Haycock, D. J., 1927–
   Eisenhower and the art of warfare : a critical appraisal /
D. J. Haycock.
   p.   cm.
   Includes bibliographical references and index.

   ISBN 0-7864-1894-X (softcover : 50# alkaline paper) ∞

   1. Eisenhower, Dwight D. (Dwight David), 1890–1969 — Military
leadership. 2. World War, 1939–1945 — United States. 3. World
War, 1939–1945 — Campaigns — Western Front. 4. World War,
1939–1945 — Campaigns — Africa, North. 5. Strategy. I. Title.
E836.H34   2004
940.54'0092 — dc22   2004013467

British Library cataloguing data are available

©2004 D. J. Haycock. All rights reserved

*No part of this book may be reproduced or transmitted in any form
or by any means, electronic or mechanical, including photocopying
or recording, or by any information storage and retrieval system,
without permission in writing from the publisher.*

Cover photograph: General Dwight D. Eisenhower (NATO)

Manufactured in the United States of America

McFarland & Company, Inc., Publishers
   Box 611, Jefferson, North Carolina 28640
   www.mcfarlandpub.com

Contents

Preface	1
Introduction	3
Chapter 1 — The Decision to Invade North Africa	15
Chapter 2 — Supreme Commander Eisenhower and the Landings in North Africa	16
Chapter 3 — The Battle of Kasserine Pass	29
Chapter 4 — Post-Kasserine and the Casablanca Conference	42
Chapter 5 — The Sicily Invasion	45
Chapter 6 — The Invasion of Italy	54
Chapter 7 — Operation Dragoon — The Landing in Southern France	60
Chapter 8 — The Invasion of Northern Europe	74
Chapter 9 — Caen and Operations Goodwood and Cobra	82
Chapter 10 — The Campaign Following Caen	92
Chapter 11 — The Problem of Appointing a Ground Commander	118
Chapter 12 — Antwerp	123
Chapter 13 — "Market-Garden"	128
Chapter 14 — West of the Rhine	132
Chapter 15 — The Germans Strike in the Ardennes	138

Chapter 16 — The Final Assault Against Germany		154
Chapter 17 — The End of the War in Europe		168
Chapter 18 — Eisenhower's Errors		180
Chapter 19 — Montgomery		191
Chapter 20 — U.S. Chief of Staff George C. Marshall		195
Chapter 21 — Eisenhower's Qualifications		198
Chapter 22 — Conclusion		213
Notes		215
Bibliography		221
Index		227

Preface

I have two friends with whom I meet frequently for lunch and conversation. At one of our lunches, when the subject of World War II was raised, it was stated that Dwight D. Eisenhower was a brilliant general. Unable to refute such a sweeping statement, I decided to do some reading on the subject and discovered that there were few authors who were objective, but many who praised most of Eisenhower's decisions.

It soon became apparent from reading that Eisenhower had a charming personality, but his experience and his qualifications for commanding armies in battle were much less in evidence. The more I read, the more convinced I became that too few authors had given an objective portrait of Eisenhower's wartime accomplishments, and too few had credited Montgomery for his achievements. Many seemed intent on denigrating Montgomery purely because he lacked the social assets of the Supreme Commander.

This book attempts to provide the balanced coverage that other works lack, and to answer, as objectively and completely as possible, the question with which my research began. Was Eisenhower a brilliant general? History provides the answer.

Eisenhower had no prior experience of warfare and no prior experience of commanding an army. Despite his assertion that he had read Clausewitz's *On War* more than once, his tactics and strategy showed no indication of this. He was selected by Marshall simply because he was one of the names in a book Marshall kept, listing officers he believed were deserving of promotion — a bizarre method of selecting one to fill such an important position as Supreme Commander, and later ground commander. Both Eisenhower and Gen. George C. Marshall appeared to make too many decisions which were based not on solid military grounds, but rather on nationalism.

Eisenhower had no easy task. The GIs in Africa had had no prior fighting experience and suffered from a lack of intensive training. These shortcomings were made patent in the battle of Kasserine Pass. It must be also emphasized that Eisenhower was given insufficient pragmatic support. Too frequently he was subjected to unjustifiable interference from Marshall, who, being 3,000 miles from the fighting, could not have had a complete understanding of the front-line situation.

One wonders why the U.S. government did not appreciate the logic of appointing to the post of ground commander a man who possessed the essential military experience and talent, even had such a person not been an American, and why Marshall did not appreciate the disadvantages of one person simultaneously holding two positions, those of Supreme Commander and ground commander.

I am indebted to the staff of the Los Angeles Public Library, Branch ER32, for their invaluable assistance during the four years of researching the subject.

Introduction

In a large army training camp in the north of England, the morning service in the garrison church proceeded normally. The soldiers who had been selected for church parade indulged in their usual spate of coughing as the senior padre entered the pulpit. The only indication this was no ordinary Sunday was the padre's announcement there would be a short sermon so the congregation could leave early to be home in time to hear Prime Minister Neville Chamberlain broadcast to the nation. The speech, from the Cabinet Room of 10 Downing Street, announced that Britain had given Adolf Hitler, the German dictator, an ultimatum that if by 11:00 A.M. of that day he did not assure His Majesty's Government that German troops had begun to withdraw from Poland, then a state of war would exist between the two countries. Chamberlain continued: "I have to tell you that no such assurance has been received" and consequently the two countries were at war with each other.

This declaration of war, on 3 September 1939, was made at the wrong time from the point of view of the country's military strength. Britain's armed forces were unready for a modern conflict, while Hitler had been preparing for many months and had used the Spanish Civil War as a training and testing ground for his armed forces and equipment. The speed with which the Germans advanced, the extremely low morale of the French population and the reluctance of the French government to prolong the fight surprised the Allies. The withdrawal from Dunkirk left only Britain and her Commonwealth and Empire free to prolong the struggle against the combined strengths of Germany and Italy, which had allied itself with Hitler.

Despite being forced out of the mainland of Europe, the British continued the land war in the Middle East; later it was here in North Africa that the first Anglo-American operation, under American command, was mounted. In the meantime, the British Imperial Forces, after defeating the weaker Italians, were faced by the German Afrika Corps under Irwin Rommel and withdrew to Egypt, taking up positions at El Alamein, just 70 miles west of Alexandria.

Winston Churchill was in Washington for a conference with President Franklin D. Roosevelt at the time Tobruk fell to the Germans. When this news was announced, Chief of Staff George C. Marshall generously ordered 300 Sherman tanks and 100 self-propelled guns, intended for the U.S. Army, to be sent to Egypt as soon as possible; he later had replaced those guns and tanks which were lost when a supply ship was sunk by German U-boats. This equipment was to prove of great value later in ensuring the defeat of Rommel.

The following month, Churchill, having become disenchanted with the lack of progress in the Middle East, appointed Lt. Gen. Bernard Law Montgomery to command the Eighth Army, with Gen. Harold Alexander as Commander in Chief in the Middle East. Montgomery was not widely known before taking up his new assignment. Furthermore, he was not Churchill's first choice for Eighth Army commander. The Prime Minister had preferred the South African Lt. Gen. W.H. Gott, but on a flight from Libya to Egypt to start leave before assuming his new assignment his unarmed plane was shot down by a Luftwaffe fighter and Gott was killed.

Montgomery asserted that he had not been in Egypt for more than a day before he became aware of the urgent need for a more positive attitude in the army, from the general staff to private. He instituted a rigorous system of training; he moved vital transportation from the rear to more needy areas at the front; and he made it clear to his officers that orders were not to be discussed, but obeyed without question.

On 31 August 1942, Rommel attacked the British position at Alam Halfa, and his objective was to take Alexandria. Montgomery had anticipated the move and had carefully prepared a static defense and the Germans were stopped, costing them 3,000 killed, prisoners and missing, as well as 50 of their precious tanks. Field Marshal Alfred Kesselring was of the opinion that the significance of this British victory was far greater than the immediate achievements; he was correct, for it was the first defeat suffered by Rommel, and it came at a time when his supplies, especially of fuel, were insufficient and when there was little hope of soon being resupplied. Rommel's attack began just 16 days after Montgomery officially took command of the Eighth Army; two months later, on 23 October 1942, Montgomery opened his own offensive in what was to become known as the Battle of El Alamein. This was the news the British had long been waiting for, and the B.B.C. interrupted a nighttime program of dance music to announce some of the greatest news of the war — the Eighth Army was on the move again.

Introduction

A warning to the advancing Eighth Army in Libya.

After 12 days of hard fighting, the advance to Tripoli began with the Axis forces losing 30,000 prisoners, including 9 generals. In 27 days, the British and Commonwealth army covered 1,200 miles. Considering the one tarmac road, of indifferent quality, was along the coast and consisted of two lanes only, the rate of advance was remarkable, and by January 1943 the Afrika Corps had retreated to the outskirts of Tripoli, having made a stand outside that city at Castel Benito, Azizia and Garian. Fortunately for the curious and the art lovers the mural known as *The Lady of Garian*, supposedly done by an American merchant seaman while a prisoner of war, was unscathed.

Bad weather delayed the capture of the important port of Tripoli by Montgomery. With the junction of the Afrika Corps and the German army in Tunisia, Rommel accomplished what Eisenhower's headquarters felt was impossible. This might have been prevented had the Americans reacted more speedily to cut off Rommel's escape via the Gabes to Sfax road.

Montgomery had kept Rommel on the move, making no attempt to destroy his army despite the fact the Afrika Corps' tanks had been reduced to a total of 11 and it could field only about 25 antitank guns. The Eighth Army's superiority in men was greater than 2:1, and of the Panzer Army Africa's 98,000 men a little more than half were German. The Germans fielded the Mark III and Mark IV tanks against the indifferent Grant and the more modern Sherman, which was the result of an American tank built partly to British specifications, one of which was a power-operated turret capable of traversing 360 degrees. It has been called a superb tank, but that opinion is one with which few Sherman tank crews were likely to agree, for once hit in the area of the fuel tank it had the distinct disadvantage of catching fire very easily and the unfortunate crew then had barely a minute to bail out with any hope of saving themselves. The tank also had a high profile which made it a very easy target to hit. However, it did have two assets: it was very reliable and it was faster than the German Mark III and Mark IV tanks by about 10 mph. There the advantages stopped. Until 1944, the Sherman mounted an inferior gun, the shell from which was incapable of penetrating the frontal armor of the German Mark IV tank. The Mark IV 's shell, from its 75 mm gun, could penetrate 92 mm of armor at 500 yards and 84 mm at 1,000 yards. On their later model tanks the Germans mounted the very effective 88 mm, firing a 21-pound shell.

Despite these handicaps, Montgomery was forever conscious of the need to be balanced (in contrast to Eisenhower), constantly trying never to give the Germans the opportunity to surprise him. He was adept at changing the axis of his attack, if necessary, and always ensured his troops were rotated out of the line to rest as often as possible. Rommel believed that El Alamein was not only the turning point for the campaign in North Africa but for the entire war, and an officer on his staff went further contending the Battle of Alam Halfa foreshadowed the defeat of Germany.

At the outbreak of war in Europe, the United States' army ranked 17th in the world; with a strength of 210,000 men not only was it below the maximum specified by the National Defense Act of 1930, but it also came behind both Portugal's and Spain's in size. The task of increasing its numbers and refitting it with modern weapons was enormous, and for this achievement Marshall must be given credit. He had to work with a Congress which was both parsimonious and shortsighted; it refused to allot funds for the revitalization of the army since it felt that the war in Europe was of no concern to the United States. Not until July 1941 did the American army reach more than 1 million in strength.

Marshall was made Chief of Staff in September 1939 and promoted to the rank of general. Despite his efforts to prepare the army for war, he was initially unsuccessful for he could not arouse the needed political support until the Japanese attacked Pearl Harbor in December 1941. Field Marshal Sir John Dill, later the British member of the Allied Combined Chiefs of Staff created in January 1942, reported from Washington that the United States had no idea of the effect war would have on it and its armed forces were ill-prepared for combat, added to which they knew little about the British.[1]

Despite this, the European conflict was taken seriously by the U.S. armed forces and almost a year before Pearl Harbor the Joint Army-Navy Committee considered its position in the event that war was declared. The committee issued a warning that the United States could possibly be drawn into placing the country's future in British hands and this resulted in the U.S. Navy stressing the need for a "Pacific First" policy.

The army had visions of being able to field 210 divisions, plus supporting planes and shipping, to fight the European war. By September 1941, the estimate of the number of troops which would be available for transporting to the United Kingdom, should the U.S. be drawn into a European conflict, was subject to frequent change and this unrealistic optimism was to continue for some time before eventually the realities of the situation were better appreciated. Despite a later assessment by the U.S. War Department that it would need 215 divisions to defeat Germany, Italy and Japan, the forming of new divisions was stopped when the total number in the U.S. army reached 90,[2] and the effect of this was adversely felt later by the American armies in Europe.

Since Churchill was anxious to meet Roosevelt so they could co-ordinate Allied efforts to defeat the Axis powers, preparations were made for a conference at the beginning of 1941. Secret talks were held in Washington between U.S. and British representatives at which it was agreed should the United States enter the war there would be set up a unified command of the two countries' armed forces in case joint operations were conducted. It was also agreed Europe would be given priority over the war in the Pacific; to this end, the first objective would be the elimination of Italy from the conflict. On 22 December 1941, Churchill went to Washington to confer with the American President. Among the understandings reached was that the United States would relieve the British in Iceland, which resulted in opposition from some American officers, including Eisenhower, who wrote in his desk diary that he had been insisting the Far East was critical and no other operations should be started in the West until air and ground forces were better prepared.

In the following year, on 25 March, Marshall had a meeting with Roosevelt and they resolved the United States would first concentrate on helping to finish the war in Europe before dealing decisively with Japan. The mustering of American servicemen in Britain was given the code name Bolero, and Marshall was therefore sent to England to discuss with the British ways in which the U.S. armed forces could become engaged in the European conflict.

At dinner with Field-Marshal Alan Brooke, the two considered the possibility of an invasion of Europe by the Allies. It was here that Marshall's limitations were exposed. He demonstrated that he believed that most, if not all, the problems could be solved by the application of sufficient manpower and industrial resources, two elements found in reasonable abundance in the United States, but neither of which during the war did it ever develop fully or sufficiently. What Marshall overlooked was the need for prudence and pragmatism. His previous experience in World War I had been as a staff officer and, like Eisenhower, he had no prior experience of commanding armies in battle. His strength lay in his ability to raise armies, rather than having any thought of how such forces should be employed. He was quite convinced it would be a simple matter to stage a landing on the north coast of France in the near future. He believed it possible, he told Churchill, that the Allies could establish a bridgehead on the Cotentin Peninsula of Normandy and hold it for a year, until U.S. reinforcements assembling in Britain were sufficient for the invaders to go over to the offensive. Marshall's plan was for a combined force of British and Americans to be landed in 1942, a total of six divisions, three of which would be British. This force, according to Marshall, could hold the beachhead until the Americans had accumulated in Britain five divisions, two of them armored and three infantry, to act as reinforcements. He believed that about this time the British would be able to field another seven divisions.

By propounding his plan, Marshall showed his failing which was to predominate his future thinking. He was impatient for action and adept at moving nonexistent armies across the Atlantic and Europe, all the while giving little or no consideration to the fact that these armies existed only in theory and there were many shortcomings, not least of which was the troops all too often lacked adequate training. His scheme also ignored another fact. The majority of the air support for such an operation would have to come from the R.A.F. which did not have the essential air superiority over the Luftwaffe, the Germans having an estimated 20% more front-line aircraft than the R.A.F. At the time, the U.S. Army Air Force in Britain could provide only 100 planes, totally inadequate for the needed support. The Luftwaffe had used its superiority in numbers to do heavy and widespread damage to Britain during 1940 and 1941. It needs little imagination to appreciate the damage it could have done to Cherbourg, easily making the harbor unusable and depriving the Allies of essential facilities for landing men and supplies.

Marshall had failed to do any investigation into the strength of the German forces in northern France; had he done so he would have realized that twenty-seven divisions, many with recent combat experience, would have been more than a match for a mere six Allied divisions even had they been battle hardened. He also failed to appreciate that there was a critical shortage of infantry landing craft, there being only enough to carry one division. Added to these drawbacks, Admiral Ernest King (U.S.N.) believed that his navy could not transport sufficient troops for the proposed operation. In view of King's preference for a "Pacific First" policy, it is possible he was deliberately pessimistic.

Marshall apparently assumed no special training for the ground forces was needed and the British would be able to provide administrative support for all troops involved in the landing and the later reinforcements. He had evidently made no investigation into the capabilities of Britain's industry and armed forces to supply these needs.

Marshall's next proposal was an operation code-named "Sledgehammer"; this was to be contingent upon either Russia or Germany collapsing. Marshall and special envoy Harry Hopkins went to London to put forward this plan to the British. Both Alan Brooke and the South African Prime Minister, Jan Smuts, two very astute generals, were certain any invasion of Europe at that time would fail, and Brooke informed the Americans that no more than nine divisions could be landed in France during 1942, and even if the attempt were made the Germans would destroy them. Marshall's plan had Eisenhower's support because he felt it was quite feasible to hold a bridgehead in Europe just as Tobruk and Malta had been held under siege by the British against the Germans, thereby demonstrating his grasp of strategy was faulty, for the capture and defense of Tobruk had been accomplished from the land by the Eighth Army, and Malta was already in British hands when the Germans began their aerial siege of the island. In neither case was the defense an easy matter and in neither case was an invasion by seaborne forces necessary, whereas an invasion of Europe obviously required an amphibious assault in order to establish a foothold on French soil. Eisenhower also suffered from Marshall's failing; he gave no consideration to the need for intensive training before committing forces to an invasion of France, nor did he appreciate the need for landing craft and air superiority. When Gen. Sir Hastings Ismay of the British Chiefs of Staff heard of this plan he was unimpressed by Marshall apparently always wanting to attack head-on, giving no thought to strategic requirements, a conclusion which was supported by later events.

Another proposal from the Americans was to invade the northwest coast of France sometime in 1943, and the majority of the invaders were to have been Americans. It was to be an invasion in earnest, but where the troops were to come from Marshall did not reveal. By the end of 1942, there were only 170,000 U.S. troops in the United Kingdom, which was reduced to one combat division in the first half of 1943, and the standard of training of these soldiers was known to be low; this shortcoming was not something which Marshall was ready to acknowledge, for in a meeting with Gen. L.K. Truscott early in 1942, he mentioned the U.S. troops were well trained and lacked only fighting experience. These figures of available forces must be compared with the 600,000 highly trained men, some with combat experience, which the Allies were to put ashore in France by D-Day +12. Marshall ought to have been quite aware of the poor state of the American army, since in early 1941 it consisted of little more than twenty divisions. Size, however, was not the sole factor to be considered; modern equipment and a high standard of readiness were other essentials, which were not immediately forthcoming. In late June 1942, Ismay, Brooke and Dill visited Fort Jackson in South Carolina to watch an exercise involving U.S. units of armor, infantry and paratroops. None of these generals was impressed by what he saw, concluding that there was much to be done to bring them up to a reasonable standard.

Marshall's arguments for an immediate European invasion did not sway Brooke who eventually told his American counterpart quite bluntly that if the Americans were going to mount a cross-Channel invasion then they would have to do so alone, because the British armed forces were not yet ready for a full-scale amphibious operation. Marshall seemed incapable of appreciating that the Americans were even less prepared. Their troops lacked proper training and there was an acute shortage of landing craft, which had been designed by the British and tested by them in 1940 during the Battle of Britain, adding strength to the contention that the British were not opposed to an amphibious assault on Europe. The design of these craft had been given to the U.S. since it had greater production capacity than had Britain. The Americans were quite unable to make a reasonable assessment of the type and number of landing craft needed. Originally this figure was estimated to be 7,000, later raised to 8,000 by the Operations Division, but Lt. Gen. J.T. McNarney, Deputy Chief of Staff, believed 20,000 was a more realistic figure. To add to the difficulties, the U.S. Navy relegated production of these vessels to tenth in order of priority.

Toward the end of April 1942, the U.S. Navy decided it would require about 4,000 of these craft and even this would supply only about half of Sledgehammer's needs. The problems of production were not eased when the British informed the Americans that the landing craft were unsuitable for use in the English Channel because of the stormy weather which could be expected in the autumn and winter. A new program of construction was introduced and overseen by the British. These vessels, too, underwent a design change and delivery in time for "Sledgehammer" looked doubtful.

The attitude of the U.S. Navy was, in some instances, a negative factor. The British sent several missions to the United States in order to improve co-operation between the two countries. Unfortunately there were occasions when the U.S. Navy appeared unable to fully appreciate the potential difficulties involved in a cross-Channel invasion of Europe. This limitation was not something which helped to create a good working relationship between the two allies.

Notwithstanding all the difficulties leading to the obvious conclusion that an invasion of Europe was impractical in the near future, Marshall, with a lack of logic which he displayed on more than one subsequent occasion, became convinced the British were not serious about returning to the Continent, regardless of all the evidence showing such a project was impossible at that moment, and he turned in favor of the major effort being concentrated in the Pacific. The justification for this switch was that the British refused to commit themselves to a firm date for the assault against Europe, while the Americans felt unless a date was set it would be infeasible for them to gear their industry to special war needs. This erroneous conclusion was to be upheld by many post-war American writers who also ignored the important fact that Britain, being a maritime nation, was much more aware of the difficulties facing it in an invasion of France than were the Americans and, far from being reluctant to return to Europe, their prime concern was where the main effort should be launched — northern Europe or the Adriatic — and also to ensure the assault was a success. A failure would have drastically reduced the chances of the Allies ever being able to return to Continental Europe. Before and after the invasion of Normandy the Americans showed a preference for the saber whilst the British choice was the rapier.

Despite Marshall's display of naïveté, his earlier assessment of what the Russian army should do, if that country were invaded by the Germans proved correct. He said if he were commanding the Russian army under those circumstances he would conduct a strategic withdrawal into the heart of the country, which is exactly what the Russians did. His recommendation contrasted with the later reluctance of other American generals who found a necessary withdrawal to be distasteful. Unfortunately for Anglo-American relations, Marshall seemed not to understand that a cross-Channel combined operation was not quite in the same category as a crossing of a still pond during a military exercise held in the United States.

Gen. Mark Clark contended that the only available unit which the U.S. could provide for a European invasion, should Russia collapse, was the 34th Infantry Division and that was on the assumption there would be no such invasion prior to 15 September 1942. Nevertheless, the division had undergone very little amphibious training, and there were neither anti-aircraft guns nor tanks to support it. The U.S. First Armored Division was also in Ireland, but it too was not fully equipped, and no U.S. troops scheduled to arrive in the United Kingdom before 15 September would be immediately ready to for action. Clark believed it would be 1943 before the Americans would be able to contribute anything of value and he observed that, by comparison with their British counterparts, the American GIs were overweight.[3]

Marshall's understanding of strategy did not impress Brooke in the least; it was evident that such plans as the U.S. Chief of Staff had put forward presumed the Germans would react moderately, if at all, to an attack on occupied Europe. There was absolutely no justification for such a conclusion. Marshall could not have given his ideas serious consideration, for the assumption the Germans would sit idle while the Allied troops landed in France was simply preposterous. Further, in reply to a question from Brooke, he showed how hazy his planning was when he admitted, regarding Sledgehammer, he had given no thought whatsoever to the direction of the advance once the breakout from the bridgehead had been accomplished. To add to the feebleness of his arguments for an early European invasion, in July 1942 Gen. John Hull, Deputy Chief of the Operations and Planning Division to Eisenhower, stated all the landing craft which were then available and in the process of being delivered could carry only 5,000 men and over 2,000 tanks below the estimated minimum needs.

In Sledgehammer, Marshall had the general support of Adm. Ernest King. Eisenhower, too, had caught invasion fever and in 1942 he made two revealing entries in his diary. The first was in the second week of June when he wrote that if the U.S. and Britain showed determination in mounting Bolero, then it would be "the biggest American job of the war." Ignoring the obvious display of chauvinism, one is tempted to believe Eisenhower was unable to distinguish between the meaning of "job" and "catastrophe." The second entry was made the following month, after he had been ordered by Marshall to prepare a plan for Sledgehammer, and he proposed a landing near Le Havre, which was to include two U.S. divisions (thereby dismissing Clark's assessment that only one division was available) and which he admitted had only a 20% chance of success. He supported this depressing conclusion by asserting it was essential to keep 8 million Russians in the war. According to this thinking it would have been acceptable for both the Russians and the Western Allies to have suffered crippling defeats, and the intervention of the British and Americans, even though futile, would not have been judged by history to be a gross blunder. Eisenhower's diary entries cannot be termed hastily made,

Introduction 13

for they were often recorded a little after the actual events, giving ample time for reflection. He showed how oblivious he was to the fact had Sledgehammer been launched in September 1942, as he proposed, it would have been no more damaging to the Germans than was the Lilliputians' attack on Gulliver.

Consistency was not one of Eisenhower's strong characteristics, for he had once stated that in the process of planning the invasion he did not want to be swayed by the mere desire to do something—yet his support of an operation which had no chance of success showed he possessed the very fault he abhorred. Eventually, Marshall admitted that the U.S. had little of substance to offer in the planning of a major operation in Europe, thereby tacitly conceding that the British were right in objecting to his proposed 1942 cross-Channel invasion. If Marshall was wrong in his assessment of Allied capabilities in 1942, he was correct in his preference for concentrating the Allied forces in one attack, a preference which, regrettably, he never succeeded in conveying to Eisenhower.

John D. Eisenhower has written that throughout the numerous discussions by the Allies on the subject of the invasion of northern Europe, the Americans frequently placed greater emphasis on the 6 June 1944 invasion of France than did the British. This is at best a distorted conclusion, one which ignores Churchill's assertion: "We shall not fail or flag." It ignores the cost of the air raids which resulted in the destruction of thousands of homes (civilian casualties by the war's end totaled more than 92,000, compared with the U.S. civilian casualties numbering less than one-tenth of that total). The British had suffered the indignity of withdrawal from Dunkirk, Greece and Crete, not to mention several reversals in the Western Desert; at the same time a study of British history shows that the British have never displayed any reluctance to fight on the European Continent. The civilians as well as the military were resolved to defeat Hitler ("Alone, if necessary," as the caption to Low's famous cartoon stated), but both Churchill and Alan Brooke were determined any landing on the Continent was not going to be a fiasco. Nothing would have been achieved by sending men across the channel in the knowledge that their only purpose was to fill graves, hospital beds and prisoner-of-war camps. Fortunately, the United States agreed to a more practical course of action.

Where was the weak place in George Pontifax's armour? I suppose in the fact that he had risen too rapidly.
(Samuel Barber, *The Way of All Flesh*)

1
The Decision to Invade North Africa

The Anglo-Canadian raid on Dieppe, in August 1942, had clearly revealed the problems involved in an amphibious assault on German-held Europe. It was, nevertheless, obvious that the northern coast of Europe offered the easiest area for a landing and the question was precisely where and when that landing should occur. British objections to such an operation were based upon Marshall's impractical ideas and not reluctance on the part of Churchill, or the British nation, to become involved in the fighting to liberate Europe, which is substantiated by the British having designed a landing craft, the flail tank and other specialized vehicles, in addition to the Mulberry harbor and the Pipe Line Under the Ocean ("PLUTO"). The differences of opinion between the U.S. and British chiefs of staff were eventually settled by an instruction from the President to Gen. Dwight D. Eisenhower, appointed Commander European Theater of Operations on 14 August 1942, to get U.S. forces into action, giving him the options of northern Europe, with or without British involvement, the Near East in order to help the Russians in the Caucasus or North Africa. Since the British were disinclined to commit suicide, northern Europe was out of the question, the Americans being unable to mount a successful invasion on their own; the Russians were far too xenophobic to allow Western troops on their soil, leaving North Africa the only alternative. November 1942 was agreed to as a tentative date for the invasion.

The possibility of using American troops in Egypt and Libya was vetoed by the Americans because it would have automatically meant a British commander in chief, the thought of which was seemingly objectionable to them, whereas if the invasion were mounted in northwest Africa the Americans felt they would be able to appoint their own candidate.

2

Supreme Commander Eisenhower and the Landings in North Africa

It was Marshall's plan to appoint a "supreme commander" in each theater of war; Churchill eventually agreed to the arrangement on 29 December 1942. Excellent though this was, the choice of Eisenhower to command the Allied forces in North Africa is questionable. It is difficult to understand how it can be supported on the basis of both his qualifications and his vacillation with regard to many of the problems involving the conduct of the war. One example of his indecision was shown on 17 January 1942 when he stated the situation in the Far East was far more serious than that in Europe. Therefore, he suggested, all operations scheduled for Europe should be canceled and the British should withdraw from Libya.[1] The British and Americans should then assemble forces to be sent to Burma and the Netherlands East Indies.

This recommendation ignored the obvious fact that the Germans' supply of oil depended on Romania, and a welcome supplementary source would have been the oil fields of Iraq and Iran; with these under their control they could easily have created a very serious threat to the oil fields of southern Russia. To have voluntarily withdrawn from Libya would have resulted in disaster. Clearly Eisenhower had given no thought to the consequences of his suggestion. Five days later he had changed his mind. Giving no reasons, and making no reference whatsoever to his previous entry regarding the relative importance of the Far East versus Europe, he made a diary entry stating the Allies must invade Europe in order to fight the Germans. This was not his final opinion, for on 30 January 1942 he was pessimistic about the Far East situation, believing the Americans would soon feel uneasy at having sent troops to Ulster; that conclusion lasted 20 days. The entry of 19 February noted the U.S. must send more troops to Britain to prepare for a European invasion. This ambivalence was one of the causes of later friction between himself and Montgomery. From the time of his appointment as army commander Eisenhower showed his lack of qualifications for the position. It is surprising that Churchill, after reading a summary of Eisenhower's career, approved his appointment; he did so because he said the British liked Eisenhower and he was impressed by Eisenhower's dedication to the Alliance.

The plan for the invasion of North Africa was given the code name Torch and it was to be the largest amphibious operation so far mounted. With the proposed Sledgehammer operation the Americans advocated it despite the fact that it would have been almost a certain failure, whereas with Torch they were suddenly beset by caution, Marshall being opposed to it on the grounds that the British estimate of the number of troops needed was too low, an opinion which contradicted Truscott, who served on the planning staffs of Sledgehammer and Husky; he contended the British were prone to overestimate their needs. It cannot escape attention that Sledgehammer was to have been a mainly British invasion, while Torch, so far as the ground forces were concerned, initially was principally American.

The Americans ignored many things when planning Sledgehammer, but became almost obsessed with the prospect of strong French opposition to the Torch landings. They feared the possibility of Spanish opposition, apprehensive that Spain would feel its North African colonies were threatened and would then give the Germans free passage through Spain, thereby threatening Gibraltar.[2] As the British pointed out, had the Germans wanted to take over Spain they had plenty of opportunity to do so long before Torch was mounted, and by doing so they would have stretched their lines of communication to a dangerous extent. In addition, Spanish Morocco would obviously have been threatened with an Allied attack; the Americans, spurning logic, would take no chances.

Both Roosevelt and Churchill were eager for an early start to the invasion, and therefore Eisenhower moved D-Day forward to 7 October, but there were many who felt the revised plan was not feasible. Ernest King believed 24 October would be more workable and the British Chiefs of Staff thought the revised date gave insufficient time for adequate preparation. The biggest problem facing the planning staff was the scarcity of shipping; LST (tank landing ships) never were available for this operation; this shortage caused Eisenhower to suggest on 21 August that the area of the landing should be restricted to the Mediterranean, but there was little support for his proposal. Instead, the Washington planners wanted to limit the landings to the Atlantic coast of French Morocco, consolidate the position, wait about 90 days, and then invade Algeria and Tunisia. What the Germans were supposed to do during the intervening period the planning staff did not reveal.

Fortunately, the British opposed this pause and stressed the need to reach Tunis as soon as possible. They wanted landings at Casablanca, but believed the other landings should be well within the Mediterranean Sea, preferably close to the Tunisian border. These, and other major positions, were to be captured, ideally within two weeks, but no later than four weeks from the time the invasion fleet passed Gibraltar. Eisenhower agreed to this plan. Later, when Marshall and the Washington planners raised strong objections to the main beachhead being in the Mediterranean, Eisenhower characteristically switched sides, implying the first plan had been totally British in concept and he had not approved it. The British also preferred the early October D-Day, despite the fact this would have given little time for combat-loading the transports and even less time, if any at all, for a preparatory exercise. The British favored speed at the sacrifice of efficiency in order that the Allies were first into Tunisia. Eventually the Americans obtained more time to hold amphibious exercises, a delay which did not take into consideration the forthcoming North African winter.

The British prevailed to a limited extent, and Eisenhower's staff began to draw up plans which first canceled the Casablanca landings and advanced the date for the other landings. The U.S. forces were to land at Oran, about 250 miles east of Gibraltar, and the British were to land at Algiers and Bône. Upon reviewing these plans Eisenhower felt the right flank would be exposed and Marshall agreed, adding the restriction that a landing should be made at Casablanca and no landing should be made in the Mediterranean further east than Oran. This was in agreement with the U.S. Navy, which believed that any landing in the Mediterranean would reduce its strength in the Far East. Yet a third group, the U.S. Joint Chiefs of Staff, presented their version of the proposed operation, which was extremely limited in scope and would very likely have accomplished absolutely nothing.

The British objected to Marshall's undue caution and, when he heard the plan, Churchill relayed his concern in a long cable to Roosevelt dated 27 August, stating that the advocated changes would endanger the whole operation. Roosevelt replied that the initial American landings must be made on the Atlantic coast, leaving it to the British to make their own arrangements for landing further eastwards. He also stated that the enemy would not be able to reach Tunis for at least two weeks from the date of the Allied landing. Gen. George S. Patton joined the optimists, for he believed no enemy tanks would be encountered until 30 days after the landings; he therefore advocated only light tanks should initially be put ashore. Too often, during the campaigns in the Western Hemisphere, the Americans were guilty of underestimating the enemy's capabilities. German units were airlifted into Tunisia beginning the day after the invasion commenced; by the end of the month some 15,000 of their troops had arrived, together with 100 tanks. These forces were later reinforced by the 9,000 Italians who had escaped from Tripoli before the Eighth Army captured the city, and were used to cover the southern front. The Allies were fortunate, for had Hitler paid heed to one of Italian dictator Benito Mussolini's rare accurate assessments Tunisia would have been occupied by the Axis in October 1942, because Il Duce felt there was a strong possibility that the Allies would invade Tunisia and Algeria.

Since Churchill did not share the American optimism, he again cabled Roosevelt accentuating the necessity to capture Algiers at the same time as Oran and Casablanca, contending the failure to do so would jeopardize the entire Allied operation. Unfortunately, he omitted to mention the need for a landing near Bizerta. On 3 September Roosevelt cabled his agreement to the proposal that British forces should land one hour after the Americans, instead of a delay of a week as had originally been planned. Churchill agreed, but wanted the troops designated for Casablanca diverted to Algiers, but the President would only compromise by agreeing to switch one regimental combat team from Casablanca and another from Oran.

Because the planners were given insufficient time, the navy personnel were inadequately trained in the handling of specialized craft to be employed in the landings. Eisenhower observed amphibious maneuvers conducted by U.S. forces in West Scotland and concluded that there was a lack of enterprise among some officers who often were at a loss to know what to do once their men were ashore. He took no steps to correct this fault. Before the invasion, he stated he would do all in his power to make it a truly allied force. He grandly announced that previous alliances had inadequately defined a common enemy, and a united command had been an empty hope which failed to conceal nationalism and other flaws of some officers who reluctantly served under a commander of a different nationality, or one of a different service. Such high ideals, so soon to die on the battlefields of Tunisia and Normandy, were matched by those of Edward Stettinius, the U.S. Lend-Lease administrator, who believed "Torch" would prove to be an excellent example of Allied co-operation. In an address to the American Academy of Political Science, Marshall, too, joined in this wave of optimism; despite the many differences he had with the British, three days after the landings, he drew attention to the fact that the operation was Anglo-American, and he commended the British Cabinet for approving the appointment of an American commander when the ratio of British to Americans in the Eastern Task Force was 2:1. Later, when the Eighth Army arrived in Tunisia and reinforcements reached Lt. Gen. Kenneth A.N. Anderson's army, the British forces in North Africa would greatly outnumber the Americans. This must be compared to the reaction of the British serving under a foreign commander, and Eisenhower's later assessment of the American public's reaction to the possibility of Montgomery commanding an Allied force to stage a single-front offensive in northern Europe.

During the planning of the invasion, Eisenhower gave a long dissertation on the requirements for creating an adequate staff, capable of conducting the campaign in a satisfactory manner. One point he made was that a person's attributes are of extreme importance in modern warfare. He continued by giving two examples of unfavorable personal characteristics: (1) a blatant eagerness for public praise, offensive behavior, and (2) the mistaken belief that resolution had to be accompanied by conceit or insufferable behavior. Regardless of what prompted this observation, these were the very elements displayed by Patton, yet Eisenhower appeared to have little difficulty enduring them.

Believing they had a political advantage, the Americans initially felt they alone should make the landings, convinced these would not be opposed. Hearing of this, Clark expressed his objections because he could not believe the French would be in the least impressed by what, of necessity, would have been a limited operation. He admitted there was a risk involved in the use of British forces, but he felt it was worth taking if North Africa were to be used as a base for the invasion of Europe. Washington eventually agreed to the use of British ground forces, but felt it would be expedient for them to wear American uniforms. A strange suggestion, for most of the shipping, naval and air support was to be British, all of which would be clearly visible to the defending French long before any troops wearing American uniforms were put ashore. In the event, the British wore their own battledress and the French, as might be expected, opposed the Americans just as strongly as they did the British.

The landings, which took place on 8 November 1942, were in three major areas, involving a total of 51,500 men, of whom more than 42,000 were American formed into four divisions; these landings were met with strong resistance in some locations, but within 76 hours the Allies had gained control of about 1,300 miles of coastline, from Safi to Algiers. The success reflects the low standard of French opposition rather than any display of skill by the Allies, for in keeping with Eisenhower's military phi-

Chapter 2—Supreme Commander Eisenhower 21

losophy, the Allied troops were scattered and the density of the invading forces varied from a mere 175 men per mile to 600 men per mile of front, and the Free French were poorly armed, some of their transportation consisting of commandeered civilian vehicles, much of it obsolete.

The political situation soon degenerated to near chaos, culminating in the murder, on Christmas Day 1942, of the French Admiral Jean François Darlan, appointed by the Allies to head a provisional government. The murderer was a French student, an ardent royalist, Bonnier de la Chapelle. Following a hurried trial, the assassin was executed by firing squad 36 hours after Darlan's murder. Thereupon Eisenhower assumed responsibility for handling the political situation in Algeria; he made Patton accountable for Spanish Morocco, with the specific object of showing force to the Spanish there, thus compelling him to employ about 120,000 troops who could have been more usefully used against the Germans.[3]

Neither Patton nor Eisenhower had any experience or training in dealing closely with politicians; a month after the landings, *The New York Times* was expressing doubts about the wisdom of Eisenhower holding two jobs, one military and the other political, but as was demonstrated later in northern Europe, Eisenhower could be selective in paying heed to the criticism of the press. He ignored the reproof and it is not surprising things did not go well. Patton essentially became governor of French Morocco, and was soon deeply involved in both politics and the social life.

Marshall expressed his concern for possible confusion which could have arisen from the political situation in North Africa, and on 22 December 1942 he cabled Eisenhower instructing him to delegate his political problems to others and concentrate on the fighting. Marshall did not enforce these instructions and Eisenhower did not comply with them, resulting in too much of his time being taken up with internal affairs rather than military matters; he proved just as mediocre at performing the one as he was at performing the other.

Once the assault was underway, the Americans had trouble with their supplies. Their equipment in Britain had been stored in warehouses, and it was discovered that materiel was often shipped from the U.S. when in fact the identical items were actually in stock in England. Marshall blamed the British, contending they did not have the American experience of operating large warehouses.[4] True, perhaps, but why the American forces did not keep their supplies under their own control is hard to understand, since in a directive to Eisenhower from the Combined Chiefs of Staff it was made clear the U.S. War and Navy Departments would be responsible for American supplies stored in England, which plainly negates any blame Marshall attached to the British. Despite this handicap, the Allied forces reached Tunisia in time to find the Germans had begun landing, with orders from Hitler to eject the Allies and return the country to Vichy control. By early December more than 20,000 first-class German troops and armor had arrived in Tunisia.

The command arrangement for Torch showed Eisenhower's lack of pragmatism. The initial landings were under the command of Maj. Gen. Charles W. Ryder, U.S. Army, and it was agreed that once the landings had been secured Anderson and Ryder would exchange positions. There seems to have been no sound reason for playing musical chairs, other than once again to assuage American national pride.

"Bladeforce," a British unit led by Col. Richard Hull, had landed in advance of the British First Army, with the object of taking Tunis and the nearby airport. This force covered 150 miles in three days over some very rugged terrain. Intelligence reports revealed the Germans were reinforcing their troops by both air and sea, and it was obvious Bladeforce alone was not strong enough to counter the newly arrived German forces in the area. Had Eisenhower been shrewd enough from the very beginning he would have realized that French opposition was likely to be weak, and it would thus have been worth the risk to have landed the British 78th Division at Bizerta. He refused to do so, and on 11 November 1942 it went ashore 100 miles east of Algiers, where it could subsequently give no help to Bladeforce whatsoever.

Anderson's forces were dispersed over a 50-mile front and were being committed piecemeal into action. It took a week to correct the confusion and prepare for a concentrated attack on Tunis, but his efforts were not helped by Eisenhower refusing to allow him to advance on to Bône until Ryder was thoroughly established at Algiers. It was not until 9 November 1942 that Anderson was able to set up his headquarters; only then did the British First Army become operational and Anderson take command of the Eastern Task Force. It was too late to achieve any notable results, for the rains prevented further action. Air support was difficult to provide because of the shortage of hard-surfaced landing fields.

The failure to take Tunis early in the campaign was not due entirely to military shortcomings. The Americans showed political ineptness, being slow to recognize Gen. Charles de Gaulle's government in exile, preferring to deal with the German-supported Vichy government. At the same time, they were unwilling to take the French North African politicians completely into their confidence, with the result they were trusted by neither Vichy nor de Gaulle. Such political simplicity did nothing to assist in the speedy conquest of North Africa. Darlan did little to help the Allies, and Eisenhower did the Allied cause no good by becoming personally

Chapter 2—Supreme Commander Eisenhower

involved in the political situation, to the detriment of the military operations he was supposed to be controlling; his political naïveté can be judged by the fact that after Darlan's death he installed Marcel Peyrouton as governor-general of Algeria. Peyrouton had a major shortcoming as successor to the late admiral—he was an incompetent politician and he too had been a member of the Vichy government. This appointment had been presented to neither Roosevelt nor Churchill for approval, a gross breach of courtesy and protocol, thus placing Eisenhower at a disadvantage in relation to the German commander, Kesselring, who was not only a far more astute soldier, but had no political problems to distract him.

The Americans failed to heed the British, for had they agreed to land further to the east inside the Mediterranean the problem of supplies may not have been so critical. As it was, it took the British a little more than a month to take Bône, which was intended to be an initial target for their invading forces, and their administration problem can be appreciated by the fact that even in December it still took seven days for supplies from Algiers to reach the front line. The American landing at Fedala, French Morocco, suffered heavily. Many of the troops were drowned in the surf, which rose in places to a height of six feet, and on one beach 75% of the landing craft were lost due to the heavy swell. At Lyantey, further north, the sands were too soft to support any vehicles except those with tracks, and these landing sites were soon in a state of confusion which was not helped by the high surf. By the time darkness fell on the first day, almost no supplies had been put ashore and barely one-fifth of the transport and artillery had landed. The high surf is customary for the area, and totally unrelated to the weather; it was not to be the only time in the following 40 years that the Americans chose to ignore the forces of nature. To add further to their problems, Patton, spurning the advice of the British, who had gained earlier experience from their commando raids and other amphibious operations, did not employ a separate headquarters ship from which to control his landing forces, and he soon regretted his error when the warship he was aboard, U.S.S. *Augusta*, was withdrawn to support another sector, putting him out of action for over five hours.

The U.S. consul in Tunis was vigorously urging the Allies to make quicker progress, paying little heed to the fact that there was only one rail line to the front, which started in Algiers. On this line only nine small trains a day could run, two of which had to haul coal to supply fuel for the other seven; one had to be used to haul food for the civilian population, leaving six for the transportation of troops and supplies. The rail line from Constantine to Tebessa, the major supply dump for the U.S. II Corps, could carry only one-third of the American daily needs and road trans-

North Africa (sketch map by author).

portation had to be used to make up the difference.[5] By the end of January 1943, about 75 trucks a day were needed for the supply task and the breakdown of even one of these vehicles was a serious matter. A shipment of 5,000 trucks arrived too late to relieve the situation. There was also a chronic shortage of spare parts, due mainly to the lack of base repair facilities. Eisenhower was slow to ensure that the supply service was reorganized and not until March was there a reasonably efficient system in use; this failure to secure his administrative services was a fault which surfaced again in northern Europe. In Algeria and Tunis, he had plenty of resources to tap for information concerning the conditions of roads and the rail system. There were many Frenchmen who had lived in these countries who were serving with the Allied armies, and the American consuls in French North Africa should also have been able to provide useful information prior to the invasion. This showed how slow the Americans were to use the knowledge and experience of their allies, even though the omission resulted in decreased efficiency and fighting ability.

Eisenhower believed if Anderson had been prepared to take risks in an attempt to take Tunis he would have succeeded; nevertheless, he made no attempt to order Anderson to move more rapidly, and he made no attempt to resupply and reinforce Bladeforce. His opinion ignored the fact he was the one who had insisted upon landing so far to the west, making it obvious that Tunis could not be taken in the first rush. He criticized Anderson for not taking a risk, yet he refused to land further into the Mediterranean because he thought it perilous—an excellent example of the pot and the kettle.

The original plan had been to give Anderson command of the Free French forces, in addition to the British First Army and U.S. II Corps, which was to be used as a mobile reserve. Although he criticized Anderson but gave no additional support, Eisenhower was very complimentary in describing the achievements of the First Army, initially an army in name only, consisting of three infantry brigades and a brigade of obsolete armor. It is likely the Supreme Commander was comparing them with the poorly trained Americans, for throughout the war the best men were drafted by the navy, air force, technical corps and parachute regiments. In addition, the U.S. army lacked combat experience and it seemed to take their generals a long time to appreciate the value of well-trained, battle-hardened troops. To add to their problems, they had an inefficient radio system. Their communications to the U.S. or Britain had to be routed through Gibraltar, using British facilities which were subject to availability. That defect was eventually corrected, after a great deal of inconvenience had been experienced.

The planners, specifically Marshall, had delayed Torch and in doing so had not taken into consideration the winter weather and the consequent need to make provisions for the capture of hard-surfaced landing grounds. The result was that during the rainy season Allied air coverage was virtually nonexistent, for the ground was turned into a treacly composition over which no wheeled traffic could move with ease. To make matters worse, when aircraft were able to give support to the army there was a risk they would be incorrectly identified by the ground forces, for the antiaircraft crews, American in particular, were poor at differentiating between Allied and German planes. On one occasion a plane carrying Patton came under friendly fire. Patton's comments are not recorded.

The hope of capturing Tunis was not abandoned and another attempt was made by the V Corps of First Army, when on the night of 22/23 December 1942 the Second Battalion Coldstream Guards attacked Jebel el Ahmera, known to the British as Long Stop Hill, which cricket term was completely misunderstood by the Americans. The hill, which is about six miles northeast of Medjez el Bab (literally and aptly "the Medjez door") was of strategic importance for it overlooked the Medjerda Valley, which was the only route available to armor. It was partially occupied, with fairly heavy casualties, and there followed three days of torrential rain. The Guards then handed over their position to Regimental Combat Team 17 U.S. First Division, which was subsequently forced to withdraw after a strong counterattack by the Germans; by sticking to the lower reaches and making no attempt to gain control of a commanding hill, the Americans had shown a lamentable understanding of tactics. The following day, having marched 30 miles with only a brief stop, the Guards returned and again recaptured the hill, but the Americans were unprepared for their new responsibilities for upon relieving the Guards they were reluctant to make preparations to defend their position against a probable German counterattack. That attack came and after three days of hard fighting, with the Guards suffering many casualties, the Allied forces had to withdraw. Two officers of the First Division were subsequently relieved of their command.

The failure to hold Long Stop Hill prevented an attempt to take Tunis, though the chances of that assault succeeding must have been few, for the Allies were suffering from a shortage of supplies and the Germans were not unaware of the importance of their main port of entry. This incident revealed a radical difference in the standard of training between the British and American troops in North Africa; it could have done nothing to inspire confidence in the Americans by the British.

Soon two German armies were opposing the Allies: the army in the north commanded by Gen. Jurgen von Arnim, who was nominally in charge of all Axis forces in North Africa; and the Afrika Corps, consisting of a total of 78,000 men of whom 30,000 were German and the remainder Italian. Inside the Tunisian border, facing Libya, was the Mareth Line, which had been constructed by the French in the 1920s as a defense against a possible Italian invasion. Dismissed by Gen. Omar N. Bradley as something "known too grandly as the Mareth Line"[6] and described by John D. Eisenhower as "antiquated,"[7] it was in fact a strong defensive position, despite its age, sited on a natural barrier. It reached from the coast 22 miles inland, was four miles deep and had its right flank in the Matmata Hills, which was an area the French believed impassable. The terrain on this flank was hilly and although there were a few tracks through the narrow passages they were thought to be impassable to wheeled traffic. On the east end of the line was a wadi (dried-up river bed), the Wadi Zigzaou. To create a tank obstacle it had been increased to about 60 feet in width and its depth varied from 8 to 20 feet, and the banks had been dug into steep slopes. The whole length was covered by a complicated system of concrete and steel pillboxes and gun emplacements. Further work had been done first by the French, under the direction of Gen. Maxime Weygand following the Franco-German armistice of 1940, and second by the Italians under the supervision of the Germans, before the arrival of the Afrika Corps. Antitank ditches had been added as well as barbed wire entanglements and minefields, in which there were an estimated 100,000 mines.

All this was protected by a series of well-placed outposts and a variety of other emplacements. An additional position covered the bottleneck between the sea and Shott el Faraj, approximately northwest of Gabes. On the far side of Dahar was the Tebequ Gap, through which could be reached the plain of El Hamma and the Mediterranean Sea at Gabes. This gap was defended by wire and mines,[8] although these were not as densely laid as in the main line.

Such, then, was the defensive position belittled by John D. Eisen-

Chapter 2—Supreme Commander Eisenhower

hower and dismissed by Bradley in such an offhand manner. One is left to wonder if Bradley's opinion would have been any different had he commanded the army given the task of breaching it, and if John D. Eisenhower's appraisal would have been more objective had his father been in Montgomery's position.

In December 1942, a unit of the Long Range Desert Group, under Vladimir Peniakoff, was sent to confirm information gained from a French army captain, Paul Mezan, former garrison engineer at Mareth; he contended that the right flank of the line could be penetrated and turned. Peniakoff found this route, which was used later in Montgomery's assault to outflank the line.

Eisenhower eventually moved his HQ from Gibraltar to Algiers. Soon after arrival he discovered deficiencies in the Allied armies to the extent that, on 7 December, he wrote to Brig. Gen. Tom Handy in Washington, stating the Allied operations to date had violated "every recognized principle of war."[9] A strange admission for any commander-in-chief to make, and it raises the questions, "Why did he allow it to happen?" and "What did he do to prevent a repetition?" To the first question the answer will never be known, and to the second the reply is "Nothing."

Two days before Christmas 1942, Eisenhower visited the front and encountered more problems. The French would not accept orders from the British, and Gen. Lloyd Fredendall, commander of the U.S. II Corps, was an Anglophobe who was reluctant to co-operate with Anderson and frequently at loggerheads with Maj. Gen. Orlando Ward, commanding the U.S. 1st Armored Division. Eisenhower also learned that the French general Henri Giraud had modified his conditions for going to North Africa, but refused to be subordinated to a British commander; such a position was beneath a man of his rank and prestige. In an attempt to assuage his feelings, Eisenhower set up his own forward HQ, appointing Truscott as his representative, so Giraud would report to the American officer instead of to Anderson, the putative ground commander. Eisenhower, from his experience as a staff officer, ought to have known better than to create such a chain of command, for instead of simplifying the system it only created confusion; his own headquarters were situated 400 miles from the front line while Truscott was only a little nearer, being 200 miles away at Constantine.

In II Corps' sector Eisenhower was surprised to discover that Fredendall's command post in Tebessa, Algeria, had been dug and blasted out of rock over a period of three weeks—the work of some 200 U.S. Army engineers. The Allied commander commented it was the only time during the war, to his knowledge, that any officer commanding at least one division had been so concerned for his own safety. Eisenhower discussed the general situation with the G-2 (Intelligence Officer) who informed him he expected an attack through the Kasserine Pass. However, no mines had been laid and no defensive positions created.

This was another example of the inadequate training given to the Americans at the time. It was estimated that upon capturing an objective they would take two to three days before setting up their defenses, whereas the Germans took just two hours to prepare for an anticipated counterattack. Eisenhower stated he gave orders to take immediate defensive measures, including the laying of mines in the pass. If this work was ever started it was woefully incomplete when the enemy attacked.

It is astonishing that Eisenhower never questioned Fredendall's intentions, for he had prepared for static operations despite commanding Orlando Ward's 1st Armored Division of 15,000 men, a variety of tanks and other vehicles. With this mobile force Fredendall had no reason not to mount more active operations.

3

The Battle of Kasserine Pass

The Germans began their assault by taking Faid, Sbeitla and the village of Kasserine. They made the mistake of dividing their forces in an effort to capture Tebessa and to continue on by taking Thala, Le Kef and Souk el Arba, in order to cut off the British First Army. The Jebel in this area resembles an inverted "Y," and on Christmas Day 1942 von Arnim attacked the Eastern Dorsal and took two passes. There was good reason for this German nibbling at the French line — the French lacked both equipment and training, and by taking such action von Arnim was forcing the British and Americans to reinforce a threatened area. The Allied commanders suspected a major attack was pending, but they could not agree where the main assault would be made.

The II Corps commander, ignoring Anderson's instructions and Ward's objections, prepared a static defense based on Jebel Ksaira and Jebel Lessouda, which were situated one on either side of the road to Sbeitla. Fredendall continued his defensive preparations by placing Combat Command A — too small to be of any use — in reserve at Sidi bou Zid. He then issued very detailed orders to Ward regarding the defense of the road to Sbeitla, but made only one short visit to Sbeitla and was in no reasonable position to issue such specific instructions. These two hills were too far apart to be mutually supporting; the result was Ward was hamstrung and found it extremely difficult to arrange an effective defense receiving no help from Fredendall, who refused to visit the front to see for himself how futile were his dispositions.

On 3 January von Arnim struck Fondouk. At the end of the month he turned against the French with a force of 30 tanks which was stopped at Faid by the defenders making astute use of their artillery. Simultaneously, a mixed force of enemy tanks and infantry moved through the

Rabaou Pass to the southeast of Faid and attacked the rear of the French positions; the defenders were outnumbered and surrounded.

After some delay, Fredendall sent reinforcements from Sbeitla to Faid, with the proviso that this transfer was not to weaken Sbeitla's defenses. Therefore, only light forces were sent and following a reconnaissance, which showed the Eastern Dorsal had fallen to the Germans, the reinforcements were heavily attacked from the air. The intended U.S. counterattack had to be postponed. A day later, at sunrise, von Arnim mounted an assault in the area of Pichon, northwest of Fondouk, causing Anderson to send British reinforcements there to assist the French. Although von Arnim was close to succeeding, he canceled his offensive principally because he discovered the Americans at Sbeitla had more tanks than he had anticipated. Anderson also ordered a halt to offensive operations and during the resulting respite the Allies reacted with self-criticism. Eisenhower was sufficiently stirred by the events to question Fredendall's abilities. Had the Commander-in-Chief done but a little soul-searching he might have concluded that part of the blame was attributable to himself, for he had created an incredibly cumbersome command organization.

Originally it had been intended that Orlando Ward would command all U.S. ground forces in Tunisia, but when Eisenhower discovered the British had decided to give their forces the designation of First Army, he felt something must be done to boost the status of the Americans in Tunisia. He therefore made the error of putting Fredendall in direct command of II Corps with Ward as his subordinate. It was nothing but a cosmetic change designed to pander to egos and was a thoroughly inefficient arrangement. Fredendall and Ward could not tolerate each other and Fredendall often bypassed Ward in issuing orders. Among Fredendall's failings was his refusal to delegate authority to Ward, who was the closer to the fighting, and his instructions were anything but precise. As though the American command was not complex enough, Eisenhower allowed a mixing of the three nationalities, giving no consideration to such things as their differences in organizations, equipment and supply arrangements.

The theoretical commander of this assortment was Anderson, but although Eisenhower was 400 miles from the front line he accorded Anderson the position of nothing higher than adviser, allowing him such limited authority he even had to obtain Eisenhower's permission to close down the Allied counterattack. Eisenhower did little to ensure the French XIX Corps was adequately armed, leaving it to the British to provide it with uniforms and light weapons. At the end of the North Africa hostilities, there were supply dumps and vehicle parks full of U.S. equipment which, even if originally intended for II Corps, could easily have been used

Chapter 3—The Battle of Kasserine Pass 31

to provide greater support for the French, who had fewer than 100 prewar vehicles.

In an effort to forestall the anticipated attack on Kasserine, the Americans mounted their own at Gafsa on 1 February. Despite the capture of Sened, which cut the rail line from Gafsa to Macknassy, the American position was weak; there were insufficient men at Sened and the lines of communication were vulnerable to attacks from the Luftwaffe, since the nearest U.S. air base was Tebessa. As a result of this success the Germans developed their assault against the French at Faid. After the fall of Faid, the Americans at Sbeitla, attacking a numerically inferior force of German tanks, showed yet again how slow they were to learn not just from the British but also from their own experience. The Shermans charged in the best cavalry tradition and before the tank commanders realized they had been trapped, it was too late; the German 88 mm antitank guns had eliminated more than 70 of their tanks. The Americans pulled back to the Kasserine Pass and destroyed their stores at Sbeitla, overlooking large stocks of fuel and several Sherman tanks which were only slightly damaged. Kesselring called Rommel and von Arnim to a meeting on 9 February to discuss his proposal for an attack against the Americans. To von Arnim it was evident the Americans were not well led and lacked battle experience. Kesselring, acceding to this assessment, proposed an attack designed to eliminate the U.S. II Corps and which entailed Rommel capturing Gafsa from the Americans while simultaneously von Arnim was to launch his offensive in the north against Sbeitla. The hope was that von Arnim and Rommel would advance beyond the passes and be able to reach flatter terrain in Algeria; then, with the addition of Italian armor, they would be able to join forces to attack Bône, thus isolating Anderson's First Army. Because of the shortage of fuel, von Arnim obtained approval to delay his offensive.

Eisenhower toured the U.S. front on Saturday 13 February. Anderson warned the weather was favorable for an enemy attack and was sure it would begin the next morning; also there could very possibly be a diversionary attack made somewhere along the line, though exactly where he was not sure. He stated Fredendall's G-2 felt certain the assault would come from the Faid area. Eisenhower heard of how Anderson had arranged his forces and agreed with the disposition, but he also agreed with Truscott, who, unlike Anderson, wanted to hold the forward areas—just one example of Eisenhower's inability to arrive at an unequivocal decision.

That afternoon, the Germans began to shell Jebel Lessouda and after nightfall Eisenhower and Truscott went to visit Orlando Ward. Gen. Paul Robinett, commanding Combat Command B, informed Eisenhower the two Jebels were too far apart to support each other, despite Fredendall's contrary opinion. Eisenhower appeared to agree, but he did nothing to correct the situation. In preparation for an offensive, Rommel transferred 26 tanks to assist the Italians holding the Gafsa road in the south. Von Arnim's main attack opened on Sunday, 14 February 1943, at 6:00 A.M. with the 10th and 21st Divisions, which included Tiger tanks. The Americans were surprised, and before the end of the day the enemy had routed Combat Command A and had taken their first objectives, Sidi bou Zid and Bir el Afey. One U.S. tank battalion had been wiped out, some 44 tanks, 60 halftracks and more than 25 guns had been abandoned, and the remaining defenders had withdrawn toward Sbeitla, leaving Jebels Lessouda and Ksaira surrounded.

The Americans casualties were heavy and Fredendall appealed to Anderson for help, but the British commander felt this attack was simply a feint and sent only a battalion of Shermans to assist the U.S. First Armored Division. Anderson was wrong in believing the attack on Sidi bou Zid was a diversion simply because the 10th Panzer Division had not been reported in action there, and he believed it was going to be used for the main attack in the north. His conclusion had an adverse effect on the defense of the Kasserine Pass. To add to their problems the Americans had little air support, due partly to a lack of forward air bases. The next day, the U.S. First Armored counterattacked south of Sbeitla, but it advanced with no prior reconnaissance and was caught in a carefully prepared ambush by the 10th and 21st Divisions and heavily defeated. Lt. Gen. Heinrich Zeigler had been instructed by Rommel to press his advantage by continuing the advance, but Zeigler felt it was essential to obtain confirmation from von Arnim. This action delayed the advance to Sbeitla, which did not begin until the next day. When Zeigler's forces attacked they encountered strong resistance, but by late afternoon the place fell with a loss to the defenders of 3,000 prisoners and 100 tanks.

Rommel had begun his own attack against Gafsa on 15 February, only to find the Allies had abandoned it. Taking advantage of the situation and believing his rear to be secure, he advanced as rapidly as possible, giving instructions that his commanders were to avoid any engagements likely to delay their progress. After Gafsa, the Afrika Corps pushed on to Thelepte and found the Americans had set fire to 30 of their aircraft before withdrawing, but had left 20 tons of aviation fuel and a large quantity of ammunition. By the second day following the fall of Gafsa, Rommel's forces had advanced 35 miles against little resistance from the retreating Americans. At the very moment when its services would have been invaluable, von Arnim refused to allow 21st Panzer Division to remain with Rommel. He

Chapter 3—The Battle of Kasserine Pass 33

reasoned it was to have been used in the capture of Gafsa, which had already been taken, and felt the division could be used more profitably elsewhere.

Confusion in the Allied forces resulted from Rommel trying to exploit his advantage; he planned to make a deep thrust into the Allied defenses in an attempt to sever their main line of communications by taking Tebessa and continuing to Bône. Rommel argued such an attack would be so far behind the Allied line that it would impede the use of their reserves. Von Arnim was not so bold and disagreed with the proposal. Rommel therefore obtained approval from Commando Supremo in Rome and was placed in command of the operation. There was a slight difference, however, in Rome's plan compared with Rommel's. The former wanted to strike northward to Thala and Le Kef instead of northwest to Tebessa and beyond. Rommel was unhappy with this limitation and contended it would result in the very thing he wished to avoid, which was the commitment of the Allied reserves. The difference between the two German generals broadened after the fall of Sbeitla. Von Arnim was disinclined to take more risks and halted his northern offensive, except for minor operations conducted by the 21st Panzer Division. Rommel, however, feeling the time was ripe for action, on 19 February attacked the Americans at Sbiba and the Kasserine Pass. Initially, the Americans held their own, but the enemy changed tactics by infiltrating the U.S. position and making good use of the commanding heights. Before nightfall, about 100 Americans had been taken prisoner and with the increased German pressure the ill-trained GIs showed signs of nervousness. One company turned and fled the battlefield.

Earlier the 21st Panzer Division had moved from Sbetla towards Sbiba, but it encountered a minefield and this, combined with heavy artillery fire, caused it to halt. A later attack was unsuccessful and the division withdrew to a position seven miles away, south of Sbiba. Rommel now changed his line of attack to concentrate on Kasserine; by so doing he gave Eisenhower a lesson which was too soon forgotten.

Anderson moved armored units to protect Thala from any enemy attempt to cut the Thala-Tebessa road. Due to the loss of Sbeitla and Kasserine, Sbiba was threatened and its capture by the Germans would have given them control of the road to Le Kef. Anderson took the precaution of moving the balance of 29th Armoured Brigade and the Brigade of Guards to Sbiba. Here, the Guards took command of the high ground and were supported by tanks of the 16th/5th Lancers. Three U.S. regimental combat teams were also in position to give added strength to the sector. At Tebessa, Gen. Ernest N. Harmon, sent by Eisenhower to bolster a failing Fredendall, made it clear to Ward that there would be no retreat by the American defenders; a stand had to be made and the German advance halted. Harmon continued on to Thala to meet Brigadier Cameron Nicholson, second-in-command of the British 6th Armoured Division. While this meeting was in progress, Brig. Gen. S.L. Irwin arrived with an assortment of guns after covering 800 miles in four days, an admirable achievement given the condition of the roads. No sooner had he arrived than he learned Anderson had ordered him north to Le Kef; following his strong objections to such a move, Harmon gave him instructions to stay and support the defense of Thala. The addition of his guns was welcome. The battle opened with a flank attack by British tanks supported by American artillerymen, who proved to be good students after being given a quick lesson in how the British gunnery system operated. The Germans withdrew through Kasserine to Sbeitla, having misjudged the Allied ability to counterattack and fearing an assault on their left flank.

Anderson now met Eisenhower at Tulergma airfield and pointed out that by the Americans having to move from the south to the north, the line was very thinly held, jeopardizing the plan for a narrow front offensive in the north to capture Tunis. Nothing was done to correct the problem; eight days later concern was again expressed that the line was dangerously extended. This tactic of holding the line with insufficient numbers was to be repeated by Eisenhower, with even more serious results, almost two years later. The Americans defending the Kasserine Pass were untried, lacked adequate training, were poorly led and, as Eisenhower admitted, they were too few in numbers. To add to the problems of the defenders, Ultra signals had been misinterpreted by II Corps to indicate an attack would come from the direction of Faid and, to confuse the matter more, Anderson's G-2 believed the attack would come from Fondouk. That was why Anderson placed the U.S. 1st Armored Division near Fondouk, which action led to criticism from Eisenhower. The move, however, was based on incorrect information given to the First Army by Eisenhower's G-2 section. The result was that the defenders were taken by surprise and fled, and the demoralizing of the Americans was partly due to the first use by the enemy of their six-barreled rocket launchers.

Fredendall commanded the center of the line. Eisenhower had known this officer slightly before his appointment and found him to have a good record in training and organization. Such qualities, however, do not necessarily make a competent field commander, as was demonstrated not only with regard to Fredendall but also with regard to Eisenhower. Fredendall had been instructed by the Allied Commander to hold the line with a screen of reconnaissance forces operating in front of a mobile reserve. Instead, the infantry was scattered in penny packets on isolated hills along the length of the entire front, and the mobile reserves, too, were spread out in small groups. Despite the fact the front was now 80 miles away, Fredendall did not move his command post nearer to the action, and Eisenhower paid him a visit on several occasions in an attempt to straighten out the chaotic situation on the II Corps front. He tried to persuade Fredendall to go to the front to observe the situation for himself, but in the absence of definite orders Fredendall stayed in Tebessa and, when the attack came, refused to take personal control of the battle. Obviously he could have had little idea of what was happening as far away as Kasserine Pass, and yet he was trying to conduct the defense with maps spread out in front of him, using information from the front which was so old by the time it reached him that it was useless.

As a result of this lack of cohesion and leadership, the Americans had been thrown into a great deal of confusion; they were forced to retreat in such disorder that one American general called it a rout. The defenders had again failed to gain control of the high ground on either side of the Pass, and, as at Long Stop Hill, the Germans used the higher elevations to their advantage, hammering the Americans with artillery and mortar fire. The defenders left behind a large amount of equipment, including some undamaged tanks with engines still running. In one sector, the Germans took over this armor and, giving the impression they were Americans, infiltrated the American line.

The low standard of collaboration between the Allied armies was a great help to Rommel. His forces knocked out nearly half of the U.S. 1st Armored Division's tanks and guns, and the Pass remained in enemy hands for a few days until Gen. Harold Alexander, perhaps the best British strategist, took over direct command of the operation. One omission he discovered was the absence of any plan for the final defeat of the Germans in North Africa, a neglect Eisenhower repeated in northern Europe. Six days after the initial assault, the Germans mounted a second attack, and by late afternoon had committed all of their infantry, including a battalion of the elite Italian Bersaglieri. Enemy patrols broke through the American lines, some reaching Sbiba. Had that village remained in German hands for any length of time it would have created a very serious situation for the Allies, for it was through there that the main road passed between Le Kef to the north and Sfax on the coast; had the Allies been deprived of the use of this road it would have slowed down communications between their forces in the north and south. The following day, a column led by about 14 tanks attacked the position but, unknown to the enemy, the U.S. 34th Division had been reinforced by a detachment of Welsh Guards and the 26th Armoured Brigade; the enemy attacked in strength, but despite some initial success, which included the surrender of Sbiba by Anderson, the Germans were forced to abandon their efforts. On the third day they withdrew with little interference from the Allies, who proved slow to follow up their advantage.

The British had used a degree of cunning to defeat the Germans. The Panzer forces had been allowed to pass through the Guards' position, thus exposing themselves to short-range fire from 6-pounder anti-tank guns. Behind these were the 25-pounder field guns which soon destroyed many of the enemy's self-propelled guns. The retreating Germans left behind eight tanks and a few wrecked guns, but the Lothians of the 26th Armoured, too, had suffered quite heavily and to counter any further German success a defense of Le Kef was hastily arranged. By the end of the month, all ground lost in the offensive had been regained by the Allies, but the cost to the Americans had not been light, for although Rommel had failed to capture Bône, his ultimate objective, which would have severed the Allied lines of communication between Tunisia and Algiers, he had inflicted on the Americans heavy losses of over 6,000 killed, missing and prisoner, and the loss of equipment was extremely heavy. So badly mauled was the 1st Armored Division, having lost two thirds of its tanks, that it virtually ceased to exist. These losses and the performance of some of the tank crews emphasized how lacking the U.S. II Corps was in battle experience, and Marshall felt many of the American troops sent overseas were lacking adequate training.[1] No timely steps were taken to rectify the omission. For once, however, the British were near to agreement with their Allies. After Kasserine, Alexander visited the battlefield and it was evident the Americans were ill-trained; they were, among other things, too defensive in outlook. They also lacked the necessary sense of urgency when attacking and did not seem to appreciate that if their first attack failed the success of a subsequent assault would be more difficult to achieve. Alexander, in a letter to Brooke, wrote that something had to be done to resolve the Americans' problems or else their army in Europe would be useless. Of Eisenhower, he commented that he was not impressed by his military intellect.

The second attack on the Kasserine Pass had caused Alexander concern and on 20 February he asked Montgomery to intervene to relieve the pressure on the U.S. front. This was done, and on 5 March Montgomery received a message saying the crisis was over and Rommel had failed to achieve his purpose; the attack on the Pass cost the Axis a little more than 1,000 casualties. Their failure, however, was not due to skillful Allied tactics, but to the German command not being co-ordinated. Von Arnim, being more cautious than Rommel, did not appreciate that in view of the

Allied disposition of forces, if Rommel's plan had been put into operation it would have had a good chance of succeeding. The Germans also made the same error Eisenhower did in late February when he gave Anderson orders to conduct a broad front offensive, using insufficient forces. On this occasion, it was the Germans who neglected to concentrate their attack, and the mounting of a second offensive while the first was still in progress was a contributing factor to their failure.

Following his appointment as commander of all Allied ground forces in North Africa, Alexander paid a visit to Eisenhower and told him the Allied forces had been too thinly deployed and could be easily destroyed by the enemy. An example of the confusion he encountered was at the Denaia Pass where there was no officer in charge of the Allied troops, an omission he soon rectified by appointing to the position the senior officer, an American. He suggested the British and Americans should each be given a sector, that all units attached to another army should be returned to their own command and, once established in Tunisia, the Eighth Army should be given its own area of operations.[2] With this done, it contributed greatly to the operating efficiency of the Allied armies, as did the creation of a plan for the final defeat of the Axis forces.

After the battle, the Americans blamed Anderson for their defeat because he had dispersed some of their units to strengthen the British and French fronts, thus preventing the Americans from creating a mobile reserve. This accusation was totally false since it was Fredendall who commanded II Corps to which the units referred to belonged.

The allegation also ignored the limited abilities of the American troops at the time, and it failed to take into consideration Fredendall's indisputable ineptitude. Eisenhower blamed him for not concentrating his forces to meet the expected attack, but not only did he fail to ensure his orders were executed, he later failed to heed his own advice in the Ardennes, showing how quickly he forgot his own recommendations.

Considering the quality of the U.S. forces and their commander, it is doubtful if Rommel could have been repulsed any earlier. A further indication of the poor discipline in the U.S. army in North Africa was shown in May 1943. During the victory parade in Tunis, the U.S., 1st Infantry Division was being moved by road from Tunisia to Algeria, and as they passed from one village to another the soldiers looted as they went through.[3]

In a radio message to the Combined Chiefs of Staff in Washington, Eisenhower displayed a remarkable ability to understate the situation. He reported on 15 February 1943, following the fall of the Faid Pass, Sidi bou Zid and the German threat to the Kasserine Pass, that the existing tactical problems were possibly the result of his trying to accomplish too much, and in his memoirs he admitted he and others shared the responsibility for the week of reverses. As was demonstrated later, he neglected to learn from his self-admitted mistakes. In another message to Washington he made a surprising admission. He stated American troops had been complacent, but were now ready to fight. His conclusion completely missed the essence of the problem which was the GIs had been given second-rate training, they were poorly led and yet they were expected to be the equal of the experienced Germans; they could not afford to be complacent when opposed by an adversary of Rommel's caliber.

Eisenhower's inconsistency as a disciplinarian can be appreciated by a letter he wrote to Fredendall on 4 February 1943. Instead of enumerating that officer's faults he indulged in much circumlocution, evidenced by his statement that some generals were inclined to stay too close to their command posts. In lieu of ordering Fredendall to correct the fault alluded to by moving his command post nearer to the front line, he simply instructed him to be careful.

Soon after the first battle of Kasserine, Fredendall was relieved of his command by Eisenhower. His temporary replacement was Ernest Harmon of the U.S. 2nd Armored Division, who was handed written instructions by Fredendall and told to assume command; thereupon Fredendall retired to his bed for 24 hours. Harmon, in turn, was replaced by Gen. George Patton, but he had shown talent in his defense of the pass during the second offensive.

Having been thwarted in his attempt to advance to Sbeitla, Rommel turned his attention to the Eighth Army at Medinine. This attack began on 6 March with two assaults taking place on the same day; each was repulsed with heavy losses, costing the enemy one third of his tank force, which he could ill afford. Following this setback, the Afrika Corps attacked the French on the west flank of the Eighth Army, under the command of Gen. Jaques-Philippe Leclerc. With the help of strong air support, the French held on to their position and by so doing were of great help to the New Zealanders in their outflanking movement. At this point, Montgomery was in need of assistance. The U.S. II Corps, commanded by Patton, on 30 March attacked and captured Gafsa, but after a week of fighting they were unable to take their next objective, El Guettar. This success, although limited, did help Montgomery, since it drew off the 21st Panzer, enabling him to contain the 10th Panzer Division and making it easier for him to prepare for his forthcoming attack on the Mareth Line. These preparations included the use of the Gurkhas of the 4th Indian Division, who were given a general assignment in the hills near Hallouf, with the object

Chapter 3—The Battle of Kasserine Pass 39

of destroying any enemy posts, any big guns found in the area and otherwise to create as much confusion as possible behind the enemy lines. One patrol returned to base and filed a terse report; it was to the effect that the enemy had been encountered and the enemy had been engaged; number of enemy killed, 10; own losses, nil; expenditure of ammunition, nil. The Gurkhas had used their kukris.

Montgomery's offensive against the Mareth Line opened on 20 March 1943 with an attack against Wadi Zigzaou, but two days later the assault was hampered by heavy rains and in the afternoon the Germans launched a counterattack. Montgomery ordered a withdrawal from the Wadi, and switched his attack to his left flank where the New Zealanders, under the command of Gen. Sir Bernard Freyburg, reinforced by the X Corps, were advancing in their outflanking movement and by the following day were within a few miles of El Hamma. To avoid being trapped, von Arnim began withdrawing from the Mareth Line on 21 March to take up a position north of Gabes at Wadi Akarit. The retreat was harried by attacks from cannon-firing fighters and fighter-bombers, which created much damage and generally stunned the enemy.

The Allied tanks now prepared for their move. British armor, with a sandstorm behind it, broke through the enemy line, reaching the outskirts of El Hamma by 27 March. Montgomery had failed to trap the Afrika Corps, but he once again demonstrated his flexibility by switching the main attack to the New Zealand column on the left. Patton had mounted his own offensive to take Fondouk, but it failed. The main U.S. assault at El Guettar began on 28 March and it, too, was halted by the enemy after making only small gains. By that time, however, Montgomery had reached El Hamma and he arrived at Gabes the following day.

Upon instructions from Alexander, Patton mounted an attack toward the coast, but he used armor alone and soon came up against strong anti-tank defenses. After three days of fighting he had made little headway. The infantry were called in to try to save the situation, but they, too, failed. The attacks did produce some positive results, for the Germans felt there was a threat to their rear and sent the 21st Panzer Division to support the threatened sector, which helped Montgomery take Wadi Akarit. Due to their tardy evacuation of the Mareth Line, the Germans had no time to strengthen their position at the Wadi, and to add to their troubles they were short of ammunition. On the night of 5 April, Wadi Akarit was attacked and the enemy defenses breached, but the X Corps was slow to take advantage of the gain and the next day Montgomery renewed the assault, with an aerial bombardment preceding the ground attack. It was too late, for the Germans had slipped away, and once again Montgomery was deprived of a decisive victory. Part of Montgomery's plan for this fight was for the U.S. II Corps to exert pressure on the enemy's right flank. On the morning of 6 April, the 10th and 21st Panzer Divisions opposing II Corps were moved eastward to reinforce Wadi Akarit, but even though this decreased the pressure against his front, Patton, commanding some 88,000 troops, gave the impression he had little idea how to use them to advantage, which contributed to the failure to take the Axis position from the rear. The Germans had reacted too slowly to achieve any positive results and, despite having stopped the attack across Wadi Zigzaou, they were unbalanced by rapidly developing events at the west end of the front. In eight days, the Afrika Corps had lost 7,000 men taken prisoner alone; this was followed by even heavier losses as the British and Americans joined forces at Gafsa, after six battalions of 4th Indian Division had mounted an attack on 5/6 April in the hills overlooking the Wadi at El Guettar, where the Gurkhas were again in action — with fixed bayonets. Fondouk was captured by the Guards and Bizerta and Tunis were soon taken in a brilliant piece of planning by Alexander, based on a narrow front assault which left behind pockets of resistance to be dealt with later. With the final surrender on 12 May 1943 of all Axis troops in Tunisia, the Allies took nearly 240,000 prisoners, including the German commander von Arnim, Rommel's replacement. The figure of 240,000 is at variance with Eisenhower's estimate of the total number of Axis troops in Tunisia, given only a week preceding the surrender; he contended that there were only 150,000 enemy soldiers in North Africa.[4]

Fewer than 700 Germans managed to escape and prior to the surrender the enemy position had been made very difficult by the action of the Royal Navy and the U.S. Army Air Force. Royal Navy destroyers and USAAF bombers were in action and by 5 May had sunk two merchantmen, loaded with supplies — the last ships of any size to attempt to run the blockade.

When he heard both Bizerte and Tunis had fallen, Eisenhower appeared to be apathetic, remarking he was not particularly interested in mere geographic locations. He seemed quite enamored of this expression for he used it later in Europe, more than once.

In the original plan for the final offensive, which Alexander presented to Eisenhower, the U.S. II Corps was to have been relegated to a holding action while the British First and Eighth Armies were to go on to capture Bizerte and Tunis. This arrangement caused Eisenhower much concern; he pointed out to Alexander that it would only result in the U.S. shifting attention from Europe to the Pacific, a curiously strong reaction since he later felt the objectives were mere geographic locations, but this was not the last time he was to object to what he believed was a minor role for U.S. units; in the final assault, the II Corps was given a larger part than was originally intended.

Eisenhower's headquarters in Algiers was not a slender one. It consisted of 1,000 officers and 5,000 other ranks; at one time the ratio of headquarters personnel to front line troops was 1:5. This liking for a bloated headquarters was a fault he repeated in northern Europe. Perhaps it was due to the size of his staff that Eisenhower exercised so little control over it. Frequently the bulletins issued by Allied Headquarters were far more optimistic than any statements made by Eisenhower to the press.

4
Post-Kasserine and the Casablanca Conference

The Allied air command was poorly organized, and much of the fault must be attributed to nationalism and a lack of firmness on Eisenhower's part. In November 1942, Air Chief Marshal Sir Arthur Tedder found the situation in Algeria far from satisfactory, with the U.S. Army Air Force operating independently of the RAF and showing no desire to co-operate. When Eisenhower was informed of this matter he promised to do something about it, but was careful not to be specific, for he was reluctant to create a unified air command; Tedder, usually no denigrator of his commanding officer, was sure the reason for this was by combining the Libyan and Northwest Africa air commands, Eisenhower felt he would lose control over the air force in Britain, the source of reinforcements and replacements. Not until the end of 1942 did Eisenhower eventually understand the need for an integrated air command.

Patton moved his Ninth Division to El Guettar in the hope of capturing it and then pushing on to the coast, but the attempt ended in failure and stalemate. This setback resulted in exaggerated accusations being made by Patton regarding the inadequate air support provided. In reply, Air Vice-Marshal Sir Arthur Coningham, R.A.F. (a New Zealander), blamed the II Corps' lack of experience for the setback. As Coningham's investigation revealed, in total the 9th Division had suffered six losses from enemy air attacks, and his assessment of II Corps' fighting proficiency was in all likelihood correct; however, it was not phrased in words which did anything but arouse Patton's ire. Eisenhower could have averted a problem had he simply passed on the grievance to his deputy commander to handle. When he heard of the bother he had caused, Tedder telephoned Eisenhower to assure him the reply had been withdrawn. That did not prevent the Allied commander from drafting a signal to Washington asking

Chapter 4—Post-Kasserine and the Casablanca Conference 43

to be relieved of his command because it was obvious he had lost control over his subordinate commanders. The signal was never sent because Brig. Gen. Walter Bedell Smith, Eisenhower's Chief of Staff, persuaded him to withdraw it. This was not the last time Eisenhower used the threat of resignation when confronted with what he felt was an awkward situation. The incident was reported by Eisenhower to Marshall in a letter dated 5 April. Why Marshall should have been involved in petty quarreling is unclear. What is apparent, however, is there were occasions when the R.A.F. did not provide the degree of co-operation which could reasonably have been expected by the ground forces. By January 1943 it had four fighter squadrons based at Souk el Arba, but the then GOC R.A.F. refused to allow them to give direct support to the armies, contending they were to be used only to destroy enemy aircraft—an extremely unco-operative and narrow-minded attitude.

In the last half of January 1943, there was a meeting in Casablanca between Roosevelt and Churchill. Each leader took with him a staff, which for the Americans included Marshall and for the British, Brooke. The U.S. Chiefs of Staff attended the meeting lacking definite objectives; however, they seemed determined to give no ground to the British, who had arrived thoroughly prepared, which caused some American officers to display resentment.

At this conference, the Allies agreed to invade Sicily in the summer of 1943, to assemble forces in the UK for a cross-Channel invasion of France just as soon as Germany was weak enough, to continue the air offensive against Germany, and to assist the USSR to the best of their abilities. It was also agreed to maintain operations against Japan, but this was to be done only to the extent that it did not jeopardize the cross-Channel operation. Brooke gave his opinion that an invasion of northern Europe would be impossible before the late summer of 1943, and even then the number of troops landed would be severely limited by the shortage of landing craft. By the middle of September 1943 he estimated that the maximum number of divisions available for an invasion of France would be 23, but he was quite confident a European invasion could be mounted in 1944.

For all the self-assurance the American service chiefs showed in the feasibility of a 1943 invasion, the number of U.S. servicemen in Britain by June of that year numbered only 65,830, more than 25% fewer than the projected figure for that time, while the Pacific theater had received more than 150% of its planned numbers. Quite evidently, the U.S. was not keeping to its part of the 1941 understanding. Another agreement resulting from the conference was the setting up of a Combined Staff in Britain, and the Supreme Commander designate was the British Lt. Gen. Sir Frederick

Morgan. Churchill agreed that ultimately the Supreme Commander would be an American.

There was a delay in the appointment of the actual Supreme Commander due to the shortage of shipping, and the Americans attributed part of this shortage to the British using too many ships for imports. Since imports into Britain were generally restricted to war supplies and food, it was not an opinion designed to make the accuser very popular with the British, whose very slender food ration was near to a starvation diet compared with the generous allowance given to the American servicemen. The available shipping was used more efficiently in the Western Hemisphere than in the Pacific, where any ship arriving there on a temporary assignment was frequently "lost" when the time came for it to be returned to the West.

5
The Sicily Invasion

The next stage in the assault against Hitler's Europe was to be Operation Husky the invasion of Sicily, but even though the planning was quite advanced, Churchill had his doubts about it, feeling it would be better to land in Italy instead. In late May 1943, there was a conference in Algiers attended by Churchill, Brooke, Marshall and Eisenhower, at which the latter stated he was not willing to commit himself to any invasion of the European mainland until Sicily had been taken. As a result, the plans for the assault on that island went ahead, and although he accepted the invasion of Sicily prior to Italy, Churchill would have preferred to have mounted the invasion in May or June.[1] Had this been done, the opposition, at least initially, would have been much lighter for at the time the island was garrisoned only by weak Axis forces. Five months before Tunis fell to the Allies, the British had produced plans for the invasion of Sicily, and there arose the question of who was to command the operation. Alexander was one candidate, but both Churchill and Roosevelt felt Eisenhower had done such a good job in North Africa he was asked to stay on another six months, and upon accepting the assignment was selected to be Supreme Allied Commander North African Theater of Operations and given the directive for planning the Sicily invasion.

If the politicians were satisfied with their selection of military commander, Patton was not. In May 1943 he noted in his diary, with commendable accuracy, that the United States lacked a potential candidate for the position of Supreme Commander, one who possessed the necessary strength of character, but he omitted the need for experience. Having received his orders in January 1943, Eisenhower set up his planning committee, which was no more than an inexpert ad hoc staff having had little or no contact with the field commanders. The committee was quartered in Algiers, where the Supreme Commander had his Western Task Force HQ. The Eastern Task Force HQ was in Cairo, and the troops allotted to

45

Gen. Dwight D. Eisenhower and Gen. George C. Marshall hold a press conference in Algeria in June 1943. (Courtesy Dwight D. Eisenhower Library.)

that task force were scattered, some in the U.K., some in Tripoli, others in the Suez Canal Zone.[2] The Supreme Commander had to approve the plan and all subsequent changes to it, but he was so involved with the complex political situation which had arisen in Algeria that he could not give the planning problems the attention they deserved; added to the difficulties was the fact the service commanders were divided between Tunisia and Malta.

There were no fewer than nine different plans for the invasion, and the confusion was not helped by Marshall's attitude. He was still irritated by the British refusal to stage a premature landing in northern Europe. He believed the United States had been outfoxed; in an attempt to regain the initiative he pressed for an invasion of Sicily to commence almost immediately following the end of the campaign in Tunisia, contending by so doing the operations in the Mediterranean could be finished quickly and the Allies would then be able to attend to operations against northern Europe. In Montgomery's opinion, no progress was being made and he obtained Alexander's approval for a conference to be held in Algiers on 2 May 1943.

Upon arrival, Montgomery discovered Alexander had been unable to take off due to bad weather; in his anxiety to settle the problems he searched for Eisenhower's Chief of Staff, Bedell Smith, eventually finding him in a lavatory. There they discussed the situation and, after some later talks in more salubrious surroundings, they agreed to the final plans. That resulted in Montgomery pushing through his own plans. He dismissed the objections of the air commanders when they pointed out to him there was to be a large number of airfields left in enemy hands after the initial landings. What they failed to appreciate then, as later in northern Europe, airfields, Allied or German, could operate effectively only if they were protected, and in the case of Sicily the enemy airfields were frequently within range of naval and shore artillery. Montgomery felt, with justification, the air force was not being totally realistic in its demands. As it transpired, the Germans made no effort to make the island a stronghold, preferring instead to save their resources for Italy, using Sicily simply as a means of delaying the Allies for as long as possible. Unfortunately, Montgomery's action in having the plan changed aggravated the strong opinion already held against him by Bradley and Patton, who both felt he was making the alterations simply to satisfy his own ego. For his part, Eisenhower accepted the Sicily campaign on the understanding that, during the campaign, he was not going to commit himself to any ill-defined strategic objectives. This showed a great difference between the U.S. and British thinking. Marshall and Eisenhower were both convinced the tactical goal was the military smashing of the Axis, and that the Mediterranean operations were subsidiary to the proposed Channel crossing.

Both Churchill and Brooke took exception to what they felt was a very narrow and extremely dangerous view. In the long term, it seemed obvious to them, any military decision which lacked political expediency would result in tragedy. The rigidity of the Marshall-Eisenhower attitude was one which the British believed would permit the Russians to occupy large areas of Europe, but Eisenhower and the other U.S. generals remained convinced intervention in the Mediterranean would be of doubtful value. In fact, at a meeting of the British and Americans in Washington in May 1943, Roosevelt made the astonishing statement that an invasion of Italy would actually free German divisions for use in Russia. Neither he nor his generals explained how this could possibly occur. Not for the first time, logic was lacking in American arguments. The higher echelon of the American armed forces, as well as some Washington politicians, seemed distrustful of British imperial designs in the area. What designs the British could possibly have had is hard to imagine. They already controlled Cyprus, Malta, Gibraltar, Egypt and Palestine, and it is extremely unlikely they would have had any intentions of expanding along the north coast of the Mediterranean. As for the Balkans, another area of concern to the Americans, Churchill made it clear at the Quebec Conference in August 1943 the only interest he had in that area was to encourage guerrilla warfare and he had no thought of sending in regular forces. It is not difficult to conclude the Americans were looking for an excuse to avoid a campaign in the Mediterranean.

When Eisenhower discovered that Field Marshal Kesselring, the German commander of Axis forces in Sicily, was planning to reinforce the island with two Panzer divisions, he expressed concern in a telegram to the Combined Chiefs of Staff in London. He said the invasion did not have much of a chance of success if the island were defended by what he termed substantial, well-armed German ground forces—there were nine Italian and four German divisions. He displayed a poor opinion of the nine Allied divisions which were going to be deployed against light Axis divisions and his pessimism contrasted markedly with his optimism with regard to Sledgehammer, where opposition would have been far more than just four German divisions. It was also a direct contradiction of a statement he had made to Alan Brooke that he expected the Sicily campaign to be over within a week from the time of the landings.

This display of despondency irritated Churchill, provoking him to write a minute contending that after adequate preparation, superiority in the air and at sea, the addition of but two German divisions was enough to cause Eisenhower to become pessimistic about the prospects of an Allied success.

The Allied invasion forces, designated as 15 Army Group, were split 55% American and 45% British and Canadians on the ground, with 80% of the air force being British. The armies were made up of the British Eighth Army, commanded by Montgomery, and the U.S. Seventh Army under the command of Patton. The ground commander was Alexander, the air force was commanded by Air Marshal Sir Arthur Tedder, R.A.F., with the naval forces under Admiral Sir John Cunningham R.N. There was inadequate co-operation between the air force and the army; the air force refused to fully assist the planners because the airmen were convinced air power alone would win the war, and by collaborating with the other two services they felt this would dilute their main effort. The evidence, however, showed that valuable though air power was, it could be totally effective only if the raids were followed up by ground forces, as was done after the Luftwaffe's bombing of Warsaw in 1939 and Rotterdam in 1940. The Luftwaffe's raids on London, Coventry and other large British cities had not resulted in any pleas from the population for the govern-

Chapter 5—The Sicily Invasion

ment to capitulate; the Allied bombing of Germany had not had any appreciable effect on German morale, nor had German industrial production been brought to a halt. Eisenhower supported his air chief on the grounds major air operations never ceased and the enemy air force was an elusive target whose whereabouts was impossible to find in advance. Even the passing of time did nothing to improve the clarity of his reasoning.

Eisenhower eventually approved the final plans and they included the significant statement that it was essential not to disperse the land forces because that would result in their collapse. The landings took place before dawn on 10 July 1943, and they were successful although not without error. The beaches had neither been bombed nor shelled before zero hour, and the enemy mobile defenses were also left untouched. The chain of air command was far from efficient. Patton's forces received very little air support until 12 July, and in order to obtain that Admiral H. Kent Hewitt (U.S.N.) had to contact Cunningham in Malta, and Cunningham had to obtain approval from Tedder in Tunis, who decided how many aircraft could be spared for the assignment. Frequently the planes arrived when the need for them had passed. Later, in the invasion of Normandy, the Allies did improve the system; however, the air force did not give the ground forces total control over the fighters. During the first two days, no more than eight Allied planes were covering the landing areas at any one time, and those that were proved to be of little use to the ground forces. Part of the problem was the navy had no air force officer aboard any of its ships.

Patton's Seventh Army landed over open beaches in the Gulf of Gela on the south coast of Sicily. Some of the II Corps was embarked using a different system from that of the Eighth Army. The Americans were loaded on the basis of one battalion per ship, leaving no capacity to carry enough landing craft to take all the troops ashore at the same time; therefore the transports had to wait offshore for the landing craft to return to carry the remainder of the battalion ashore. Had the Germans been better prepared they could have inflicted extremely heavy casualties, which would have severely impaired the success of the landing.

Patton was to hold the western flank of the 15th Army Group while the Eighth Army attempted to isolate the Axis from Messina. To accomplish this, the U.S. Seventh Army was to push northwards and cut the Palermo to Messina road along the north coast while holding the enemy on the left. As was shown more than once later, Patton was the wrong commander to be assigned a secondary role, which was clearly demonstrated when he decided to implement what he called his "rock soup" strategy. He mounted a reconnaissance in force against Agrigento on his left flank. It was successful. He then flew to Algiers on 17 July to see Alexan-

Sicily and Italy showing important battle locations.

der and requested approval to direct his main attack against Agrigento and mount a two-pronged assault on Palermo. Unfortunately Alexander agreed, for Patton's move was of little value to the Allies. Palermo was taken as a result of Patton's advance which commenced 19 July. The port was held by Italians who began to surrender long before the Americans actually entered the town, and from that point of view capture was no great accomplishment. The U.S. press apparently felt otherwise, for it was touted as a great victory, and Patton was made to appear to have conquered against heavy odds. He accepted the adulation, making no effort to minimize his achievement by admitting the indifferent opposition.

The Eighth Army landed between Siracusa and Pozzalo; ultimately the U.S. Seventh Army was to ensure the defense of captured airfields and protect the Eighth Army's left flank. Once the 15th Army Group was ashore, however, it was left to the individual army commanders to decide how operations were to proceed since the planners had not seen fit to involve themselves in such mundane details. The Eighth Army was given the exclusive use by Alexander of the four roads which led into Messina with the ultimate object of the town falling to the British. Originally, the plan was for the British to take Messina early in the campaign, but the German defense of Mount Etna plus malaria in the Catania Plain were reasons for the slow progress of the Eighth Army. Under the circumstances, he had little option but to restrict the encirclement of that point by Gen. Oliver Leese, leaving Enna to be taken by the U.S. Seventh Army. This exposed the II Corps' entire right flank, provoking Bradley to write to Leese pointing out the danger thus created. Leese corrected the situation and sent Bradley two bottles of Scotch whisky by way of atonement. In view of Montgomery's delay, Alexander gave Patton permission to go full speed for Messina, but the so-called "race" for Messina was a figment perpetrated by Patton, perhaps intended to enhance his own reputation as well as that of his army, a fact substantiated by the meeting on 25 July between Patton and Montgomery at which it was agreed that the Seventh Army would try to capture Messina as quickly as possible.[3]

By now the Germans realized their position on the island was hopeless, and early in August they began, in broad daylight, to evacuate troops from Messina to Italy, using two big train ferries capable of carrying 5,600 men or 800 tons of supplies each trip. Neither these ferries nor the port facilities on the Italian side of the Straits of Messina had been disabled by air raids,[4] despite the fact the importance of Messina was fully realized prior to the invasion when the port facilities were bombed, but the Allies wrongly believed the raids had reduced the daily capacity handled to a mere fraction of its normal 4,000 tons. As a result, the enemy managed to evacuate 102,000 men together with a quantity of tanks, guns and ammunition.

The failure of the Allied air force to intercede successfully was yet another indication of Eisenhower's lack of control over his subordinates, for Tedder was allowed to give priority to targets on the Italian mainland, paying too little attention to what was happening at Messina during daylight hours. The navy did engage in sweeps to destroy enemy shipping, but it is unclear why no attempt was made to intercept the ferries. The German navy in the Mediterranean consisted of E-boats and other small craft which alone should have been no cause for timidity. If the fear of air attacks was the reason for the Allied navies keeping clear of the Straits, then this ignored the fact the Allied air forces were far more powerful than the Luftwaffe, and any attempt by it to interfere with Allied naval operations should have been easily defeated.

The Axis defense of the island ended 17 August 1943, 39 days from the date of the landings, more than twice Marshall's estimate of time the campaign would actually last, and a month longer than Eisenhower's forecast. During the entire battle for Sicily, both Eisenhower and Alexander maintained their respective headquarters in Algiers, taking no active part in the operations whatsoever. This was contrary to the Supreme Commander's actions the following year when he assumed the position of ground commander in northern Europe. He never explained what he believed was the difference in the situation in Sicily and the later one in Italy, compared with that of France.

While in Sicily, Patton behaved in a manner which was to prove typical of him throughout the remainder of his career. He seemed incapable of appreciating that his words and actions were not always of the high standard expected of an officer in his position. In Oran, he had addressed the U.S. 45th Division, giving them a pep talk and urging them to kill the Germans unless they were certain they really intended to surrender.[5] Soon after the landing at Scoglitti, in two separate incidents, a captain and a sergeant of that division killed some German prisoners. When it came to his attention, Patton promptly ordered courts-martial for the accused. At their trials they each pleaded they had been instructed to kill prisoners of war by their army commander. Their pleas failed and both were found guilty. Upon hearing of the incidents, Eisenhower mildly reproved Patton with the simple understatement that he talked too much.

Patton often visited field hospitals on the spur of the moment to talk to the wounded in the belief it helped their morale. He called upon the evacuation hospital at Troina and there saw one soldier whom he presumed was faking illness. Infuriated, Patton slapped the patient across the face with his hand. The soldier was diagnosed with a moderately severe case of psychoneurosis anxiety state, malaria, chronic diarrhea and a temperature of 102° F. A week later Patton visited another evacuation hospital, this one at Sant' Agata, where he saw a shell-shocked soldier huddled and shivering in his bunk. This was too much for Patton's concept of an ideal soldier; he called him a "yellow son of a bitch," drew one of his ivory-handled revolvers and waved it in the man's face. He then told the doctor

Chapter 5—The Sicily Invasion

the soldier must be removed from the hospital immediately. Upon leaving he noticed the patient was weeping. Enraged, Patton rushed back into the tent and struck the man.[6] Later, he mentioned to Bradley that he had had to slap a "malingering soldier," but Bradley did not treat the remark seriously. Afterwards, when shown the report, Bradley instructed his Chief of Staff, Brig. Gen. William B. Kean, to place it in a sealed envelope which was to be opened only by himself or Kean. It was then placed in the safe. The only purpose this action could have served was to cover up the entire incident in the hope of shielding his commanding officer from possible punitive action by Eisenhower. In due course, Eisenhower did learn about the incident and seemed at first quite undisturbed by the apparent breach of discipline, simply assuming he would have to reprimand Patton once more. Nevertheless, it soon became evident the episode could not be hushed up and he ordered an investigation. Eventually, Patton was instructed to apologize to the two men involved as well as to the medical staff of the hospitals.

The apology was made at Palermo on 22 August, in his headquarters at the Royal Palace, where he delivered little more than an excuse for his behavior based on something he had witnessed in the First World War. Later he toured the divisions of the U.S. Seventh Army to apologize for his conduct, and also wrote a contrite letter to Eisenhower expressing his chagrin for the trouble he had caused. As he showed later in Normandy and Germany, Patton learned nothing from his breaches of military conduct. Eisenhower ignored the attempt by Bradley to suppress his knowledge of the incident, and seemed unaffected by the questionable conduct of his senior officers. He believed he had taken immediate and appropriate measures against Patton. These two events were reported to Marshall, but Eisenhower minimized the condition of both soldiers, describing them as suffering from "... nervous disorders, and in one case the man had a temperature." Certainly an accurate description as far as it went, but it was seriously incomplete; he omitted mention of the malaria and chronic diarrhea, neither of which is a minor complaint.

The two affairs reflected the low level of discipline enforced by Eisenhower. That a soldier should be assaulted by another is serious enough—when the assault is perpetrated by a general it surely calls for much more severe punishment than was imposed. Eisenhower contended that had the incident happened in action and in an assaulting unit, it would not have been a crime—not that such behavior is condoned by military law, but any witnesses to the incident would have concluded the aggressor was one who could tolerate no shirking. Neither his standard of discipline nor his standard of reasoning can elicit any admiration.

6
The Invasion of Italy

The Combined Chiefs of Staff gave approval for the invasion of Italy just 10 days after the landings in Sicily, on 20 July 1943, but neither Eisenhower nor Alexander would support the plea for an overall commander to co-ordinate planning and the subsequent offensive. To add to the confusion, the Combined Chiefs of Staff, displaying a degree of ambivalence, insisted men and materiel were to be transferred to the Far East after the landings in Sicily had been completed, but the British Chiefs of Staff ordered a halt to the transfer of aircraft and ships from the Mediterranean and their action resulted in strong objections being voiced by Marshall and King.

One suggestion, from Alexander, was that prior to the end of the Sicily campaign the Allies should establish a bridgehead in southern Italy to prevent the Germans from using the area to assist in their evacuation of Sicily. Churchill enthusiastically agreed, but Eisenhower and Marshall could see no advantage to the plan and refused to accept it, an error of judgment which was to be costly to the Allies. The toe of Italy at Calabria was a suitable landing area and air cover could have been provided from two Royal Navy aircraft carriers in the vicinity, as well as from the R.A.F. station on Malta. In addition, there were the captured facilities in Sicily and bombers were stationed in Tunisia, just 300 miles away and within easy range. Montgomery supported Churchill, believing if the landing at Salerno were successful the forces would be better used reinforcing that area. Eisenhower afterward admitted the failure to make a landing at Calabria was an error; he pleaded there had been no guidance from his superiors, overlooking the fact it was he who had been given the task of planning the invasion of Italy and had he, or his staff, felt an earlier assault on mainland Italy would have been advantageous, he should have put forward the proposal to the Combined Chiefs of Staff for their action. It was not for them to give detailed instructions to the planners. After the war, two German generals, one of whom was Kesselring, expressed surprise that nothing had been attempted to cut off their forces in the toe of Italy.

In the event, the overall planning suffered from much the same problems as did the planning for the invasion of North Africa and Sicily—it lacked cohesion and pragmatism and did not have the full support of the Roosevelt administration. Eisenhower showed every sign of being unable to arrive at a firm decision and it later reached the stage where Montgomery was left uninformed regarding the objectives which had been assigned to his Eighth Army.[1] Secretary of State Henry L. Stimson was convinced that if the British ever thought the Italian operation was developing successfully they would cancel Overlord and become involved in the Balkans. Marshall, in turn, appeared unable to understand that the fighting on three fronts had a common connection and were not separate wars which were being conducted.[2]

One of the purposes of the Italian invasion was to tie down German forces in the peninsula so that an invasion of France, and possibly an invasion of the Balkans via the Ljubljana Gap, would be made easier. The plan succeeded. The German Tenth Army in the area south of Rome had been reinforced by the addition of three divisions, and within nine days following the fall of Sicily, Hitler had moved some divisions from the south of France to reinforce Italy[2]; later in the same month, four more divisions were sent to Italy, two of which were SS Panzer divisions transferred from the Eastern Front. Prior to the arrival of these reinforcements there was only one poorly trained division in the center of the country, with two more in the south. By the time the Italians had signed the armistice with the Allies, the Germans fielded 19 divisions in Italy, and by October 1943 this had increased to 24 divisions, some of which were Panzer and Panzer Grenadiers. This movement of troops was a clear indication of the importance Hitler placed upon defending the country, an indication which Eisenhower and Marshall ignored when the topic of the invasion of southern France was discussed with the British.

In a prolix speech at the first meeting of the Fascist Grand Council to be held since 1939, Mussolini tried hard to assert his authority over the assembly, but he was defeated on a motion made by King Victor Emmanuel III rejecting Mussolini's pleas for support and the egotistical dictator was forced into exile on the island of Ponza. He was later caught on the mainland by Italian partisans and, together with his mistress, he was executed. The King now proclaimed himself Commander-in-Chief of the armed forces and Marshal Pietro Badoglio was appointed Prime Minister. This unexpected change of circumstances resulted in no immediate reaction from the Allies, leading to the impression they had no contingency plans to cover the downfall of the Italian dictatorship. The most Eisenhower could think of was to issue a statement which praised the Italians for ridding themselves of Il Duce and assuring them he was prepared to negotiate with the new government. His words were as uninspiring as his military responses, and these were not helped by the fact Marshall had insisted on the withdrawal of four bomber groups, greatly limiting the options available to the Allies.

There followed no immediate reaction involving the armed forces; due to Eisenhower's refusal to appreciate the need for preparedness and having no contingency plans, all that could be done, in lieu of an immediate invasion, was to hold a series of bizarre clandestine meetings between representatives of both sides. It was soon obvious the only thing the Italians were doing was successfully playing for time. One serious impediment to the acceptance by the Italians of the surrender terms was the Allies' insistence upon unconditional surrender. Another obstacle was the failure of the Allies to use the offices of the Vatican to act as intermediary. In addition, the British Embassy in Rome had only one old code book, the copy of which was suspected of being in German hands, and the U.S. Embassy in Cairo was in no better situation since the Germans were able to read its coded transmissions.[4]

The Allies lost five precious weeks and gained nothing, which was an advantage to the enemy for it gave him time to send more forces to Italy. Hitler had originally intended to defend only the northern part of the country, feeling the north was of greater importance than the south, but due to the Allied slowness to take advantage of the Italian political turmoil, the Germans were enabled to defend the entire country. The day before the capitulation there was a meeting at the 15th Army Group Headquarters in Syracuse to discuss the possible capture of Rome. It was contended this could be done with the assistance of the Italians, and it was proposed there should be a drop of the strongest airborne assault force that the air force could transport. The proposal was far too ambitious and was eventually canceled. Post-war, Kesselring said he was convinced had the Allies in fact made a paratroop landing close to Rome, followed by an amphibious landing nearby, the Germans would have been forced to evacuate the entire southern half of Italy.[5]

Once again, the initial landings on enemy soil were a success, and the invasion of the European mainland began on the same day as Italy's surrender, but this success was despite a lamentable lack of co-ordination between each of the landings. The opening barrage from Messina against the toe of Italy was completely wasted; the results of intelligence-gathering raids by commandos, which revealed the Germans had evacuated the

Chapter 6—The Invasion of Italy   57

area to form defenses in the mountains, were disregarded as was the fact that the Allied air forces were far more powerful than the Luftwaffe and any attempt by it to interfere with Allied naval operations should have been easily defeated.

The preliminary operations were followed by a landing on the drained marshes of Anzio; the preceding exercise was not successful, and during the actual invasion the U.S. Navy offloaded some assault craft too far from the shore, resulting in these vessels taking about four hours to reach the beach. Casualties were heavy, averaging 2,000 killed and wounded per week, and for this little was achieved. The U.S. Navy seemed unwilling to learn, for the following year it made the identical mistake in Normandy.

Alexander visited the front to make an assessment of the situation and conferred with Maj. Gen. John Lucas at his headquarters. He wired Brooke informing him that he was troubled by Lucas's leadership and suggested replacing the U.S. VI Corps' Headquarters with a British one; alternatively, another U.S. commander should be appointed. A copy of the message was sent to Eisenhower and it produced a characteristic reaction from him. He forwarded Alexander's signal to Marshall, admitting the existence of a problem, but expressing fervent opposition to a British officer supplanting Lucas, as though the British were not allies of the United States. Upon receiving this message, Marshall sent instructions to U.S. Lt. Gen. Jacob L. Devers, deputy to Alexander, telling him to find and appoint a qualified American replacement.[6]

While this exchange of signals was in progress, the Germans launched an attack intended to drive the Allies into the sea. For three days the battle was fought with great intensity, but finally Lucas managed to bring about order to the situation. Unfortunately, it was too late to save himself and he was replaced by Gen. Mark Clark. It seems Lucas was a victim of circumstances not of his making, for the Anzio landing was not well planned and it is to be wondered the Allies managed to retain a foothold. The removal of a senior officer was soon to be quite common in the U.S. armies in northern Europe. Any general who failed to accomplish his given assignment, whether or not due to incompetence, ran the risk of being removed from his post. He was often given insufficient time to settle into the new position, and commonly expected to produce results greater than reasonable expectations.

Eisenhower blamed inexperience and indifferent leadership for the unsatisfactory performance in North Africa, Salerno and Anzio, and attributed German success in central Tunisia to poor discipline and morale in the U.S. army, together with a lack of regular patrolling. If these assessments are accurate, it reflects adversely upon his qualifications as a leader.

He ought to have been fully aware of the shortcomings of his armies in Tunisia, and he had more than two months in which to institute the needed corrections before the assault on Italy took place. As for the Salerno and Anzio landings, neither of them achieved surprise, and the allegedly unsatisfactory performance of the army commanders was more a fault of the planners than of any one general in the field, with one important exception. It was believed that a naval bombardment preceding the Salerno landings would alert the enemy, and it was canceled.[7] Despite this omission, the enemy was well prepared for the invaders.

Montgomery, for his part, was unsatisfied with the progress of the Italian campaign for it lacked the essential element of any battle—concentration of effort. He also made the point that the 15th Army Group was not as strong as it ought to have been since men and supplies were being siphoned off to support the forthcoming Normandy invasion. In addition, he believed there was a lack of a cohesive plan. In Sicily and Italy, Eisenhower adopted the same aloofness toward the fighting as he had done in Tunisia, yet in Tunisia and Italy he saw fit to criticize others while he himself was much further from the fighting than ever Fredendall had been in his command post at Tebessa. The armies suffered from the narrow-mindedness of Marshall and Eisenhower, both of whom insisted upon the invasion of southern France, resulting in the 15th Army Group being stripped of well trained and much needed divisions and consequently having to fight with depleted forces, for the units diverted to Operation "Dragoon" were never replaced. One reason Eisenhower gave for his support of "Dragoon" was that the United States had re-equipped the French army, which together with the British and Americans, could not profitably be used in Italy. Again he offered no detailed reason for this sweeping and flagrantly incorrect conclusion.

It was during the Italian campaign that the American manpower shortage in this theater of war came to light. Eisenhower was well aware of the situation for he was concerned that if the Allies, with insufficient regard to economy, were to force the enemy to fight, it might mean men and supplies would have to be diverted from Overlord. Clark reported to Washington the existence of a shortage of replacements. It was vital to maintain the strength of all units, not only in the interest of efficiency but also for the sake of morale; two weeks later, reinforcements for the Fifth Army fell short by more than 13,000 men. This lack of reinforcements was the fault of the Selective Service; it conscripted 194,000 men in July 1944 to fill a need for 250,000. The army needed 175,000 for each of August and September, but actually received an intake of only 131,000 in August and 122,000 in September. Despite these deficiencies, the Americans went ahead with Operation "Dragoon" and by doing so they greatly weakened the capabilities of the armies in Italy, one result being in December 1944 the drive for Bologna had to be postponed due to enemy pressure on the western flank of the Fifth Army, and also the transfer of some units from the Eighth Army to Greece to assist in the suppression of a left-wing uprising.

It is hard to understand why the U.S. government did not make better use of its country's manpower supply. The reluctance to fully mobilize the nation to a wartime basis contrasted with the British efforts. In spite of full mobilization, eventually resulting in the conscription of both sexes, the British were hard-pressed to find replacements in 1945 for their army in Europe, since they lacked a pool of manpower to call upon. In the European theater, although having by far the greater population, the United States in May 1945 fielded only 54,000 men more than did the British.

The American ambivalence toward the Italian campaign was evident at the meeting of the Big Three (United States, Britain and U.S.S.R.) at Teheran in November 1943. For a time Marshall believed the Allies should advance into northern Italy, divide their forces, one branching into southeastern France, the other entering Austria through the Ljubljana Gap. He reasoned it was vital to avoid fighting on too many fronts at once, contradicting his support of "Dragoon" and overlooking the fact that as the two armies moved, each in its own direction, they would soon form two different fronts, with independent lines of communications—the precise situation he stated was undesirable.

7

Operation Dragoon — The Landing in Southern France

The original "Anvil" plan (renamed "Dragoon" by Churchill because he felt he had been dragooned into agreeing to it) had been to wait until Rome was captured and then mount the invasion, or alternatively to make a feint attack on the south of France. The entire purpose of the invasion was to provide a port for the passage of supplies and reinforcements to the Allied armies fighting in the north. Gen. Hastings Ismay of the Chiefs of Staff Committee contended that "Dragoon" was unnecessary because the Germans had transferred forces from France to oppose the Allied attack on Monte Cassino in Italy.[1]

Churchill held the firm belief that the use of the Brittany ports would be a far greater advantage to the Allies than would Marseilles, and an army landed in the north would be much more useful than one which would have to fight its way northward, resulting in more than a month's delay before it could be of any value to Eisenhower. He pointed out, during discussions with Roosevelt and Eisenhower, that the lines of communication to Marseilles were far longer than they were to Brest. Any attack from the south coast of France would be so distant from the main fighting in the north that there would be no tactical connection between the two. He went on to say Devers's men in Italy would be much more useful there to act as a threat to Germany from the south. It was known from "Ultra" decrypts that Hitler intended to make a stand for Rome, thus this decision made it very unlikely he would have also been able to defend the south of France effectively.

Eisenhower made the elementary mistake of refusing to reinforce success—an error he was to repeat in northern Europe. He tried to rebut Churchill's argument by pointing out that the distance from Brest to Metz, on the Franco-German border, was greater than from Marseilles to Metz.

Chapter 7—Operation Dragoon 61

A specious argument, for it ignored the vital fact that reinforcements landed in northern France would not have to fight their way eastward to link up with the main forces, and consequently could have been sent into action there far more quickly and effectively than those landed in the south. By November, Devers's 6th Army Group was short of supplies, Marseilles was 500 miles to their rear, and they experienced delays in transporting provisions to the front. In addition, the distance from the United States, or Britain, to Brest is considerably shorter than it is to Marseilles, and the shorter the sea journey the safer and quicker it would have been for the supply ships.

After the Channel storm, Eisenhower admitted to having supply problems, since Cherbourg and one artificial harbor in the British bridgehead were the only major unloading facilities in operation, and Marseilles was of no benefit despite all his previous assertions. Had Bradley been more astute he could have temporarily eased the problem by the rapid capture of the French Atlantic ports, but he failed to do so. Kesselring, after his surrender, stated he had been puzzled by the Allied failure to take the offensive following the fall of Rome, with the object of destroying the weaker German army, instead of invading the south of France.

Rome fell later than the Allies anticipated, and since any prior attack on the French Mediterranean coast would inevitably have involved the withdrawal of experienced troops from Italy, it is conceivable that would have necessitated the reassignment of troops in northern France. Marshall, Eisenhower and Roosevelt all agreed "Dragoon" must take place. Agreement could quite possibly have resulted from the U.S. Chiefs of Staff believing there were adequate supplies for "Overlord" and "Dragoon" to be mounted simultaneously; however, neither the British nor American planners concurred with this conclusion. Despite his support for "Dragoon," Eisenhower, on 6 December 1943, stated the most important objective in Italy was the Po Valley from which the enemy could be threatened in France, the Balkans and Germany. The possibility of a rapid advance to the Po was negated by the removal of divisions for the invasion of the south of France.

After D-Day, Marshall went to England to put his views to the British. He emphasized there were large forces accumulating in the United States, again showing impatience and an excessive concern for committing Americans to battle, regardless of their effectiveness, for he stated these forces had to be sent into action as soon as possible, either through Britain or through the yet uncaptured ports of western France. More than once he refused to consider military proposals put forward by the British. He was confident it was vital for the Allies to invade the south of France. At the

Teheran conference of November 1943, Brooke had stated such a landing would be to the advantage of the Russians (in fact, with Marshall absent from the meeting, Stalin had proposed such an attack[2]) and would cause the Western Allies to divert their efforts from the Balkans, leaving the area to be controlled by the Communists. He stressed the shortage of landing craft available for "Overlord" operations, yet many of these would have to be sent to the Mediterranean to take part first in "Dragoon" and then returned to Britain for the cross-channel invasion. All losses would have to be made good and the returned craft would be subject to repair and overhaul. He was certain the final blow would have to come from "Overlord" rather than "Dragoon." Marshall, however, predicted, with no little optimism, hostilities would end sometime between 1 September and 1 November 1944; had he seriously considered this estimate he should have appreciated it would have made "Dragoon" quite pointless, for the army to be landed in the south of France would be totally unable to influence the outcome of the war prior to his estimated date of the German surrender. Churchill was not convinced the invasion of the south of France would have any advantages, and he deplored the effect it would have on shipping shortages for the winter campaign in Italy. Because of the problems with landing craft, Bedell Smith also opposed "Dragoon" but was overruled by Eisenhower. At one time Eisenhower, too, appeared to have his doubts about the success of the south of France invasion, but it was not for strategic reasons. He wrote to Marshall in 1943 stating he did not feel the landing craft could be moved from Anzio to the south of France in time for the assault, and Marshall in his reply promised to use his influence to support any ideas Eisenhower might have in order to solve the problem. However, Eisenhower believed the obstacles were Ernest King and President Roosevelt, and he expressed doubts that Marshall would be strong enough to influence either of them. Furthermore, he felt Marshall's shortcomings included his failure to delegate responsibility[3] ... an inexplicable conclusion coming from one who was later to demonstrate his unwillingness to cede authority to those with more experience than he had. The reasons Eisenhower eventually supported "Dragoon" were twofold; firstly, he felt Marseilles could be captured much sooner than Bordeaux and an assault from Italy through the Ljubljana Gap would not divert any enemy forces from Normandy, an opinion not borne out later when it became evident German divisions were being switched back and forth between the eastern and western fronts as Hitler believed necessary; secondly, he grossly overestimated the adverse effect the June storms had on the supply situation in Normandy, and as a result he contended the ports in the south of France were essential. He reasoned supplies could be

Chapter 7—Operation Dragoon 63

shipped through these southern facilities to the armies in the north. He overlooked the very important fact that once these supplies had been landed they would then have to be transported the equivalent of over half the length of France to their final destination, an arrangement far more cumbersome and time consuming than existed in the north. One cause of strong support for the landings was that he was unable to give a date by which Antwerp would be in use, but, as the Supreme Commander, he ought to have had that project well beyond the mere planning stage, and his failure to appreciate this resulted in the expensive and fruitless "Dragoon." In the ensuing debate over the mounting of this operation, Brooke was of the opinion Eisenhower was too overawed by Marshall to disagree with him,[4] and it ought to have been obvious to him from a logistical point of view it was impossible for the Allies to maintain three major offensives in three different theaters, northern Europe, Italy and the south of France.

Marshall and Eisenhower were both supported in their contention that "Dragoon" was essential by U.S. Brig. Gen. Frank N. Roberts, who was on the staff of U.S. Army Planners. He was certain if "Dragoon" were canceled then it would have serious consequences, namely there would be political differences arising with the French, it would result in a loss of ten divisions to "Overlord," the U.S. forces would be supporting operations in the western Mediterranean, U.S. and French divisions would be committed to a slow, fruitless and costly campaign in Italy which, Roberts believed, would not be tolerated for very long, and lastly, the U.S. army in Italy would be used to invade southwest Europe and it would be difficult to stop it from then being employed as an occupation force in Austria, south Germany and Hungary.

These arguments are not impressive. Roberts did not detail the potential differences with France, nor did he explain how it was the French had suddenly become so influential in regard to planning the war against Germany. His assertion U.S. forces would be supporting operations in the western Mediterranean is indeed a puzzle; the only operations anywhere in the western part of that sea were in Italy, and if the U.S. was not inclined to give that campaign its full support it would take months before these forces could be of any value, and the very object of invading Italy was to pin down German troops to prevent their use in Russia or France. The allegation that the French and American divisions in Italy were involved in a slow and unrewarding advance was soon proven wrong by subsequent events. Mark Clark, too, was of the opinion "Dragoon" was nothing but a high-level blunder, and in a meeting with Marshall he emphasized the withdrawal of forces from Italy would adversely affect operations there.

In the course of discussion regarding the merits of "Dragoon," Eisenhower assured the British Chiefs of Staff, on 22 February 1944, that the U.S. did not look upon the operation as one which would take two divisions in the initial assault and ten divisions in the follow-up phase, although he did want a two-division assault force in the Mediterranean. He believed the U.S. would accept a diversionary operation after all requirements had been met for the Italian campaign. Subject to these conditions, the British Chiefs of Staff agreed to the invasion planning continuing on the understanding Italy was to be given overriding priority in all Mediterranean operations. On 18 April it was determined to postpone "Dragoon" and mount a full-scale assault in Italy. The offensive was successful, resulting in a breakout from the Anzio bridgehead and the capture of Rome on 4 June. During 1944, there was much disagreement between Washington, London and Field Marshal Sir Henry M. Wilson, regarding the date of the invasion of southern France and the inadequate number of landing craft for Operation "Overlord."

At a meeting of the Combined Chiefs of Staff on 14 June 1944, a proposal was made for a landing either in the south of France, the Bay of Biscay (with the object of taking the port of Brest) or on the Adriatic coast with the object of continuing on into the Ljubljana Gap. Wilson and Alexander agreed a landing at the head of the Adriatic was the best alternative and disagreed only about details. Field Marshal Jan Smuts stressed the need to take note of the opinions of these two experienced officers. Eisenhower wanted to invade southern France because he believed supplies landed in the western ports of France would take longer to reach the front line, even though these ports were closer to the point of origin, namely the United States. To this Brooke replied it was the opinion of the British Chiefs of Staff that if "Dragoon were mounted on a scale to be of any use, it would only succeed in hindering the depleted 15th Army Group, resulting in any achievements in Italy being on a modest scale. He urged that Alexander should be authorized to go ahead with his offensive with the intent of destroying the opposing German forces, while Wilson would make a threat of an attack on the south of France. When shipping and supplies permitted, Wilson would then send Eisenhower all the U.S. divisions he could spare, together with as many French divisions as Eisenhower could handle.

Montgomery agreed with Wilson and Alexander because he believed the troops in Italy were tired and, since many of them would be used in "Dragoon," he recommended this landing should be canceled and the landing craft sent back to Britain to be used in the Normandy invasion. In a letter to Eisenhower dated 21 February 1944 he advocated the Allies should concentrate on Normandy and Italy. Ultimately, Wilson's request for a

Chapter 7—Operation Dragoon

postponement was approved, but Marshall was as usual suspicious; he felt Wilson was hoping to keep the forces in the Mediterranean busy until after "Overlord," when a subsequent offensive in Italy would make the southern France landings impossible. Marshall fell back on a rather puerile conclusion. He said "Dragoon" was a test of the alliance between the two countries[5]—an illogical deduction and certainly an absurd one. His attitude seems to have been much like that of a spoiled child who informs his friends the game will be played his way or not at all.

At a meeting with Brooke, Eisenhower tried his usual conciliatory approach by proposing that Brooke should meet Marshall halfway; this recommendation was refused since "Dragoon" was not limited to a mere two-division assault but was to be followed up by the addition of eight more divisions, which represented one-third of Wilson's forces in Italy. The U.S. belief that "Dragoon" would cause a rapid withdrawal of enemy forces from Italy was obviously ill-founded. It was in direct contradiction to British "Ultra" decrypts showing the Germans could not withdraw from the north of Rome before 15 May, since Hitler intended to defend the capital, making the defense of the south of France in any strength extremely improbable.

The American opinion also dangerously underestimated the German military intellect; had Hitler given priority to southern France at the expense of Italy, it would have facilitated an attack in the rear of his army in southern France by enabling the 15th Army Group to make a rapid advance towards the Franco-Italian border. Furthermore, had the U.S. "Dragoon" forces been passed into France from the northern ports at the appropriate time, the Germans would probably have withdrawn from the south of France to avoid being attacked by far superior forces from the north.

By 24 June 1944, the U.S. Joint Chiefs of Staff were convinced the British proposal to cancel or delay "Dragoon" was unacceptable, and they so informed their ally. The latter's answer was history would not forget a commitment of a substantial force to an invasion which would take three months to reach fruition and which would take an additional three months to show results. Far from gaining anything, six valuable months would be lost, and the Italian campaign would be severely handicapped. Churchill erred by not informing Roosevelt that due to the President's stand on "Dragoon," the Russians would have to be told that the invasion of northern Europe would be postponed so the British could replace those divisions transferred from Italy. If he had done so, Roosevelt and Marshall might not then have been so determined to mount the assault. Had the "Dragoon" forces remained in Italy, that campaign would have been finished much sooner. In June 1944, the Allies in Italy were making reasonably good progress and Alexander hoped the south of France invasion would be called off, allowing him to use those divisions to reach and break through the Apennines and thereafter to go on to northern Italy. Churchill was confident this could be done and, if it were, he predicted the war would be over by Christmas 1944. The U.S. argued the Germans in Italy had reduced their army by four combat divisions which had been moved to France. Perhaps the Americans were using a different intelligence source, for the British, on the contrary, believed the Germans had reinforced their 10th Army Group in Italy by four divisions, and six more were en route. Furthermore, the British strongly supported if not an attack then at least the threat of one through the Ljubljana Gap into the Balkans, maintaining it would cause the enemy to transfer five divisions from France, thereby easing the task of the Allied armies invading northern Europe. The Americans were quite unable to believe the British had no territorial gains in mind by promoting such an attack against the Balkans. Not only was this conclusion incorrect, it also was a tacit accusation that the British had broken the terms of the Atlantic Charter, signed in Placentia Bay, Newfoundland, and made public on 12 August 1941. One of the items agreed to was that neither party would seek to augment its territorial possessions. The suspicion exhibited by Roosevelt and Marshall toward their ally was not conducive to the speedy termination of the war and was in direct contrast to Roosevelt's faith in Joseph Stalin.

Eisenhower disagreed with the British. He felt that far from causing the Germans to reinforce the Balkans, an Allied campaign in that area would release German troops from Italy for use in France. Perhaps it was just as well he did not expand on his conclusion, for it is not easy to understand this argument and the explanation may well have been even more confusing. From his own limited experience, he must have been fully aware the Germans were most unlikely to ignore an Allied attack which was obviously aimed at a vital part of the Reich. To have done so would have been entirely out of character for the German High Command, and for Hitler especially.

Even had the American assessment been correct, their military personnel showed obvious gaps in their knowledge of basic strategy, for a weakness in the enemy front should generally be exploited by their opponents. If Marshall truly believed the Germans were reducing their forces in Italy he ought to have realized that this should have been the place for the Allies to mount a powerful, all-out offensive. The defeat of the German 10th Army Group in late 1944 would have been a serious blow to German morale, aside from putting thousands of their soldiers in prisoner-of-war camps.

Chapter 7—Operation Dragoon

By now, Churchill was convinced it would be inadvisable to mount "Dragoon"; however, accepting the existence of the American forces in the south of France, it would have been far more sensible had they turned eastward toward Italy and thence into Yugoslavia and Austria.[6] The resulting squeeze between the Russians and the Western Allies would have increased the threat to Germany. In July, Smuts wrote to Churchill stressing his regret that the decision was made to proceed with "Dragoon" as it would only result in impeding Alexander's operations. Churchill cabled Roosevelt objecting to the proposed landing, since it could not influence the main battle. The Allies, Churchill maintained, ran the risk of failing to achieve victory in Italy, resulting in them having to revert to a passive role there. These were prophetic words, for to a certain extent it is exactly what happened; by this time, however, it was too late to make changes.

An exchange of messages had already taken place between Roosevelt and Churchill, the former expressing his opposition to the capture of Trieste and Istria, and stating he would suffer politically in the event of even a minor setback in the Normandy invasion should it be known that "fairly large forces" had been switched to the Balkans.[7] This was an absolute misinterpretation of the proposed attack. The forces to be used would have been drawn from the 15th Army Group in Italy and not from Eisenhower's command in northern Europe. To compound his misunderstanding, Roosevelt suggested the Western Allies should seek the services of Stalin as an arbitrator—as sensible as the devil being invited to mediate in a saint's dispute with a sinner. Eisenhower, too, tried his hand at convincing the British that "Dragoon" was the proper strategy to employ. He told Wilson the southern France invasion would have the advantage of containing and destroying enemy forces which might otherwise be used to oppose the Normandy invasion. In view of the known quality of the German forces in the south of France, this was a ludicrous argument, proven by subsequent events.

Since the United States was convinced the landings must proceed, on 29 June 1944 Churchill telephoned Roosevelt and gave his consent to the disputed invasion, in the interests of Anglo-American unity rather than because he had been convinced of the wisdom of such an operation. Roosevelt made the excuse that at the Teheran Conference the British, Americans and Russians had agreed to attack, but he seemingly failed to give weight to the fact that the agreement had been made in the last month of 1943, and much had happened in the succeeding six months to cause a reasonable revision of strategy. In addition, the understanding at the Quebec meeting stipulated "Dragoon" would only use men and materials not needed for Italy. In fact, the Americans stripped their armies in Italy of

25% of the total Allied ground forces in that country. They withdrew three of their own divisions, which were among the best they had there, in addition to four excellent Free French divisions. Upon hearing the news that his divisions were to be sent to the south of France, Marshal Alphonse Juin protested angrily that it was idiotic to stop a victorious army. Perhaps that was one thing which was not taught when Eisenhower and Marshall attended West Point. Juin's belief has been taken further — not only should one never stop a victorious army, but success should generally be reinforced, not weakened.

The Americans tried to support their arguments for "Dragoon" by pointing out the Germans were building submarine pens in Marseilles, and the capture of these would remove a positive threat to Allied shipping in the Mediterranean. The contention ignored the fact the enemy had little intention of defending the area as evidenced not only by the presence of a mere eight garrison divisions, but also, prior to the landings, by the withdrawal of front-line troops from the prospective invasion area. In addition, the Mediterranean could no longer be accurately called by the Axis "Mare Nostrum" due to the presence of the Allied navies, and in the unlikely event these installations at Marseilles did prove troublesome, a commando raid to destroy them would have been far more economical than a full-scale invasion. Such a raid had been carried out earlier by the British against the French port of St-Nazaire. The Americans contended it was essential to make a landing in the south of France because the Maquis (the French guerrillas) were fighting in that area and the French Communists were also active there. A landing, therefore, could be used to help one and eliminate the influence of the other. It was an implausible contention, for help to the Maquis could have been provided by air drops of supplies and irregular forces, as was done for northern France. American antipathy to French Communists was not shown in their dealings with Communist Russia.

As though these reasons for mounting "Dragoon" lacked conviction, the Americans tried to persuade the British it would result in the concentration of the Allied forces, but this argument absolutely ignored the unmistakable — by doing so the armies in Italy were being robbed of men and supplies where the potential for achievements already existed and did not have to be developed, as would be the case in southern France. As it happened, with Eisenhower's insistence on broad-front warfare, concentration of forces never occurred. The U.S. attempted to add credence to its support for "Dragoon" by asserting its resources were finite, and any attack on south Germany, through Yugoslavia and Hungary, would necessitate the establishment of new bases in the Mediterranean, which would

Chapter 7—Operation Dragoon

be an intolerable burden on U.S. industry and manpower capabilities. One of the aims of "Dragoon" was to establish bases in Mediterranean France, contradicting the American assertion they could not afford to expand in that area. Had the Italian campaign been permitted to continue with its original strength, unhampered by any other commitments, it is quite conceivable more could have been accomplished. It would have divided the German armies at, for them, a most inopportune time, forcing them to defend three fronts—the Russian, the Italian and the north European. Even had this assessment been too optimistic, with the capture of Italy, air bases could have been established which would have brought more of the industrial parts of Germany and occupied Europe within range of Allied bombers.

The illogical American reasoning was supported, not surprisingly, by Eisenhower, who at a lunch with Churchill in the first week of August, disagreed with the prime minister and Admiral Andrew Cunningham (R.N.), by stating the invasion of southern France was essential because it would make the Germans fight on as many fronts as possible. Churchill asserted the landings in southern France would be of no benefit to the forces in the north, and the troops to be taken from Italy for "Dragoon" would be of more use where they were.

It was at this conference that Eisenhower said the Allied supply situation would never be secure until Antwerp was captured and operating. How the Allies were to supply all their fronts pending the capture of Antwerp he did not divulge, nor did he seem to appreciate those enemy's divisions, even though of poor quality, which were stationed in the south of France could easily act as reinforcements for the main German front and would no longer hold a separate front once the two had joined forces. While the retreating Germans were shortening their lines of communications, Devers's army group had to be supplied from Italy for some time after it had passed from Mediterranean command to SHAEF (Supreme Headquarters Allied Expeditionary Force) on 15 September 1944.

The Allied forces in Italy were depleted to the extent of allowing the Germans to transfer one panzer division and two mechanized divisions to their armies in northern France. The reduction in enemy strength was the subject of a signal from Maitland Wilson to the British Chiefs of Staff on 19 June 1944. In the previous two weeks, he stated, the Allied armies in Italy had advanced 100 miles, but this momentum could not be maintained if several divisions and air support were diverted to southern France. Marshall, upon hearing this, was not convinced by Wilson's assessment, and showing how easily he could persuade himself the facts were as he wished them to be, gave his opinion that if the enemy were pushed extremely hard he would withdraw from the Po Valley to the Alps, having nothing to lose by doing so. Obviously Marshall had sunk into becoming an armchair strategist trying to conduct a war being waged more than 3,000 miles away, and his conclusions were in direct contradiction to the Allied experience of the previous year, when the Germans had fought strongly while withdrawing from Salerno; it contradicted the American experience in the Kasserine Pass; it contradicted the Allied experience at Anzio and earlier in Sicily. There was absolutely no indication that the German strategy had changed. The south of France was no longer vital to the Germans, one reason being that tungsten from Spain could no longer be imported due to Allied air attacks on the French rail system. The Balkans, however, were still of great importance to Hitler, for much of the German war industry had been transferred there and to central Europe, where it was out of range of the Allied bombers.

Another argument put forward by the Americans in support of "Dragoon" was that it would eliminate any threat from the German naval and air forces in the western Mediterranean, a feeble contention which totally lacked substance. Undoubtedly, had they had the naval and air forces to do so, Germans would indeed have done their best to create havoc with the Allied supply lines in that area; no such forces existed. The enemy lacked any naval forces of note and had a paltry 200 planes to protect them. To add to their discomfort, behind them were French resistance forces which succeeded in impeding road communications. In fact, southern France had lost its importance to the enemy, but Italy was potentially the entrance to the Balkans and southern Germany and therefore had to be defended. In coming to this contrary opinion and advocating "Dragoon" Marshall was showing the very streak of perversity which he objected to in the British. The U.S. had earlier stated it would postpone "Dragoon" and wait to see how the general situation in the Mediterranean developed. The Americans now reversed themselves and forced a decision. Despite having given his reluctant approval, in early August Churchill tried again to dissuade Roosevelt from his decision to go ahead with the landing. His pleas were unavailing, so he put his case to Harry Hopkins, one of Roosevelt's advisers, but he was again unsuccessful. In seeming desperation, he turned to Eisenhower, but although Adm. Bertram Ramsey (R.N.) and Bedell Smith both agreed with Churchill, Eisenhower was adamantly in favor of "Dragoon." He apparently did not know that Gen. James Wolfe wrote that pushing on smartly was the road to success, or if he did, he chose to ignore good advice. The French general René Chambé may have been guilty of only slight exaggeration when he stated operations were now to be interminable, and Gen. Alphonse Juin's estimation of the German

Chapter 7—Operation Dragoon

inability to defend the Po Valley was correct; Gen. Siegfried Westphal admitted the Germans had no troops capable of holding the area, Gen. Rudolf Bohmler felt the Allied failure to follow up the capture of Rome was a great benefit to both Hitler and Stalin, and Kesselring confirmed, as any student of war should have appreciated, it was in the Po Valley that the German army could have been destroyed.

In view of the American obduracy, there was little alternative, and the invasion began on 15 August 1944, with American and French troops formed into the 6th Army Group under the command of Devers; their landing was assisted by Royal Navy commandos, but once the beachhead was established, the British took no further part in the operation. These 450,000 troops met little resistance, and before they went ashore it was known the Germans did not think the area was of much strategic importance to them since they defended it with only seven divisions (as opposed to 50 in the north) which, on the assumption they were at full strength, would have numbered about 104,000 men; four of these divisions were garrison troops[1] who were considered unfit for front-line duty, and some of them had been removed from medical care to provide much-needed replacements. The defenders were thinly spread, having to protect 300 miles of coastline.

Allied intelligence must have been fully aware of the quality and numbers of the German troops in southern France; had the enemy felt the area was important to them they would have marched into it four years earlier. It was the Allied landings in North Africa which provoked Hitler to take over Vichy France. So quick and comparatively easy was the 6th Army Group's advance that just two weeks later the U.S. Seventh Army was making plans to join it. Smuts commented on the facility with which Devers's forces moved through southern France to Lyon and beyond, describing it as a "futile joy-ride."[8] Despite their optimism it was September before French patrols of First Army's II Corps from the south contacted the U.S. forces from the north, and it was mid–November before the 6th Army Group was able to give appreciable support to other Allied armies in France. In the interim, as the British predicted, the Germans reinforced their positions in Italy, contrary to Roosevelt's forecast.

What the landings achieved will no doubt depend on whose opinion is sought. More Allied soldiers were passed into France, but the important theater of fighting was still in the north and had there been need for such heavy reinforcements it would have been wiser, and cheaper in human life, to have sent them in from a point nearer to the main fighting. The German forces in the south of France were a threat to no one, least of all to the Allied armies in Normandy. The invasion certainly did not cause the enemy to move any units from Russia or northern Europe but it did prevent the Allies from exploiting their hard earned gains in Italy, where the loss was felt, and where the armies totaling about 250,000 were reduced to 153,000 and no real accomplishments resulted from "Dragoon." Far from proving useful to the Allies in northern Europe, it assisted Hitler almost immediately and Stalin later.

"Dragoon" was an unforgivable error and a superfluous operation. Too often the American-dominated SHAEF was overly optimistic, one example being the intelligence summary issued 26 August 1944. This stated the strength of the German armies in the West had been shattered, and soon afterward SHAEF operational instructions contained the information that some two and one half enemy divisions (two infantry and the balance armor) were being driven north along the Rhone Valley, evidently believing the retreat of two and one half divisions of third-rate troops, opposed by veterans of the Italian campaign, was a victory unparalleled in the records of military history. After the war Eisenhower admitted "Dragoon" was a mistake, but in mitigation he illogically pleaded at the time of discussing the operation he could concern himself only with military matters.[9]

Why did it not occur to him "Dragoon" would entail supporting an extra front when the men and supplies involved could be much better used to concentrate forces in Italy? Why did he ignore the intelligence reports showing the German defenders of southern France were not front-line troops (a report confirmed by the fact that on the first day of the landings 40% of the prisoners were Russian conscripts)? What prevented him from understanding that "Dragoon" was a military operation? How could he possibly have reached the conclusion that the invasion of southern France, to the detriment of the Italian campaign, was anything but a military matter? In addition to a lamentable absence of logic, he also displayed an abysmal ignorance of basic warfare.

By 1 September, Churchill was even more convinced that "Dragoon" was useless, and he believed it had not helped Eisenhower at all. By weakening the Allied armies there, the Germans, he concluded, had been enabled to delay the Allied advance into northern Italy, a fact confirmed as early as the end of July when the Fifth Army had to ration artillery shells.

At the second Quebec Conference, held in September 1944, Alexander was given permission to advance to Vienna, but his forces were so depleted it was not feasible. Another resulting problem was the shortage of replacements, provoking Clark to write to Marshall pointing out the increased incidence of troops suffering psychological disorders due to the excessive time they were in the front line before being rotated to rest. The

Chapter 7—Operation Dragoon

problem was primarily due to inefficiency. The system required reinforcements be sent to southern France from Fifth Army, and Devers would send back to Italy the equivalent number of men as they became available from other sources. The lack of reinforcements was a reason the Po Valley was not reached until the winter of 1944. There were subsequent disadvantages to the southern France operation. Progress of the 15th Army Group was so slow that the air force in the Mediterranean area was unable to provide assistance to the Warsaw insurgents due to the lack of forward air bases.

"Dragoon" not only denuded Italy of experienced soldiers, it was also planned before "Overlord," thus entailing the switching of forces from either northern France or Italy. It was evident "Dragoon" would make one of them nearly impotent.

8

The Invasion of Northern Europe

As the United States became more involved in Europe, more differences arose between the Allies. The Quebec Conference of August 1943 had decided upon a Supreme Commander for the Normandy invasion. The selection was made not with ability being the prime consideration but purely on the basis of U.S. numerical superiority. The responsibility for this command was given to the former Allied commander in the Mediterranean, Dwight D. Eisenhower. Upon assuming his new post he was given a directive dated 12 February 1944 which read: "You will enter the continent of Europe and, in conjunction with other United Nations, undertake operations aimed at the heart of Germany...." Unfortunately, Eisenhower's knowledge of Germany's anatomy was a little limited. His war service is highly regarded in his own country and some of the adulation may be deserved, for it is not an easy task to elicit co-operation from commanders with characters as diverse as Patton's, Montgomery's and Bradley's. Had he but limited himself to his known abilities, by war's end he would have had a much stronger reputation, based on a firmer foundation; regrettably, he insisted upon assuming responsibilities for which he had neither the training nor the talent. So the greatest invasion force ever to set sail from Britain to France was under the supreme command of a man of dubious military competence, who was promoted simply because he was a name in a book.

To command the U.S. First Army, Bradley was selected; here again was an officer who had never before commanded an army and he was chosen because Patton, his senior in rank in North Africa and Sicily, was an unreliable personality. Nevertheless, the sensible decision was taken to appoint a ground commander, Montgomery, but good judgment was negated by the appointment being only temporary. The British press, according to some American critics, hailed Montgomery as the country's greatest soldier since Wellington,[1] this hyperbole leading the Americans to the conclusion it was a semi-official opinion. Even had this conclusion been accurate it was of domestic significance only and there was no logical reason for the American military to have been disturbed by it, but it was and this contributed to further discord between the Allies.

In the final planning for the invasion, Eisenhower discovered he was not to have complete control over the bombers. Again, the Allied air forces believed strategic bombing alone could win the war and they were reluctant to see another service using planes for tactical purposes, thereby diverting them from the policy which the air chiefs felt would be more rewarding. The Supreme Commander, however, was determined to have his way, and while his reasons were sound his method of accomplishing his ends was the unimaginative one of threatening to resign unless command of the bombers was ceded to him[2] — the identical approach he also used in France. Finally the Combined Chiefs of Staff conditionally approved his request.

Fighter protection for the invading troops and assault craft was flawed. Originally it was organized strictly on the basis of unity of command; there was to be no individual protection allowed in any of the landing zones. It was much the same method as had been used in the invasion of Sicily, with no marked success, and despite that experience the air force was unwilling to give up control of the fighter cover to the ground forces. The result was that any request for air intervention at a particular location had to be sent to Uxbridge, near London, where it was handled by Air Vice-Marshal Kingston McCloughry R.A.F., who decided on the necessary allocation of aircraft. The organization of the planning staff also had shortcomings. There was a lack of speed and efficiency, which could easily have been avoided; in particular there was only a minimum of briefings and conferences for high-ranking officers. Planning problems were not eased by the U.S. diverting men and materiel to the Pacific, which it did again later in the campaign in northern Europe, despite the agreement not to allow the war in the Pacific to jeopardize the cross-Channel operation and despite the increased German war production. These obstacles did not prevent the Allied planners from learning a vital lesson from the Germans, which was the importance of concentrating forces during the attack. It was, unfortunately, a lesson which Eisenhower never fully grasped, as he later demonstrated.

Montgomery, in early 1944, made some revisions to the invasion plan by doing three things, two of which were to his advantage and the third was not. Upon hearing Rommel was in command of the German defenses, he ordered an increase in the amount of armor to be put ashore on D-Day, which proved a definite benefit to the 21st Army Group — a benefit not shared by the Americans, whose generals had refused to follow example, and their forces suffered heavily as a result.

Included in the British armor was a special unit commanded by Montgomery's brother-in-law, Gen. Percy Hobart. One of the specialized vehicles was the Scorpion, a tank which, attached to the front, had a rotating drum with fitted chains which exploded mines as the tank moved forward, clearing a path for the infantry as it did so. There were also flame-throwing tanks, bombard tanks firing mortar shells, "roly-poly" tanks for laying mesh tracks over sand or marshy ground and bridging tanks capable of laying a bridge 30 feet in length. Despite the faults alleged by his detractors, including some American officers, it was Montgomery who, on D-Day, made imaginative use of Hobart's special armor.

The Americans were offered a third of these "funnies" as they were called, but they accepted only the DD's, the amphibious duplex drive tanks.[3] The excuse for refusing the rest of the equipment was it would take too long to train their men in the use of the Churchill tanks to which some of the specialized equipment was attached. Nevertheless, the Scorpion was an adaptation of the Sherman, and once more there was evidence to believe the Americans did not want to appear beholden to the British in any way, even though it meant depriving their army of very useful items.

When Bradley was offered the special armor he replied he would have to discuss the matter with his staff, leading to the conclusion that he was incapable of making a simple decision himself or, more probably, it was a circuitous way of declining the offer. By February of the following year, Hobart's unit had been expanded into the only division of its kind in the British army, but even at this late date, the Americans never used the special armor to the same extent as did the British. The second thing Montgomery did was to alter the plans for the initial landings. He extended the beaches from 25 miles to 50 miles in length. The areas of the western flank, which the Germans had flooded to block access to Cherbourg, were to be taken by U.S. airborne forces, there was to be leapfrogging of one unit through another and each corps was to have its own beach, obviating the inevitable entanglement resulting from passing men and materiel of one unit across the beach of another. In addition, the build-up following the landings was to be increased.

The third thing Montgomery did was crucial to the initial part of the Normandy campaign and the cause of some later problems. He showed he was fully aware that, when planning amphibious operations, there is a tendency to concentrate on the details of the landings giving insufficient attention to what will happen thereafter. He held a briefing in St. Paul's School, London, on 7 April 1944, which was attended by Allied commanders and Churchill, the purpose of the meeting being to give details of the post–D-Day plan to the audience. The U.S. First Army was to take Cherbourg as soon as possible. The British Second Army was to engage in operations to the south and southeast of the river Orne with the object of taking suitable sites for airfields and protecting the American left flank as it developed an attack to capture Cherbourg. Subsequently, the British Second Army was to pivot on its left flank and prevent any enemy movement to the west.

The existence of a plan for the Second Army to execute a pivoting move has been denied by Brig. E.T. Williams of Montgomery's intelligence staff; by Bedell Smith; Sir James Grigg (Secretary of State for War in Churchill's government) and by Brig. E.J. Foord, Deputy G-2 at SHAEF. Williams did confirm the purpose of the battle for Normandy was not the acquisition of territory, with the exception of ports, but the build-up of men and supplies in sufficient quantities to give the U.S. forces enough strength to be able to break out into Brittany and the Loire.

Whether or not Montgomery intended to take Caen in the first few days of the invasion, whether or not he originally intended to pivot on Caen or some other location, is moot, but what is clear is Montgomery, long before D-Day, was emphasizing the need for the 21st Army Group to take the brunt of the German attacks during the first few weeks, so the Americans would be given full assistance to break out from the beachhead.

At this St. Paul's School meeting, Montgomery showed a map on which were drawn phase lines to indicate the anticipated progress for each day, another cause of much trouble. They were not something which originated with the British planners, but were included at the insistence of the U.S. planning staff. Montgomery was adamant he was not to be associated with these lines, since he believed them to be too imprecise and therefore worthless. So far as the planners of "Overlord" were concerned phase lines were included for the benefit of the logistics staff, which needed to have some idea of where the front line would be on a given date, how many men would be in action and what supplies would be required.[4] Apparently not knowing phase lines were standard in the U.S. planning system, Bradley raised objections to them, contending that if his troops did not attain the indicated lines on time they would conclude they had failed and morale would suffer. Not only was his judgment at fault, but also his reasoning, for the troops would only know of any long-range planning if they had been told about it; more importantly, nothing is of greater uncertainty in battle than the attainment of a given objective within a specified period

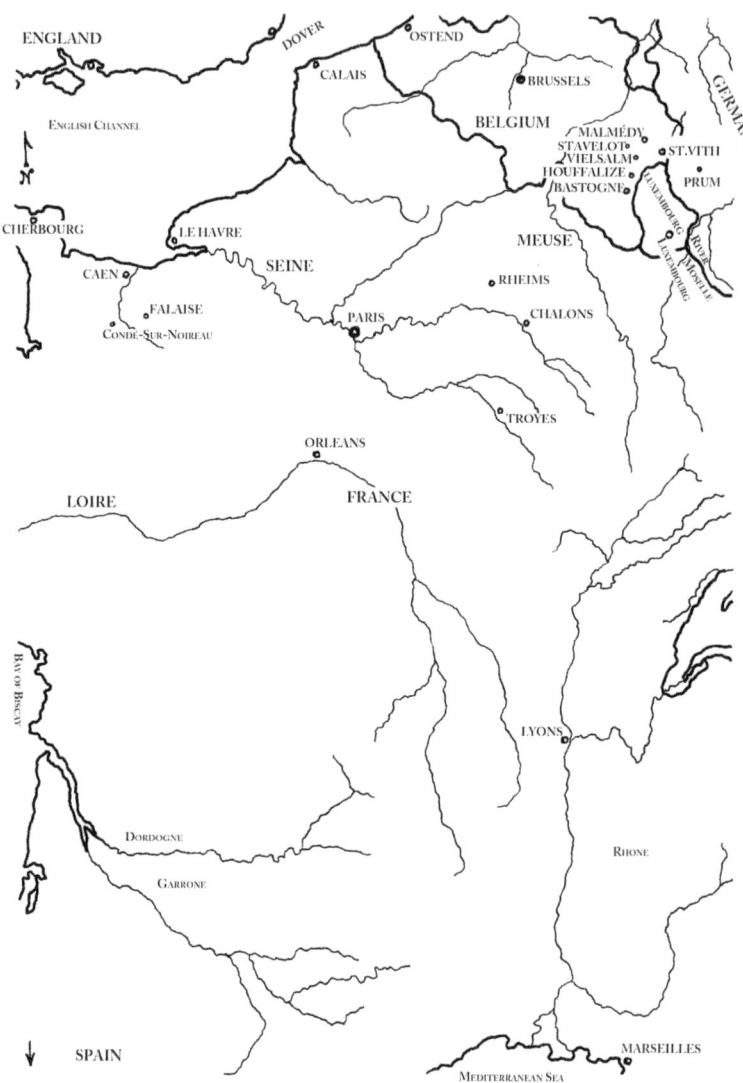

France, Belgium and Luxembourg.

of time. Such uncertainty should be well understood by the rank and file of a fully trained army. Nevertheless, it is apparent that to plan a battle without the hypothesis of achieving particular targets within a certain time is pointless. The U.S War Department contended phase lines could be useful, but were not an absolute forecast of what could be attained by a specified date. The planning never intended to suggest a failure to reach

Chapter 8—The Invasion of Northern Europe

these lines on time would be an adverse reflection on the competence of an army or its commander, and Bradley's reaction was nothing but excessive.

As a result of Bradley's objections the offending lines were removed for the U.S. forces, but Montgomery made the mistake of retaining them for the 21st Army Group, whose indicated objectives to be taken by D-Day included Caen. Bradley showed an illogical streak; having had the phase lines removed for the 12th Army Group he then maintained they were quite valid for the British and Canadians. Nonetheless, as a result of strong enemy opposition, the original concept was changed by Montgomery, and he decided the capture of the town was not immediately feasible. Since Rommel had worked hard to fortify the beaches, the planners were at fault for not realizing it would have been reasonable to have included Caen in these defenses.

It should have been obvious to the Americans that the taking of Caen early in the assault was no longer practicable. Lacking this appreciation, they reacted like a mindless claque, substituting for applause loud and ill-informed criticism of both Montgomery and the 21st Army Group, which did little to cement Anglo-American relations. Critics of Montgomery included Eisenhower, who took no steps to stop others from denigrating the British general's achievements.

Montgomery held a final briefing on 15 May 1944 at the same school, and present were H.M. King George VI, Churchill, Smuts, the British Chiefs of Staff, members of the British War cabinet, Eisenhower, Tedder and other officers on the SHAEF staff. Here Montgomery again propounded his plan for holding the enemy on the left flank while there was a breakout on the right by the Americans. The assault on the beaches began on 6 June 1944 against 600,000 Germans formed into 58 divisions; it was a success, perhaps a far greater success than many dared to hope, for never before had such a large amphibious military operation been launched across the English Channel. There were inevitably errors made, none of which proved to be a serious hindrance to the operation as a whole.

The Allied accomplishments were undoubtedly due to a high degree of training received by the majority of the servicemen, to superb planning and to excellent equipment provided to the invading forces. The pre-invasion bombing by the allied air forces was also of great importance, for with their 30:1 superiority over the Luftwaffe they were able to isolate the Normandy province by the destruction of road and rail communications, doing so with little interference from the Germans. By D-Day, rail traffic in France had dropped to less than one-third of its January 1944 level and of this only 20 trains per day were hauling military supplies; 75% of the bridges over

Eisenhower with members of 101st Airborne Division, Newbury, England, June 1944. U.S. Army photograph. (Courtesy of Dwight D. Eisenhower Library.)

the Seine were unusable and every German airfield within 130 miles of the Normandy coast was made inoperative. It was an impressive achievement, but it fell short of the prediction made by the USAAF that it could finish the war given 20 to 30 clear days to conduct raids against vital targets.[5]

At one point the U.S. forces on Omaha Beach, on the right of the British, became bogged down because their commanders had refused to pay heed to British experience, and a serious situation soon developed. Not only were the troops landed on the wrong beaches, but demolition squads were surprised by some of the explosive obstacles they encountered, managing to open only 12 lanes, a failure due in part to inadequate training and an absence of competent leadership. These demolition teams also suffered from a lack of liaison with the British. Royal Navy commandos had made several raids against the French coast and had managed to examine three types of German obstacles, but the Americans took no interest in this discovery. One other reason for the confusion on "Omaha" was the Americans, unlike the British, refused to use midget submarines to mark the limits of the beach.[6]

It can be reasonably assumed the British were more familiar with the problems of a cross-Channel invasion than were their allies. That did not

Chapter 8—The Invasion of Northern Europe

stop the U.S. staffs from believing the British grossly exaggerated the potential difficulties involved in such an amphibious operation; one American officer pointed out to a Royal Navy captain that the English Channel was only 22 miles wide, thereby displaying the identical ignorance as had Marshall earlier.

The Royal Navy had advised the U.S. Navy that it should unload the landing craft no further than eight miles from the beaches. The U.S. Navy, showing too much concern for German coastal batteries, transferred their troops to landing craft too far from the beaches.[7] In the choppy seas the extra distance did nothing to improve the fighting abilities of these soldiers, whose discomfort was not helped by navigational errors resulting in fewer than half of them being landed within 800 yards of the correct sites. To add to their problems, many of the duplex drive tanks were flooded and sank before reaching the shore, for they were not designed to survive such a long journey in heavy seas. At the eastern end of "Omaha" a total of 32 tanks launched into the sea, of which only two reached the beach under their own power and three were landed from an LCT whose commander had enough initiative to disobey orders by beaching his vessel. Some of the DUKWs, the amphibious trucks, were overloaded with supplies, sinking soon after they were launched into the water[8]

The Americans also landed with no flame-throwing tanks and in lieu of flail tanks they preferred bulldozers.[9] The choice was not a good one; on the right of "Utah" Beach, 16 bulldozers were landed, but only two were ultimately serviceable. High losses in equipment were matched by human casualties. On "Omaha" Beach alone the Americans suffered over 3,000 dead, wounded and missing. Overall, progress on the American beaches was below expectation and most of their losses were due to faults of the general staff. By the end of D-Day, the British and Canadians outnumbered the Americans and had incurred 5.6% casualties based on their numbers; the Americans had lost 10.4% of their total.

Because of what he felt was a dangerous situation, Bradley requested permission from Montgomery to use the British beaches to land men and supplies to reinforce "Omaha"; his request was justifiably refused. It would only have resulted in chaotic supply lines and benefited neither the Americans nor the British. It is surprising Bradley ever made such a request, for his common sense and military training should have told him what the inevitable results would have been. However, his forces corrected their situation and the full use of "Omaha" was eventually restored. Bradley had a short memory, for it was in Sicily that the Allies learned of the dangers of trying to pass men of one unit through the assault area of another.

9

Caen and Operations Goodwood and Cobra

The initial plan regarding Caen has been the subject of much discussion, and there are many who argue that it was originally intended to take the town within 24 hours of landing, a fact not denied by Montgomery. The difference of opinion arose when Montgomery realized the German defenses in the area were stronger than anticipated; he therefore modified his plan. This display of flexibility did not appeal to his detractors who attributed this change to failure. In fact, by holding on to Caen so tenaciously, the Germans eventually contributed to their own defeat and it was certainly not the first time that a general has been compelled to make alterations to his original ideas. Despite the fact that Bradley, at the time, felt the change of plan regarding Caen troublesome (throughout the war he rarely agreed with Montgomery) the idea was not new, and it was quite logical in view of the heavy concentration of enemy armor around the area. Indeed, Bradley, no admirer of Montgomery, afterward considered the Caen strategy to have been "brilliant"; he believed Montgomery's success should have been measured by the number of tank divisions the Germans had moved into position against him, enabling the Americans to mount their successful offensive to take Cherbourg. Contributing to Montgomery's success was the German belief it was the 21st Army Group which was to break out from Normandy and head for Paris—another reason for the increased amount of armor the Germans assembled against the British and Canadians.

Eisenhower created unnecessary difficulties for himself by showing little understanding of the very plan he had approved. Part of the problem may have been because Montgomery felt no need to explain to him what he felt was a simple strategic decision, but Eisenhower certainly made no attempt to find out what the motive was for Montgomery's actions.

Chapter 9—Caen and Operations Goodwood and Cobra

Indeed, Eisenhower's general concept of success was one measured by the amount of territory captured and subtlety was not one of his professional attributes. As a result, he reported to the Combined Chiefs of Staff on 3 July 1944 that his forces had been unable to break out in the east in the direction of the Seine; Bradley followed suit, no doubt not wishing to appear at odds with his commanding officer, contending with an army of 83,000 British and Canadians, Montgomery should have been able to defeat 15,000 Germans and accused the 21st Army Group of failing to take the initiative.

Four days later, Eisenhower wrote to Montgomery asserting that, together with his G-2 and Air Commander, he had studied the situation on the 21st Army Group's front. He warned that the limits of the build-up capabilities had almost been reached, and the enemy reinforcements were being sent to oppose the invasion. He continued by stating it was essential to obtain more room for maneuvering before the Germans were able to reach parity with the Allies, in order to protect "Sword" Beach from attacks. Airfields were needed as well as some small ports in Brittany. This fourth paragraph of his message stated he was fully conversant with Montgomery's objectives, an assurance which must be doubted in view of his later remarks. His message showed indisputably that he was ignorant of the fact that in order to create reinforcements Hitler had to strip units of men and reduce the size of a division, while at the same time he was refusing to move any forces from his 15th Army in the Pas de Calais region.

The Germans were now short of fuel by about 200,000 gallons a day and, due to lack of transporters and the heavy damage to the rail system, their tanks had to be moved to the front on their own tracks, resulting in a loss of efficiency, for this armor had then to be serviced in forward workshops before it could be committed to battle. These tanks used about three gallons of fuel per mile, which was a contributing reason for the gasoline shortage.

The Supreme Commander also showed little appreciation of the effect the bombing and Maquis interference had had on the rail system. Prisoners revealed that to travel from the Russian front to Germany's western border took five days, but from there to Normandy it took two weeks.[1] To add to the enemy's problems, in addition to fuel, the Luftwaffe was very short of spare parts. As a result, the number of planes it could put into the air at any one time was very limited.

For all Eisenhower's caviling, Montgomery's plan did succeed in disrupting the Germans, for they found it nearly impossible to rotate their troops to rest areas, and once a unit had been committed to action it was extremely difficult for the commander to create reserves. Had the 21st Army Group taken Caen earlier, the Germans would then have had no reason to commit their armored forces piecemeal to defend the town. That in turn would have had an adverse effect on the other end of the front and the Americans would undoubtedly have had a much more difficult task in their attempt to break loose. By his actions, Montgomery was keeping his opponent off balance. Eisenhower certainly ought to have understood the Caen strategy for he was present at the final meeting in St. Paul's School on 15 May 1944.

The object of the revised plan was to hold the Germans at Caen and bring onto that front as many enemy tanks as possible, relieving the pressure on the American front and allowing Bradley to fight southward to the Periers-St. Lô road, where his tanks could then prepare for the breakthrough. Apart from the consideration of the different topography on the British front as compared with that of the American front, the British Second Army was stronger in armor than was the U.S. First Army and this was therefore a logical decision. Eisenhower, post-war, stated he had hoped both surprise and speed would have resulted in the early fall of Caen, contradicting a statement he made toward the end of August 1944 when in London to give a press conference at the Ministry of Information, where he said the stand made by the Germans at Caen was a last-ditch effort and the British should be boasting about what they had achieved there, for the German determination to hold Caen against repeated British attacks had resulted in helping the Americans to break out from western France. Eisenhower's hope for speed and surprise from the British was just a little one-sided, for after he assumed command of the Allied armies in September 1944 these were the two elements which were conspicuously missing from his strategy.

Caen was important to both sides, for it was the junction of road and rail in the Cotentin area. Its value to the Allies was fully appreciated by Montgomery, who issued a directive to his troops on 18 June stating the Second Army must capture it and the Americans must take Cherbourg. The key to Cherbourg was Caen and he went on to state he expected both to be captured by 24 June. Not only was Caen vital to the army, but the R.A.F. felt it was imperative that suitable landing sites be taken in order to facilitate the provision of air cover for the ground forces; however, Montgomery correctly decided the capture of ports was more important than the capture of airfields, for the air force was strong enough to control the Luftwaffe without the immediate need of local landing facilities. Gen. Freddie de Guingand warned the air force that even should such sites be taken it would be a while before they could be made secure, especially from long-range artillery fire.

Chapter 9—Caen and Operations Goodwood and Cobra 85

Despite the grumbles of the air chiefs that the army was dilatory in capturing satisfactory landing fields, the air force was still able to do outstanding work. Such was the strength of the Allied fighter and fighter-bomber forces that the Germans in Normandy had great difficulty in bringing up reinforcements. By 18 June the enemy had lost about 26,000 men and replacements had to be sent to the front by side roads, frequently by night, in order to avoid attacks from the Allied aircraft. The men of one unit were sent into action immediately upon arrival at the front, having just cycled 65 miles from their base.[2]

Caen was eventually entered on 9 July by British and Canadians, on the heels of the Germans who had to withdraw in contravention of Hitler's orders. The town had been obliterated by both heavy bombing and shelling; it had cost the 21st Army Group more casualties than had been projected it would lose for the balance of hostilities. The heavy bombing did very little damage to enemy forces, for the only German troops in Caen were those of the 12th SS Panzer Grenadier Division in the north of the town, all other units having been withdrawn to the outskirts.

With the fall of Caen, Eisenhower again demonstrated his failings. He wrote the town had not been taken in the initial British rush as had been expected, resulting in the Allies being denied the use of the ground to the south and southeast of the town, areas strongly held by the Germans. Displaying inexcusable ignorance, Eisenhower failed to understand what the 21st Army Group had accomplished. Rommel committed to action his last reserves of armor, and had been forced to withdraw from the American front two brigades of multiple mortars. Fearing an invasion in the Pas de Calais area, Hitler had kept his 15th Army, amounting to 250,000 men, north of the Seine; Rommel was therefore compelled to make do with inadequate forces. The 15th Army was only 100 miles away and contained infantry units of far higher quality than were available to Rome. This, combined with Montgomery's strategy, resulted in Bradley's forces being given the ability to break out from Brittany.

Following the clearance of the Germans from Caen's suburbs, there began a new offensive on 18 July, code-named "Goodwood," and it was directed toward the southeast, while the Americans concentrated their efforts to capture St-Lô Montgomery was forced to act quickly as a result of Bradley's delayed offensive and the Germans moving into the line three infantry divisions in the hope of being able to withdraw the 1st SS, 2nd Lehr and 21st Panzer Divisions, which they intended to switch to the American front. A week of heavy rain hampered road transportation and limited the ability to supply by air. The Canadian First Army began its attack on 23 July along a front which extended from Caen along the road to Falaise, but the Germans countered with heavy fire and Montgomery stopped the assault after his infantry had suffered heavily. It was not only the infantry who suffered for the Germans showed their superiority in both armor and antitank guns, knocking out 413 British tanks while losing a little more than one-third of that total themselves. Only one out of four of the British tanks was armed with the superior 17-pounder gun, the remainder mounted the ineffective 75 mm. It was the unexpectedly determined opposition which led Montgomery to amend his plans and it must be noted in this offensive he did not adhere to his belief, for the tanks were used to lead the assault instead of supporting the infantry.

With the cessation of Operation "Goodwood," it was decided to concentrate on holding down as large a German force as possible to assist the Americans in their break-out attempt. The Germans, however, thinking "Goodwood" was the main effort and "Cobra" (the break-out operation mounted on 25 July) a diversion, did not transfer any armor; they counterattacked with forces which included three divisions which had been intended for the American sector. The enemy's reaction clearly indicated Montgomery's plan of deception was working, for all Eisenhower's reservations; but Eisenhower was not alone in thinking "Goodwood" was a failure or that it was deliberately mounted by Montgomery to demonstrate the superiority of the 21st Army Group over the 12th Army Group, as some Americans believed, although not Bradley.

In reality, "Goodwood" was both a success and a failure for, while it did not achieve its tactical objectives, it did prevent the Germans from withdrawing both men and armor to create a reserve. Had they been able to do so, there is no doubt Bradley's offensive at St-Lô, which opened a week after "Goodwood," would have miscarried or at least have encountered much stiffer opposition.

Eisenhower and SHAEF staff failed to interpret the results of "Goodwood" correctly and also failed to interpret the "Ultra" signals correctly; they therefore consigned "Cobra" to a premature failure. Despite these difficulties, the efforts of the British and Canadians at Caen did have beneficial effects, even though unappreciated by Eisenhower. The operation ended with part of the Bourgébus Ridge occupied, all of Caen in Allied hands and the 21st Army Group controlling the rivers Odon and Orne. "Goodwood" had succeeded in wearing down the enemy reserves and the number of German tanks on the 21st Army Group's front was 500 on 15 June, as opposed to a mere 70 deployed against the U.S. First Army. Little more than a month later, on 25 July, the enemy fielded 645 tanks against the British and Canadians compared with 190 on the U.S. front; in addi-

Chapter 9—Caen and Operations Goodwood and Cobra 87

tion, most of the German 88 mm guns were opposing the 21st Army Group.

Between 15 June and 25 July, the Germans had reinforced their infantry opposite the Americans from 63 to 85 battalions and from 43 to 92 battalions against the 21st Army Group, an increase of nearly 114% on Montgomery's front as opposed to a moderate 35% gain on the U.S. front. Such was Eisenhower's lack of comprehension that these statistics were simply not understood. On 7 July he wrote to Montgomery stressing the need for a determined effort against the enemy, pointing out Bradley had not had a great deal of success on the western flank and what was needed now was a "major full-dress attack" by the British which would be given priority over supplies.

Eisenhower cannot be excused for failing to grasp what was happening at Caen. If Montgomery's plan was too complex for him, he should have visited his deputy in order to be given a detailed explanation. He was still headquartered in England and could have had no clear idea of either the detailed progress of the battle or of Montgomery's plan. Not for the first time and not for the last, he was trying to conduct operations from a distance. While Eisenhower failed to appreciate fully the significance of the events which took place at Caen, the radio correspondents definitely comprehended what Montgomery was doing. In a report to London on 29 July, CBC's Bill Downs gave a lucid description of what had led the Germans to believe that the attack, following the fall of Cherbourg, would be on the British front. He made the point that by a series of Allied assaults in the general area of Caen, the Germans had been duped into concentrating their strength in this sector when, in fact, the main blow was to be launched by the Americans. He ended his report by stressing that Rommel was compelled to fight the battle the way the Allies wanted him to ... exactly what Montgomery intended and what Eisenhower failed to understand.

After "Goodwood," the antipathy toward Montgomery increased and on 23 July, Sir Arthur Tedder, who appeared to think he was a better soldier than Montgomery, wrote to Eisenhower expressing the opinion that the situation around Caen was the cause for concern. He urged the Supreme Commander to move to Normandy and there set up his tactical headquarters as quickly as possible and then assume command of the ground forces.[3] Such an unwarranted interference on Tedder's part demonstrated how little he understood the presentation of the plans given by Montgomery in May of that year.

It was not the first time he had criticized Montgomery's handling of the Normandy battle. At a meeting on 14 June he had said the situation had the makings of a crisis, and his only attempt to substantiate this gross exaggeration was to point out that Caen had not yet been taken. If he thought the delay in capturing that town also delayed air operations he was mistaken. The taking of secure landing sites would certainly have been useful, but not a necessity.

Some of the reasons for which Montgomery was censured after halting "Goodwood" were of his own doing. He had requested Eisenhower to provide maximum air support for the operation. Due to rare imprecise phrasing, Eisenhower assumed that "Goodwood" was also to be a major offensive. He wrote to Montgomery in flowery terms on 13 July 1944, referring to the VIII Corps' "plunging into the enemy vitals" and expressing the opinion that he would not be surprised if this offensive made some of history's great battles look like a "skirmish between patrols." [4] This was a plain indication he had failed to understand the object of the attack and addition he showed his lack of clear recognition of the overall strategy, for if "Goodwood" were to have been the main assault in conjunction with a secondary American operation, then it would have negated the plan for the creation of the Falaise Pocket.

Montgomery did not correct Eisenhower's error, fearing it would result in the curtailment of his requested air support. The fact that there was no intention of breaking out from Caen is supported by a personal note he wrote to Gen. Sir Richard O'Connor, former commander of the Eighth Army and in July 1944 commander of the British VIII Corps. O'Connor was instructed to wear down the enemy armor and to expand the bridgehead to the east of the Orne River. Montgomery specifically stated there was to be no advance beyond the Bourgébus Ridge and in the event of an enemy withdrawal O'Connor was to follow up with patrols only.

Despite his clumsiness in handling the controversy, Montgomery had attempted to delay the release of the report on "Goodwood," but the public relations section of SHAEF was not helpful and the press was given the impression the operation would achieve far greater results than was ever intended.

Operation "Goodwood" was followed by Operation "Cobra," planned by Montgomery and launched on 25 July after a week's delay due to adverse weather. Some of the worst storms in many years were responsible for destroying the Mulberry harbor in the U.S. sector. These harbors, a British invention, were towed in sections across the Channel where they were assembled on site. They proved a great asset, for in a little more than the first three months of the invasion from them were landed 17,000 tons of supplies, 2 million men, and 500,000 vehicles of all descriptions were

Chapter 9—Caen and Operations Goodwood and Cobra   89

landed from them; however, with the loss of the American Mulberry, Bradley's army group had to ration ammunition and fuel and the necessary build-up of supplies was delayed seven days.

This Mulberry being out of action was due to the Americans having been less successful in anchoring it than the British had been with theirs; the British took longer to get their harbor into full use, but despite it being subjected to the same intense storm during the period 19 to 22 June, it was still serviceable thereafter.

The day "Cobra" was launched, Eisenhower visited the front, exhorting his commanders to take aggressive action. His headquarters were still in England and he was thus in much the same situation in relation to the fighting in Europe as Fredendall had been to the fighting in Tunisia, yet Eisenhower had objected to Fredendall being so far removed from the front line. Operation "Cobra" succeeded, despite the supply shortage, mainly because Bradley, upon Montgomery's suggestion, concentrated his forces, but even though this was a success there were some Americans who were unwilling to acknowledge it as such.

Montgomery's policy at Caen achieved its goals by keeping the enemy occupied in that area, while the main offensive was mounted by Bradley. The German Seventh Army had most of its tanks already committed and could field only half a Panzer division, so there were none available as reinforcements, while Panzer Group West was too far to the rear to be of any assistance, since Allied air forces controlled the road and rail systems making any movement by these tanks difficult if not impossible.

The Supreme Commander and the Prime Minister had lunch together on 26 July. Eisenhower told Churchill he was concerned the entire front was not in action and the U.S. press would see Caen as an attempt by the British to leave the fighting to the Americans. He apparently little realized if the American news media had that impression it could only have been as a result of faulty work by Supreme Headquarters' public relations staff. He went so far as to allege the British were not doing their share of the fighting, quoting comparative casualty figures in an attempt to support his accusation, forgetting the mathematical rule which states there are lies, damned lies and statistics. The following day Churchill again met Eisenhower and others, and the discussion continued. Eisenhower once more emphasized his disappointment at the entire front not being in action. It was pointed out to him he was in essence criticizing the very strategy he had approved. He sidestepped that rebuttal by enquiring why it was not possible to attack all along the line, just as the Russians were doing in the East. He was told the Russians had a 300% numerical superiority over the Germans, compared with the Western Allies' 25% superiority, and the enemy density on the Western Front was 25% greater than on the Eastern Front.[5]

These figures, since they were obviously of military significance, should have been known to him before he passed judgment on Montgomery. Furthermore, Eisenhower showed ignorance of the fact that Germany fielded 133 divisions against the Western Allies, only 32 fewer than against the Russians. Had he kept himself better informed of the disposition of Hitler's armies he might have appreciated that the forces under his command were doing a commendable job by engaging nearly 45% of the German active army.

Apparently unable to comprehend the predicament he had created for himself, on the evening of 26 July Eisenhower wrote to Montgomery to assure him Churchill knew that Montgomery understood the need to "keep the front aflame" while the main offensive was in progress.[1] It is fair to say Montgomery understood nothing of the sort. Eisenhower was exaggerating Churchill's opinion; furthermore he was essentially contradicting his prior approval of Montgomery's strategy. Eventually he was told if he had any complaints about Montgomery's conduct of operations he should confront the ground commander with details, which was the correct procedure to follow from the beginning. This suggestion was declined, thus reinforcing the suspicion Eisenhower had no clear understanding of the very plans he had endorsed. Certainly he gave the impression he did not understand the Caen strategy and his accusation that the British and Canadians, on the basis of casualties, were not doing as much as the Americans, was both insulting and unfounded. Why Eisenhower equated high casualties with success he did not explain, and his lack of experience in the First World War was patent. Nevertheless, his arithmetic was as weak as his knowledge of warfare, for by the end of the battle of Normandy the 21st Army Group provided 43% of the total Allied armies and had incurred 40% of all casualties. Broken down to a national level, up to 11 August, the 21st Army Group had suffered an average of 4,250 casualties per division since D-Day, compared to U.S. casualties of 8,500 per division for the same period. If Eisenhower was willing to accept heavy losses by attacking all along the line Montgomery was not, for he had clear memories of the slaughter which had been all too prevalent during the previous world war. As a result of Eisenhower's complaints, Brooke ordered Montgomery to instruct Gen. Miles Dempsey, commander of the British Second Army, to mount an offensive on as large a scale as possible; the Germans were to be prevented from moving troops onto Bradley's front. Dempsey was to attack without regard to casualties and his immediate objective was the capture of Vire.

Chapter 9—Caen and Operations Goodwood and Cobra

The offensive achieved Montgomery's purposes, for the enemy suffered heavy losses in armor and the 2nd Panzer Division especially took a heavy pounding. This was in accordance with Montgomery's approach, set out in a letter to Eisenhower, in which he stated he was quite satisfied to see Rommel using his strategic reserve to plug holes in the line. Eisenhower could never understand the simplicity and effectiveness of this plan. However, Montgomery made a serious error of judgment.

In the middle of the battle he changed army boundaries, taking away the town of Vire from the British sector and giving it to the Americans. He can have had no idea that on 2 August tanks of the 11th Armoured Division were in Vire following up a retreating enemy. They were forced to withdraw to comply with Army Group instructions, resulting in the Americans taking four more days and using five divisions to clear the town, which in the interim had been reinforced. It also cost them 3,000 casualties. Had Vire remained within the 21st Army Group's boundary there is every possibility it could have been taken quite easily and its capture would have posed a threat of encirclement to the German army.

While Montgomery produced satisfactory results from the operations around Caen, the same cannot be said of Bradley's misguided determination to capture the ports of Brest and Lorient. He showed he was quite incapable of arriving at a balanced decision, for he gave priority to the capture of these Atlantic ports giving no consideration to the fact they were now of diminished value to the Allies. Montgomery did not approve of the diversion of men and materiel from the main fighting, believing it could only result in delaying the advance eastward; Patton was of limited help, for he detached only one corps for the attack on these ports and on 6 August 1944 announced Brest had been taken, basing his statement solely on the erroneous report of a solitary tank commander. It was 19 September before Brest was finally captured, and the delay was due partly to the Americans stopping to mop up a pocket of bypassed Germans, which gave the defenders of the port time to organize their defenses. Patton played into enemy hands by keeping the 4th Armored Division in the area of Lorient, which served no obvious purpose. He made no better use of this division when he later committed it to the attack on Brest, Lorient and Vannes. If the Americans were deceived into believing the Brittany ports were vital, Montgomery was not, for it was he who prevented the U.S. from reinforcing the sector. During the period that Cherbourg was being attacked by the Americans, the Germans, in anticipation of a landing which never materialized, were still holding more divisions between the Scheldt and the Seine than were committed to battle in Normandy. For this the Allies must thank their program of deception and Hitler's intuition.

10

The Campaign Following Caen

Once Cherbourg was occupied a combined force of British and Americans set to work to clear the harbor and repair installations damaged by German demolitions. The task was completed 21 days after the garrison surrendered, and by November the facilities were handling 15,000 tons per day, enough to supply the equivalent of about 20 divisions. After the Cotentin Peninsula was cleared, the U.S. armies then swung around the German left flank and rear, setting the stage for the Falaise Pocket. The Brittany peninsula was cleared of the enemy in August, with the exceptions of the ports of St-Malo, Lorient, and St-Nazaire.

Patton had been given command of an army and was in the open country, well suited for tank warfare. The Canadians had attacked toward Falaise, found themselves opposed by strong Panzer formations and incurred 1,000 casualties. Their action achieved its goal of again preventing the Germans from moving forces to the American front. For all the Supreme Commander's carping on the subject of Caen, Montgomery never complained about Bradley's tardiness in seizing Cherbourg, which had been scheduled to be taken 10–30 days after D-Day. In the event, the Americans were about three months behind expectations.

Although tactically the 21st Army Group failed to achieve its objectives, Montgomery had managed to deceive the enemy, for Field Marshal Guenther von Kluge thought that after Goodwood the main attack would come from Caen. Montgomery disagreed with Eisenhower that he should always attack. On the contrary, he stuck to his plan of holding the enemy at Caen, thereby helping Bradley to swing around from Brittany to Paris. Churchill believed Eisenhower fully understood the British objective of providing a pivot for the U.S. armies to hinge on in their advance to the Seine; however, Eisenhower's ambivalence was clearly demonstrated, for

Chapter 10—The Campaign Following Caen

having complained about Montgomery's slow progress in Normandy, in his official report he praised the British achievements at Caen. Tedder, leader of the anti-Montgomery faction in SHAEF, felt Montgomery should be relieved of his command and reportedly offered, rather pompously, to intervene with Churchill on Eisenhower's behalf.[1] Before the crisis reached a climax, Bradley broke free and headed for Paris. The American contribution to "Cobra" was originally planned for 30 June, but was rescheduled by Bradley to begin 3 July. He assembled a large force, consisting of three divisions plus the U.S. 82nd Airborne, all of which was opposed by three understrength German divisions. The American forces, under the command of Troy Middleton's VIII Corps, were confident they could advance at the rate of 20 miles per day against slight opposition. There were optimistic reports from the U.S. intelligence services concerning the poor state of preparedness of the German infantry and these evaluations proved quite correct.

The Germans had suffered heavily in previous fighting, their divisions consisting largely of mauled units, and their situation was not helped by them receiving insufficient replacements for their casualties—only 17 tanks for 225 destroyed by Allied action. In spite of these disadvantages they fought stubbornly and retreated slowly, inflicting heavy casualties on Middleton's men, the 82nd Airborne suffering so badly it was withdrawn from the front line and sent to England to rest and refit.

Notwithstanding the initial expectations, Middleton's corps had managed to advance only four miles in five days with the loss of over 2,000 men, and in the first three days of the offensive had captured fewer than 600 prisoners. Success did come on other parts of the front. Due to lack of reserves, the enemy was unable to stop the American advance to the river Vire, which they crossed, then continued toward St-Lô. Bradley was too concerned with the kudos he felt was associated with the capture of the town to realize his preoccupation was hindering the general advance. Once outside St-Lô, he spent needless time and lives in an attempt to take a town which was of limited value; he would have done better to have bypassed it to continue his southward advance, as the Germans had expected him to do. When the town was eventually entered on 19 July, it was found to be nothing but a mass of rubble, the result of the heavy shelling and bombing. The cost of capturing it was not cheap, for more than 5,000 Americans were casualties after six days of fighting; within the first 16 days of the offensive, the 12th Army Group had lost 40,000 men, killed, wounded, missing and prisoner, and Bradley was still not out of the bocage and into the open country.

In conjunction with the 21st Army Group's offensive, Eisenhower urged Bradley to mount a large-scale attack, but due to bad weather the assault was delayed until 25 July and its start was then supported by an attack of fighter-bombers, followed by a very heavy artillery bombardment; three days later Coutance fell to the Americans.

It was decided on 28 July that the U.S. Third Army under Patton would become operational on 1 August, and in the meantime Middleton's VIII Corps was given instructions to take Brittany. The command organization, even though in existence for only a few days, was far from efficient. Patton commanded the Third Army, which was not yet operational. He was Deputy Commander of the First Army over which he was given no control whatsoever. He did have tacit control over the VIII Corps, but its actual commander was Troy Middleton.[2] Patton's immediate objective was the capture of Avranches, which controlled the road and rail communications between Normandy and Brittany. A supporting attack opened on 25 July and was part of Operation "Cobra." The Canadian II Corps went on the offensive against the Falaise road, but the Germans had prepared their defenses in depth, and the attack was halted on the night of 25/26 July. Nevertheless, it had succeeded in keeping the German armor concentrated at Caen, in accordance with Montgomery's plans. Montgomery regrouped, and sent six divisions to attack the area between Torigny and Caumont, while the Canadians and the balance of the British Second Army maintained pressure on the remainder of the front in order to keep the enemy occupied. On 30 July, the XXX Corps opened its attack at 6:00 A.M., moving toward Villers-Bocage along the Avranches-Caen road. Commencing its attack an hour later, the VII Corps, on Lt. Gen. Brian Horrocks' right, advanced along the same road but went as far as Le Beny Bocage. In the meantime, Patton was advancing, together with other units of the U.S. First Army, causing Field Marshal von Kluge to write to Hitler expressing his doubts that the Americans could be stopped. His assessment, disbelieved by the Fuehrer, was ultimately proved to be correct.

The Germans began an offensive on 7 August in the area of Mortain, and it was one of Hitler's inspirations. Looking at a map showing the relative positions of the opposing armies, the Germans appeared to have a salient established deep into the Allied front; in fact it was the stronger Allies who had advanced on either side of a weaker enemy leaving him in danger of being encircled. Perhaps this mistaken interpretation stimulated Hitler to order the attack which was intended to break through the American defenses, reach the Atlantic coast, isolate the Cotentin Peninsula, and divide the U.S. forces north and south of Avranches. In the process, Hitler hoped to impose crippling losses on the Allies, especially upon the Americans.

Chapter 10—The Campaign Following Caen

If Hitler ever possessed intuition, this was not one of the better examples of his fertile imagination. The Luftwaffe committed 300 fighters to this folly to provide cover for the ground forces, but within two days it had lost 190 planes.

Unluckily for the Germans, their plans were soon known through "Ultra" decrypts, and by the end of the first day of the assault they were defeated. What was, up to then, the largest tank battle of the Western Front was successfully concluded with the assistance of R.A.F. rocket-firing Typhoons. Fighter-bombers very effectively attacked German reinforcements being sent to the front, with one unit losing 30% of its men and equipment, and these attacks succeeded in delaying the arrival of fresh troops. The intervention of the air force, and the effectiveness of Montgomery's Caen strategy, resulted in the Germans being unable to disengage five Panzer divisions, which were to have been transferred to the American front.

Only one Panzer division could move and only four out of an anticipated eight armored divisions were able to go into action against the Americans, and these four could muster a mere 250 tanks.[3] With an absence of gratitude, the Americans publicized the battle of Mortain as a purely American victory; their military believed that the U.S. public needed a boost to its morale. Apart from the assistance of the R.A.F., the Guards Armoured Division and 11th Armoured Division, from the 21st Army Group, were in action against the German flank southeast of St-Lô and as a result the Germans lost very many tanks.[4] The Allied drive for Falaise continued.

One consequence of the offensive was that the Germans had their left flank unprotected, and Bradley decided that the enemy position was ripe for encirclement. He telephoned Montgomery to obtain approval for this, and the British commander agreed to it and gave orders for all armies to conform to Bradley's plan, the outline of which was Haislip's XV Corps, coming from the south, was to link up with the 21st Army Group from the north. During this Allied advance, Montgomery imposed a surprising prohibition on R.A.F. bombing of the retreating Germans. Just three miles north of Argentan, the road to Falaise was blocked by a variety of enemy equipment and men. Because the Allied air forces had earlier inflicted losses on the Canadians and Poles due to inaccurate bombing, no air attacks on these targets were allowed, and it seems strange that rocket-firing Typhoons and fighter-bombers were forbidden to go after such a prize. The risk of making an error is always present. Nevertheless, there is a distinct possibility that had this Canadian attack shown signs of success, the German commander, von Kluge, would have immediately withdrawn from the Pocket, with the result that when the gap was finally closed enemy casualties would have been much lower and fewer prisoners would have been taken.

The Falaise Gap was closed with the capture of 50,000 Germans and the burial of about 10,000, although the exact total of German dead is not known. In addition, a great deal of equipment was destroyed or fell into Allied hands. The Germans estimated that 20–40,000 of their men escaped, but even if this estimate is accurate, after Falaise the number of men in each division of German Army Group "B" was reduced to one-third, and the number of tanks per division to about one-half.

With the Falaise Pocket now sealed, Bradley permitted himself to be persuaded by Patton to amend his plans. Without consulting Montgomery, he moved two divisions and 15 artillery battalions from the XV Corps to try another encirclement in the area of the Seine and, by weakening the lower jaw of the Falaise trap, the closing of it was not entirely a success; the attempt at the larger encirclement failed. Had Bradley been a little more astute he could have made better use of a captured Seine bridge, just 36 miles west of Paris. With proper planning and execution he could have cut off more than 20,000 Germans (some estimates go as high as 50,000) retreating from the Falaise Gap. However, Bradley was ill-served by an air force which had not fully learned the benefits of tactical ground support, and he was misled by his own intelligence reports. These stated most of the Seventh and Fifteenth Panzer Armies had already escaped from Falaise, thus giving some reason for the XV Corps' move. Another factor to be considered in assessing the failure to finish the encirclement of the Germans at Falaise was the extremely strong enemy resistance; they were well aware that by holding the mouth of the Gap open they would be maintaining their own escape route. Bradley ought to have informed Montgomery before ordering Patton to advance to the Seine. By his actions he displayed inexcusable impatience, and a lack of discipline and co-operation. From the time he was elevated to command the U.S. 12th Army Group he showed reluctance to co-ordinate his moves with those of Montgomery, a weakness well illustrated by his behavior at Falaise, for Montgomery had agreed to attempt the encirclement, subject to Patton's advance being temporarily halted. With the absence of the Americans in sufficient strength, it was impossible for the British and Canadians to close the Gap alone, and the entrapment of the enemy was therefore delayed and not as successful as it might have been.

Patton believed Montgomery wanted all the honor by claiming victory for the 21st Army Group. Since this proved impossible, he halted Patton at Argentan, thereby preventing the U.S. Third Army from achieving

Chapter 10—The Campaign Following Caen

Patton, Bradley, Hodges during conference with Eisenhower in Germany, March 1945. U.S. Army photograph. (Courtesy Dwight D. Eisenhower Library.)

success. It was an opinion written several days after the halt, and although it shows a streak of paranoia, it is reasonable to assume Patton was trying to relieve his frustration at having been stopped so near to success. To believe his assessment one must believe Montgomery, besides suffering from a strong attack of xenophobia, would have deliberately exposed himself to virulent criticism and a severe reproof at the very least from Alan Brooke, the Chief of the Imperial General Staff, as well as from Churchill, for the decision would not only have risked increased casualties for the Allies, it would have intentionally delayed the end of the war which, quite obviously, would have been unacceptable to the British. Such a conclusion presumes Montgomery acted like a spoiled child when it came to military matters. For all his faults, he was a perfectionist and it is most unlikely he would have intentionally lost an opportunity for victory, even had the victors under his command not been British. In support of the contention he had nothing to do with the halt at Argentan, in addition to Bradley's own admission, Horrocks has stated unequivocally it was on 13 August that Bradley gave Patton orders to stop the XV Corps.

There is one explanation for the apparent slowness of the 21st Army

Group by comparison with the Americans. The British and Canadians were still fighting an organized enemy, whereas the Americans had broken through the German defenses and the enemy on their front was retreating in some disarray. The Poles of the Canadian First Army were very eager to get into battle, too eager as it transpired, for their tank crews could not wait to refuel and take on fresh supplies of ammunition. There was also the tendency for the Canadians to attack in unconnected assaults, which frequently failed to achieve results. There is yet another factor which cannot be ignored. On 13 August 1944 a Canadian officer drove through the German lines, having lost his way, and was killed by enemy fire. On his body was found the full plan to close the Falaise Gap. As a result of this information the enemy was able to reinforce his position.

Following Falaise, one important difference between Bradley and Montgomery was made clear. Bradley declared the German army on the Western Front had been reduced to a corporal's guard, and estimated in the area north of the Ardennes there were only eleven German divisions. With regard to the number of divisions, he appears to have been accurate, but those Germans who managed to escape from the Falaise trap to the Seine arrived with only their rifles. Five of these divisions were returned to Germany to refit; eleven others, which had been badly mauled, were barely enough to create four re-formed units each with very little supporting artillery.[5] The result was the Germans had eleven brigades, none with more than ten operating tanks and with only a few artillery pieces. Bradley was so optimistic he was already planning an army of occupation.

Montgomery, by contrast, was not so sanguine and he began to look to the future. Eight days before the fall of Paris, on 17 August, he flew to Bradley's headquarters north of Fougéres and proposed a plan which would essentially keep the 21st Army Group and the 12th Army Group together as a 40 division force and be used to launch an offensive in a northeasterly direction. The plan called for the 21st Army Group on the west flank to clear the Pas de Calais area, West Flanders, then take Brussels, Antwerp and the south of Holland, while the 12th Army Group was to be on the eastern flank of the advance and move toward Aachen and Cologne with its right flank on the Ardennes. The entire operation was to pivot on Paris, with a powerful holding force provided by the 12th Army Group to be located in the area of Orléans-Troyes-Châlons-Rheims, having its right flank spread out along the River Loire at Nantes. Should the enemy attempt a strong counteroffensive, this force would be in an excellent position to strike back. The Franco-American 6th Army Group, coming from the south, was to move northeast to the Saar, but the 12th Army Group was not to stretch itself in order to meet the approach of Devers' forces. The

Chapter 10 — The Campaign Following Caen

Northern Germany, Holland and northeastern Belgium.

objects of the proposed offensive were the destruction of the German Fifteenth Army, clearing Belgium of the enemy, the capture of the deep-sea port of Antwerp, the destruction of the V-1 and V-2 launch sites and the establishment of bridgeheads over the Rhine, culminating in a drive for Berlin. All this was to be accomplished before the onset of bad weather. The plan was not original; it was the German Schlieffen Plan of 1914 in reverse.

Montgomery was under the impression Bradley had agreed to this proposal, but Bradley believed he had suggested a modification to the plan which was a double thrust mounted by the U.S. Third Army, reinforced by two corps from the U.S. First Army, and aimed at the Rhine; another corps from the U.S. First Army was to reinforce Montgomery's drive in the north. Bradley's idea would have achieved little except the weakening of the U.S. First Army, and his amendment of Montgomery's recommendation was evidently designed to ensure all the U.S. armies were in action at once. What would be accomplished seemed to be of secondary importance.

Eisenhower held a staff meeting on 20 August at which he announced he would take over direct command of the ground forces effective 1 September, 1944 — the worst of the many errors he made while in command of Allied troops during the war. This change was provoked by an incident which was given far more attention than it deserved. An aide on Eisenhower's staff, Capt. Harry Butcher (U.S.N.), believed there was a public misunderstanding with regard to the command organization; he therefore set about rectifying the misconception. At a press conference he announced Bradley and Montgomery were equals. Regrettably, the Royal Navy's maxim, "It is better to keep your mouth shut and be thought a fool than to open it and remove all doubt," had apparently not been adopted by the U.S. Navy and this statement created an uproar in the British press, which deplored the apparent demotion of Montgomery; the American press somehow found in it an implied criticism of Bradley and Eisenhower, all of which again showed how lax was Eisenhower's control over his subordinates in Supreme Headquarters. When Marshall heard of Butcher's gaffe he instructed Eisenhower to take full command of the ground forces in northern Europe, thereby giving substance to the old German saying that the further from the battle, the greater the general. For his indiscretion, Butcher was moved to London to become head of SHAEF's Public Relations Department, a seemingly inappropriate position if the error he made was as great as the press made it appear.

At this staff meeting Eisenhower also announced the 12th Army Group was to push toward the Saar and Metz in order to join the "Dragoon" forces, in direct contradiction to Montgomery's recommendation, who sent de Guingand to meet the Supreme Commander on 22 August and discuss the matter. De Guingand spent a couple of hours trying to obtain Eisenhower's approval for a concentrated attack in the north, with the purpose of establishing the Allied air forces in Belgium, and then to turn to the Ruhr. He stressed there must be a single commander for these operations. Despite all de Guingand's charm, Eisenhower could not be persuaded to change his mind, while with characteristic stubbornness Montgomery would not leave the subject alone; he invited Eisenhower to lunch with him at his headquarters in Condé-sur-Noireau. On the morning of 23

Chapter 10—The Campaign Following Caen

August, Montgomery went to visit Bradley at Laval, to discuss the matter further, and here he learned Bradley had changed his mind.

Upon his return to Condé for lunch, Montgomery, with great foresight, stressed in his discussion with Eisenhower that the available supplies were limited; it was therefore dangerous to stretch them in order to provide support for a wide front offensive. If Eisenhower insisted on this, Montgomery believed the attack would die out and the Germans would be given the opportunity to recover, resulting in the war continuing into the following year. He contended it was essential to appoint a single commander, subordinate to the Supreme Commander, and emphasized the success in Normandy was in large part due to just such an arrangement. Should the Americans be opposed to the appointment of himself as ground commander Montgomery stated he would willing serve under Bradley, which offer has been confirmed by de Guingand.

All this did was to provoke Eisenhower into denying he had any intentions of appointing a single ground commander. He agreed the 21st Army Group was not strong enough to carry out his intended assaults on the northern end of the line, so it would be given to the U.S. First Airborne Army assisted by the 12th Army Group. When he heard this, Montgomery informed the Supreme Commander he would need at least 12 U.S. divisions, but Eisenhower jibbed saying that if this were done then the U.S. public would object. Montgomery asked, quite reasonably, why the American public would be opposed to the making of a sound military decision, but he received no reply. His suggestion that Patton should be stopped, so that supplies could be diverted to the north, was also rejected.

The eventual agreement was while the 21st Army Group took the offensive in the north, Bradley would advance on Montgomery's right to support the 21st Army Group. It was also understood that Montgomery was to have authority to achieve co-ordination between the U.S. First Army and the 21st Army Group's right flank. One day later, Eisenhower wrote to confirm the understanding of the 23 August conference, sending a copy to Bradley. The message consisted of six paragraphs and repeated the instructions that Montgomery had received the previous day. The issuance of relevant instructions to army commanders was delayed five days; in the meantime, Eisenhower had changed his mind. Montgomery was given no control whatsoever over the U.S. First Army[6] and, prior to this, Eisenhower had written to Marshall to inform him he had decided for the time being that no transfer of American units would be made to help Montgomery.

At the same time that Eisenhower had promised Montgomery he would be given limited control over elements of the 12th Army Group,

SHAEF was planning to move some divisions from the U.S. First Army to assist the Third Army in its drive to the Saar and Rhine. It is hard to believe this move was made without the Supreme Commander's knowledge and at his instigation, leading to the conclusion that Eisenhower was deliberately deceiving Montgomery, although he may have meant only to placate all army commanders involved.

Why Eisenhower reversed himself is not known and, on the surface at least, his agreement to give Montgomery some control over U.S. units is even more of a mystery, for he was sufficiently upset with the British commander to write in his desk diary that Monty wanted everything, which was crazy. This was nothing but a gross distortion of the facts, for it was obvious that while Montgomery was logically stressing the need for a single ground commander, he showed a measure of altruism by volunteering to serve under Bradley. Nevertheless, not once did Montgomery offer to relinquish command of the 21st Army Group in exchange for command of the ground forces, and had Eisenhower agreed to appoint him Deputy Commander in charge of ground operations, he would have been in exactly the same situation which he found objectionable with regard to Eisenhower, namely he would have held two positions at the same time.

Eisenhower's refusal to yield control of the ground forces to a single commander revealed his desire for authority. Butcher on more than one occasion urged him to take over the ground forces, but each time Eisenhower contended that if he did so it would mean he would have to relinquish the position of Supreme Commander. The situation was changed by Marshall's directive, and the problem of command appeared to be less important once it was clear he could now hold two jobs, even though his qualifications and experience suited him for perhaps one but certainly not for the other.

With the implementation of this broad front offensive, the Supreme Commander demonstrated he had only one strategy in his inventory. At the same time he had overlooked, yet again, the very problem he knew existed, brought to his attention earlier by Montgomery, which was that of supplies. There was insufficient maintenance to support two concurrent offensives. It is astonishing that Eisenhower did not fully comprehend the problem of logistics and his actions gave all the appearance of one who was unwilling, or unable, to face reality. Having ordered the U.S. Third Army to go over to the offensive, he took no account of the fact Patton's fuel dumps by September were down to almost one-third of his minimum daily requirements. After Patton had given orders to move the XX Corps to Verdun, he went to visit Gen. Manton S. Eddy to discuss oper-

Chapter 10—The Campaign Following Caen

ations with him, and there received a message that the expected fuel ration of 140,000 gallons had not arrived. The Third Army was eventually so short of fuel it resorted to siphoning it from vehicles belonging to other units[7]; throughout this period of shortages Eisenhower made no attempt to solve the problem which his own actions had exacerbated.

The advance of the 21st Army Group along the north coast of France was done with greater alacrity than SHAEF had anticipated; as a result, on 4 September 1944, the decision was made that Patton's drive to the Saar need not be slowed down. So convinced was Eisenhower that Germany was conquered he wrote an unjustifiably optimistic memo on 5 September, stating that the enemy was completely defeated.[8]

An unexpected rising in Paris by the French resistance movement resulted in troops being sent to help the insurrection. It had not been intended to liberate the capital so early in the campaign, because that would have necessitated diverting supplies from the front line to feed the civilian population. The city was finally cleared of the enemy on 25 August, a little more than two months from the date of the Normandy invasion, and after the event, Eisenhower felt it would have been better to have left it entirely to the Free French to liberate. Perhaps overtaken by euphoria, Eisenhower attended a parade celebrating the capture of the city, but Montgomery felt it was no time for rejoicing and declined to participate. Between 23 August and 3 September, SHAEF intelligence reports were grossly optimistic, stating that the German army was no longer an integrated force and the enemy position had deteriorated to the point where it was beyond recovery. The reports stated that organized resistance after November was unlikely and the enemy might possibly surrender. Other reports forecast political disturbances within a period of two months following the invasion of Germany.

In a statement to the press delivered on 20 August 1944, Eisenhower, however, showed more caution than his G-2; he announced the Allied armies had advanced so rapidly a strain had been placed on the supply system; as a result, it would be nearly impossible for the armies under his command to attack even the weakest German unit. Here, finally, was an admission that he understood the immediate problem of logistics, but his appreciation lasted no more than 18 days and he had made no mention of the need to capture and utilize a large port. If Eisenhower showed little optimism he was in good company, for Patton's G-2, Col. Oscar W. Koch, was cautious in his assessment of the enemy's ability to resist. He correctly pointed out the German withdrawal from Normandy had not been a rout, and the Nazis appeared to be ready to make a last-ditch stand.

Following the fall of Paris and the reaching of the Seine, Eisenhower's strategy again showed its flaws. The original plan had been to pause once the bridgehead had been thoroughly established. Events had not followed expectations and the Germans, although not trounced, had been roughly handled and were retreating. Unfortunately, Eisenhower lacked the necessary imagination and strategic skill to appreciate that what was then needed was a continuation of pressure to be applied to the withdrawing enemy. Instead, he instituted the planned pause in his operations.

After its capture of Brussels, the 21st Army Group was halted. The reason given was lack of supplies, but Eisenhower had taken no account of the fact that the capital's airport could have been used to shuttle supplies from Britain to Belgium and that the main opposition, in the area of Brussels, was 719th Division, a "stomach" unit.[9] Eisenhower's indecisiveness was quite evident in his handling of the campaign from August onward. The capture of a large port was something the Supreme Commander had considered important. Following the loss of the Mulberry harbor on "Omaha" beach, he had wired a report to Marshall in which he stated the destruction of the harbor had resulted in a shortage of supplies, which in turn had impeded the rate of advance and had also revealed the need to capture a large port. Although he did not specify which port would satisfy requirements, it was obvious the first one to fit the description was Antwerp, and the armies in Europe were to suffer because of his lack of foresight.

Once again there was an absence of co-ordination between the Allied armies, a fault which must be attributed to Eisenhower's muddled concept of strategy. He wanted a major attack on the Ruhr but, with his illogical fixation for a broad front offensive, he also wanted a secondary assault to be mounted south of the Ardennes, contending this would stretch the enemy defenses so that he would have to transfer troops from the Ruhr. He completely overlooked the obvious fact that enemy forces withdrawn from east of the Seine were those which had been mauled in the Mortain offensive and in the defense of the Falaise Gap; the result was they were no threat at all to any Allied offensive north of the Ardennes.

As SHAEF intelligence reports stated, it was essential not to give the enemy an opportunity to regroup and prepare a defensive position. Unfortunately, Eisenhower had a tendency to ignore any proffered opinion which was in conflict with his own preconceived ideas. He appeared to be trying to find the point of least resistance in the enemy defenses, but he overlooked the need to find the point which would produce the greatest results.

Having ordered a broad front offensive in the east, Eisenhower instructed Bradley to take the Atlantic port of Brest, the battle for which opened on 25 August. The assault was not essential, for by now the port was of no value to the 12th Army Group and the attack resulted in a further strain on the logistics situation, since supplies had to be diverted from the main front to support this action. As a result of the diversion of air power to the west, Patton's attacks were slowed down by his having inadequate air cover.

The dock facilities at Brest had been destroyed by enemy action, and the operation to take the port cost the Americans 10,000 dead and wounded. Nothing was achieved but the capture of more real estate. Even had the port been in perfect working order when captured, its use to the Allies would have been a diminishing asset as their armies advanced eastward, lengthening as they did so their lines of communication.

Both Eisenhower and Bradley should easily have foreseen all this. In the original plan, the capture of Brest had been projected to occur much earlier in the campaign, and it was anticipated it would then have been of some short-term value to Bradley's armies. By the time the port fell, Middleton had about 25,000 tons of valuable ammunition in his corps depot, ammunition which could have been put to better use on other fronts by supporting a division for at least 30 days. Patton alleged Bradley's fixation with the capture of Brest was due to his desire to demonstrate the U.S. army could not be beaten — the Battle of the Ardennes was still to come.

Bradley maintained his reasons were the commander of the Brest garrison, Gen. Bernhard Ramke, was a fanatic and his aggressiveness was not to be overlooked. Bradley felt it would have been too expensive to besiege the port. Aggressive though Ramke may have been he did not possess the capability of conducting a mobile offensive, for he was cut off from his source of supply, Germany (the Allied navies being in command of the seas), and the Luftwaffe was too weak to transport supplies by air. Bradley had something in common with Patton, Hodges and Eisenhower, for they all too often failed to appreciate the value of a strategic objective.

Eisenhower was certain the 12th Army Group would be able to reach the Franco-German border, but he wrote to Marshall on 24 August stating he could see no reason to do so until he was in a position to make such a move. A very imprecise reservation, but one can reasonably surmise he actually had no idea what his next step should be after the Allied armies had reached the German frontier. Once the collapse of the enemy in Normandy was apparent, there was no reason why he, emulating Montgomery, should not have begun to make long-term plans for the ultimate defeat of the German armies.

On 2 September there was a meeting at Bradley's headquarters in Chartres; in attendance were Bradley, Patton and Eisenhower, who had informed Bradley and Patton it was essential to capture a satisfactory port, and therefore priority would be given to the 21st Army Group's offensive in the Pas de Calais region and Belgium. This priority was to last until Antwerp was taken. The need to clear the approaches to that port was brought to Eisenhower's attention the following day by a message from Admiral Bertram Ramsey (R.N.), warning him Antwerp and Rotterdam could both be easily held by the Germans and it was essential the enemy coastal batteries be taken in order for the approaches to the river routes to be usable. His concern was especially valid with regard to Antwerp, where the approach from the sea is 65 miles long.

Because their own supplies would have to be curtailed in order to support Montgomery's operation, both Patton and Bradley objected to the new arrangements, but in so doing they showed they were guided solely by selfishness. Patton pointed out he had patrols on the Meuse, patrols inside Metz, and his main army had been forced to halt on the Meuse for two days due to lack of fuel. With that problem corrected, he felt he could break through to the Rhine. He was supported by Bradley, who rarely disagreed with the man who had once been his commanding officer.

Eisenhower was unconvinced there was any possibility of the war ending soon, in direct contradiction to his assertion to Montgomery that the enemy was virtually finished. He had doubted Montgomery's claim that he could capture the Ruhr, and was even more skeptical about his ability to capture Berlin. The result was one more of his infamous compromises, although he conceded Montgomery disagreed with his plans, for the U.S. Third Army's ability to mount a successful offensive was contingent upon Montgomery's offensive in the north succeeding, and the 21st Army Group had priority over supplies.

At this Chartres meeting, the Supreme Commander was easily persuaded to agree to an offensive by the Third Army, reinforced by the V Corps from the First Army, which was to be an attack on the Siegfried Line. These forces were later strengthened by the addition of the Free French 2nd Armored Division and the U.S. 79th Infantry Division, weakening the First Army and ensuring Hodges could not keep pace with the 21st Army Group on his left flank. That was in violation of Eisenhower's previous agreement with Montgomery, as was the fact he diverted supplies to Patton which had been earmarked for the 21st Army Group.

Once the northern flank was stabilized, Bradley visited Patton at Chalôns to give orders for the start of the offensive; his instructions to Patton were that the Third Army was to cross the Moselle after the situation in the north had settled, whereupon he would be given half the available supplies. Patton was to advance as far as the Meuse and no further.

Chapter 10—The Campaign Following Caen

This did not prevent Patton from exceeding his orders, for he had already decided to implement his beloved "rock soup" trick. He had been promised fuel sufficient to commence battle but insufficient to win it; had Eisenhower only shown firmness and grounded the Third Army it would have been far more sensible. The Supreme Commander was not unaware of the logistical problem, for on 4 September he declared the closer the Allies got to the Siegfried Line the more strained their lines of communication would become. He went on to the strange conclusion that it was imperative to keep the enemy extended all along the line. Wisely, he did not clarify how the already insufficient supplies for his own armies were going to be increased in order to exert the increased pressure on the enemy.

Still displaying concern for the lack of an adequate plan, Montgomery sent a message to Eisenhower on 4 September, the date Antwerp fell to the 21st Army Group, in which he made the point that the time had arrived for a "full-blooded" attack toward Berlin, and with the capture of the German capital the war would end. There were, he stressed, insufficient supplies for two different offensives; the one selected must be supported by all possible resources and all other operations on the front must be halted. In his opinion, there were only two logical options. One was to head for Berlin via the Ruhr and the second was to proceed via the Saar and Metz. He believed better and quicker results would be obtained by using the northern route. He contended even if Berlin were not taken the offensive would result in the capture of the Ruhr, which was of vital importance to the enemy. It would cause the loss to the Germans of about 50% of the production of crude steel, and about 50% of the total coal output.[10] There was limited time, Montgomery said, and an immediate decision was essential so that supplies could be sorted out; if a compromise were enforced then it would split the available maintenance and no front would receive sufficient materiel. However, Patton's advance was already under way and could not be stopped.

Eisenhower's reaction to Montgomery's plan was to admit the supply situation was not good, but he maintained the suggested single thrust was incredible; he contended that those divisions which were relegated to an active defense would not have sufficient maintenance to defend themselves against a flanking attack. This revealed he was unaware that a division engaged in an active defense needs less administration than one on the offensive. By heavily engaging the enemy in the north Montgomery, in all likelihood, would have ensured the Germans would not have been able to mount a counteroffensive on another part of the front.

Another reaction to Montgomery's proposal came from Maj. Gen. Sir John Whiteley of SHAEF staff. He inquired why three-quarters of Allied troops should be sitting on their fannies[11] while Montgomery did all the fighting. Whiteley numbered among Montgomery's detractors, and he was not the only British officer to denigrate the 21st Army Group commander. As a literal quote, however, it must be suspect; "fanny" in English slang is not synonymous with "backside" in American terminology.[12]

At this time Eisenhower's headquarters were in Joullouville, near Granville, on the west side of the Cotentin Peninsula, isolated from the front by a distance of some 400 miles. Eisenhower apparently had never heard that Napoleon contended, "You cannot command an army from the Tuileries," and the deterioration in the quality of command was soon evident.

The Supreme Commander had postponed his move to France until an adequate system of communications could be set up at his new headquarters. His idea of "adequate" was such that he had neither telephones nor radiophones at the new headquarters—astounding omissions for such an important element of the Allied organization. The means of communication with the armies was by letter or radiotelegraphy. His reply to Montgomery's signal was sent 5 September at 7:45 P.M., but was received by Montgomery in two parts; the final two paragraphs arrived 7 September and the first two arrived 9 September. Eisenhower's answer was he agreed with Montgomery's concept of a single, well-supported thrust to Berlin; he disagreed that it should be started immediately to the exclusion of other operations. He believed the bulk of the German forces in the west had been destroyed (although he offered no substantiation for this conclusion it was true the enemy, from June to September, had incurred losses equal to twice those of the Allies) and he intended to exploit success by breaking into the Siegfried Line and crossing the Rhine on a broad front, following the capture of the Saar and the Ruhr. This would cut off the Germans withdrawing from the southwest of France, and result in the enemy being dispersed over a wide area.

The reason Eisenhower was unable to substantiate his belief that most of the Germans in the west had been destroyed was made painfully obvious three months later. He was either rash in arriving at a hasty conclusion, very ill-informed, or was deplorably lacking in a grasp of elementary strategy, for he made no obvious attempt to cut off those Germans who were retreating from the southwest of France. In any case, the loss of these forces would not have been crucial, for they were not first-class soldiers. It is a fact the enemy was thinly spread on the west side of the Rhine but was not annihilated; it was only Eisenhower's tardiness which prevented

Chapter 10—The Campaign Following Caen   109

a crossing of the river being made sooner than it was. After the war, Gen. Gerd von Rundstedt, supported by Gen. Hans Speidel, stated that a concentrated attack in September by the Allies would have succeeded,[13] for they had a 20:1 superiority in tanks and a 25:1 superiority in the air. The concept of a concentrated attack was supported not only by Montgomery but also by Patton, the Canadian general Guy Simonds and the German general Westphal. According to Gen. Gunther Blumentritt, at the end of August 1944 the front was wide open, but Eisenhower, based on his military knowledge and proficiency, proved incapable of taking advantage of the situation.

The Supreme Commander seemingly gave no thought to the fact if the Allies forced the enemy to stretch his forces over a wide area, the Allies in turn would also be extended, and given the supply problems they would quite likely suffer the same fate as a piece of elastic subjected to the same treatment—their line would snap. He believed there would be no need for any reallocation of supplies for the advance to Berlin, and thereby made a fundamental mistake. He stated it was his intention to occupy the Saar and the Ruhr first, and then the ports of Le Havre and Antwerp would be in use so they could supply one or both of Montgomery's intended offensives. He maintained he had always given priority to the capture of the Ruhr, and went on to assure Montgomery the rail system was already operating to supply both the 21st Army Group and the 12th Army Group.

Eisenhower's conviction the war was almost over was demonstrated when he wrote to his commanders on 29 August 1944 giving his opinion that the enemy was close to collapsing. Unfortunately, his prognosis was not borne out by events, for the German resistance died almost as slowly as the consumptive Mimi in Puccini's *La Bohème*. This conclusion was followed by an even more optimistic and equally erroneous belief, given on 5 September, two days before he replied to Montgomery; he noted in his diary the defeat of the German army was complete. The only thing needed was speed and that depended on maintenance, which was strained to the limit.

To keep four advancing armies adequately supplied with fuel required about one million gallons a day, and from the beginning the potential logistics problem had been appreciated by the planning staff which stressed the need to capture a suitable port. The drive from the Seine to Germany came at a time when supplies were inadequate to support a broad front offensive. Distance from the front had obviously done nothing to enhance the quality of the Supreme Commander's meager comprehension of strategy. Uppermost in Eisenhower's mind was his obsession to emulate the Russians who, under different conditions, were able to mount two or more huge offensives at the same time. He ignored the facts that the Russians had a greater superiority in numbers over the Germans than did the Western Allies, and the Russians were willing to accept far higher casualties than were the British or Americans. He never appeared to fully understand there were not many large ports on the Channel coast of France which could be put to good use by the Allies; that made it essential to capture at least Antwerp and have it working as soon as possible. Why he took so long to order the capture of that port is unclear. Before Normandy was invaded, the planners had noted that without Antwerp being taken and in full operation, the progress of the Anglo-American armies would be limited by the quantity of supplies which could be landed over open beaches and through the smaller ports on the French north coast. Eisenhower's instruction to capture the Breton ports did nothing to solve the supply problem.

Much of Eisenhower's obduracy was based on an inaccurate conclusion. He was convinced, in contradiction to his belief the enemy was finished, that the Germans had considerable reserves in the center of their occupied territory, and therefore any "pencil-like" thrust, as he erroneously insisted upon calling it, would meet with failure. Again, he did not support his belief by quoting any sources of information. Had he troubled to refer to intelligence reports he would have found they did not give force to his conclusions. His assessment of the enemy's strength directly contradicted his G-2's report. Kenneth Strong wrote on 9 September 1944 that the Germans would not transfer any divisions from either Russia or Italy for fear of endangering their already precarious positions on both these fronts. He summarized his opinion by stating that the German Western Front could not expect more than a dozen divisions by way of reinforcements within the next six months. That this assessment believed the enemy could raise more divisions only with difficulty should have persuaded Eisenhower his conclusions were wrong. Added to his incorrect assumption regarding German reserves was Eisenhower's opinion that a single offensive could not be adequately supplied.

Montgomery's answer to Eisenhower's reply was dated 7 September, and responded to paragraphs three and four of Eisenhower's message. He pointed out his maintenance was extremely extended, and the first installment of 18 locomotives had just arrived and the arrival of the remainder seemed uncertain. He needed an airlift of 1,000 tons a day, and so far he had received a total of 750 tons. His transportation was based on operating 150 miles from his ports of supply, and as of 7 September he was 300 miles from his main base at Bayeux. In order to conserve transport, he had reduced his maintenance from France to 6,000 tons a day, about half

Chapter 10—The Campaign Following Caen

his needs; he warned he could not continue on this basis for much longer. It was now quite likely it would be impossible for him to take the Ruhr and Berlin. He ended his message by expressing disagreement with the Supreme Commander's statement that supplies of every description would have to be reassigned in order to support one push for Berlin.

Three days later Eisenhower flew to Brussels to meet Montgomery and discuss future operations. The two deliberated at length, and Eisenhower assured Montgomery he had always intended to give priority to the Ruhr assault and the northern route, but when Montgomery pointed out that this was not being done, Eisenhower indulged in a game of semantics. By priority, he explained, he did not mean absolute priority, and he had no intention of reducing supplies to the Saar operation which was being conducted by Patton.

Montgomery claimed the advance was being carried out in an erratic manner and, so long as there were two offensives to support, the maintenance would have to be shared, resulting in neither receiving sufficient materiel and neither succeeding. It was essential, Montgomery contended, to support the proposed the 21st Army Group assault on the left, which would, among other things, result in the clearing of the approaches to Antwerp. Eisenhower disagreed; he was quite sure the Rhine had to be reached all along its west bank first of all, necessitating an advance on a broad front. When this goal was accomplished, only then would he be prepared to concentrate on a single offensive. He did agree with the plan for the attack to take Arnhem, but he never kept his promise to mount a single concentrated offensive once the Rhine had been gained. The following day, Montgomery sent Eisenhower a signal stating as a result of Eisenhower's decision not to give the Ruhr offensive priority, this would cause the Arnhem operation to be postponed for several days, allowing the Germans to improve their defenses. What was needed was more supplies. This had the desired effect, for Bedell Smith visited Montgomery to let him know the Saar offensive had been closed down and transport from three U.S. divisions was to be used to supply the 21st Army Group. In addition, most of the supplies for the 12th Army Group were to be given to the U.S. First Army, fighting on Montgomery's right.

These arrangements were satisfactory to Montgomery, and he went ahead with the final plans for Operation "Market-Garden," the attack on the three river crossings. He was unaware at the time that Patton had taken exception to the changes instituted by Bedell Smith and, with Bradley's connivance, had become so involved in an attack on his front that SHAEF was unable to stop this offensive. It is indicative of Eisenhower's ambivalence that he should have given Montgomery the clear impression "Market-Garden" had the full support of SHAEF, yet at the same time he supplied Patton to allow him to mount an offensive, one which Bedell Smith genuinely believed would not take place. In fact, Patton's pleas for administrative support were answered in the first week of September, and by 12th September he had been given a quantity of fuel which was more than adequate for his needs; all his fuel storage tanks were full, as were his auxiliary tanks. He also, by that date, received 3,554 long tons of Bailey bridging to support his forthcoming offensive. Neither Bradley nor Patton was reprimanded for his behavior.

While concentrating on the pointless capture of Le Havre and Brest, Eisenhower had ignored the urgency for clearing Antwerp and having it in operation. One of the worst affected by the supply shortages was Patton. The port of entry for the Third Army's maintenance was Cherbourg, more than 600 miles by rail from Nancy. The main supply center, Cherbourg, could support 21 divisions using both road and rail transportation, whereas Antwerp could supply about 54 divisions by rail alone.

There had been a meeting, convened by Eisenhower and attended by Bradley, Montgomery and Ramsey; afterwards Eisenhower issued a directive on 13 September which stated in part, with a little hypocrisy and somewhat belatedly, that the goal was the capture of deep-water ports to support an invasion of Germany, and this necessity had been appreciated from the beginning of the Overlord planning. It continued by declaring the general plan was to secure bridgeheads over the Rhine, take the Ruhr, and concentrate forces for a final non-stop drive into Germany. His directive definitely stated the Allied left would have priority of logistical support, and confirmed while the drive for the Rhine and the Ruhr was in progress the Allies had to take the approaches to Antwerp and Rotterdam so one of these ports could give sufficient support to the Northern Group of armies as they advanced into the heart of Germany. The directive also provided, should the supply situation be adequate, the Third Army would be given permission to advance through the Saar and across the Rhine. Eisenhower's concern for the capture of a deep-water port was a little late. His tardiness did not go unnoticed by the Combined Chiefs of Staff, for on 16 September he received a signal from them stressing the need to open both Antwerp and Rotterdam before the onset of bad weather.

Eisenhower, on 15 September, wrote to Montgomery to assure him the objectives set forth in his 5 September directive would be accomplished, and he was therefore considering his next move. He believed the Germans in the Ruhr and Frankfurt would be defeated as a result of them defending the area, and he was sure the enemy would try to reinforce these positions. By attacking the two objectives, the Allies would be creating opportuni-

Chapter 10—The Campaign Following Caen

ties to deal with the remainder of the German forces in the west. He continued by assuring Montgomery that Berlin was the objective.

There was no doubt in his mind the Allies should concentrate all their resources and energies to mount a swift thrust to take Berlin, and his strategy would be co-ordinated with that of the Russians, so alternatives had to be considered. These were Kiel, Hamburg, Lübeck and Bremen, and the capture of these ports would seal off the Germans in Norway and Denmark, giving the Allies the advantage of providing flank protection for their drive to Berlin. In addition, he maintained, it should be remembered that the areas of Hanover-Brunswick and Leipzig-Dresden would be held by the Germans to cover Berlin. There might also be sound reasons for the Allies to occupy the areas of Nuremberg-Regensburg and Augsburg-Munich in order to cut off the Germans retreating from Italy and the Balkans.

Eisenhower went on to say that since it had played a significant rôle in Nazi history, Munich was of great importance from the political point of view, and he continued by making the astonishing statement that it was impossible to determine clearly what the future objectives would be—therefore the Allies had to be prepared for more alternatives, which were to go to Berlin with both army groups via the Ruhr and Hanover, or by Frankfurt and Leipzig, or possibly both. The northern army group was to be prepared to take the Hanover area and the German North Sea ports in the event that the Russians were first into Berlin, in which case the U.S. armies in the center of the line would take as much as possible of the area of Leipzig-Dresden, depending upon the speed of the Russian advance. As for the armies in the south, they would in any event take the Augsburg-Munich area.

In this letter, more than in any other communication oral or written, Eisenhower showed his deplorable lack of clear thinking. He was attempting to anticipate, and react to, every conceivable enemy move without appreciating he was attempting the impossible. He succeeded only in tying himself into knots with none of the skill of a circus contortionist. He failed to determine the best move the Germans could have made given a specific Allied attack. Had he, as Montgomery was urging, prepared his forces so that they would have been capable of mounting an offensive, and had he concentrated divisions to defend against a likely counterassault by the Germans, he would have been "balanced," to use a favorite Montgomery expression.

If Montgomery's plan for a northern offensive had been adopted, it is quite possible the Germans would have been unable to counter with an attack on Bradley's Army Group; had they done so, nevertheless, Montgomery's disposition of the Allied armies would conceivably have resulted in such an attack being defeated, without disrupting the Allied operation to any great extent. Post war, von Rundstedt expressed the opinion that the Allies should have attempted to take the Ruhr and Aachen. He stated that there were no German forces in the area capable of defending it; he was supported by Gen. Hasso von Manteuffel, who contended that, after the Ardennes collapse, Hitler was lacking in any pragmatic plans.[14]

It is noticeable that Eisenhower, in this 15th September letter, made much of the political importance of Munich, on the basis of the part it played in the rise of the Nazi Party. He did not mention any strategic importance it might have had, yet when it came to Berlin, which had both political and strategic value, he showed no interest in it whatsoever.

Montgomery replied to Eisenhower's letter three days later. He, not unexpectedly, disagreed with the Supreme Commander's proposals, especially with the plan to move into Germany by a broad front offensive, and he gave as his reason the known problem of logistics. He dismissed the idea of going for Nuremberg, Augsburg and other cities, and expressed preference for taking the Ruhr and continuing on for Berlin, but he was emphatic that such an offensive had to be provided with all the needed administration, and the other armies would have to be satisfied with whatever remained. In the event that Eisenhower disagreed and felt Frankfurt would be the correct axis for the advance, the 21st Army Group would make do with any surplus of supplies.

Eisenhower answered on 20 September, making the astonishing assertion he could not believe there was any great difference between the two of them. He assured Montgomery he had never considered moving into Germany with all his armies advancing in line abreast, but later in the letter he dissented from this disclaimer. He stated it would be impossible for Bradley to remain stationary while the 21st Army Group and nine U.S. divisions attacked along the northern route, offering no explanation for this conclusion.

Following Montgomery's response on 21 September, in which he warned that if Eisenhower wanted a left hook along the northern route he would have to stop the 12th Army Group's offensive, Eisenhower called a meeting at his headquarters at Versailles. Again he brought up the need to capture a suitable port, a prerequisite to the advance to Berlin. This, however, was not enough, for he continued by stating the main effort was to be directed at the encirclement of the Ruhr by the 21st Army Group with the U.S. First Army in support. Bradley was to assist Montgomery's operation against the Ruhr by taking over the British VIII Corps' sector and, to the extent resources allowed, he was to continue his thrust toward Cologne and Bonn. He was also to be ready to cross the Rhine and attack

Chapter 10—The Campaign Following Caen

the Ruhr from the south, supplies permitting. As for Patton, he was to take no more aggressive action than his logistical situation allowed, which was seemingly designed to encourage him to resort to "rock soup" tactics.

De Guingand attended the conference as Montgomery's representative, and on the night of 22 September sent a message to Montgomery assuring him Eisenhower had now accepted his plan for the attack by the 21st Army Group plus the nine U.S. divisions, but it was too late in Montgomery's opinion, for the battle of Arnhem was not going well, and the problem of supplies was becoming progressively worse all along the line. An assessment of the situation was sent to Eisenhower, and Montgomery reported he would not be able to mount the planned offensive toward the Rhine unless his maintenance improved.

The Supreme Commander did not object to this postponement and emphasized both the 21st Army Group and the 12th Army Group must still give priority to the advance to the Rhine north of Bonn, which was to be done as quickly as possible. Montgomery and Bradley agreed this was not possible, and Montgomery reported to Eisenhower he had stopped operations aimed at the Ruhr and was now devoting his efforts to opening the Scheldt and to have Antwerp working. This elicited the strange answer dated 9 October that failure to have Antwerp operating by mid-November would result in the cessation of all operations, as though he had for so long been pleading with a deaf Montgomery to take the port. He continued by stating that of all the operations from Switzerland to the Channel, he considered the opening of Antwerp to be of prime importance.

In this protracted exchange of messages, it was the first time Eisenhower mentioned the need to open Antwerp. Even long after the war had ended, in the course of defending his support for Operation "Dragoon," he supported the necessity for this landing by contending the American Mulberry harbor had been lost, communications out of Cherbourg were inadequate to handle the tonnage which could be unloaded in the harbor, Brest was useless because the enemy had destroyed the installations and repairs would take about a year to finish; therefore the capture of Marseilles was essential.

This might have been a convincing argument except for three important omissions: (1) it needed no crystal ball to foresee the Germans would do their best to destroy the harbor installations of Brest, or any other port, before surrendering it, (2) there was no mention of Antwerp and (3) as anyone using a school atlas could have told him Marseilles did nothing to shorten his lines of communications as did the capture and use of Antwerp. Sir Edward Bruce Hamley wrote that a general " ... probably directs a hundred glances, a hundred anxious thoughts, to the communications in his rear."[15] If Eisenhower ever did either of these, his sight and perception were both extremely poor.

All Montgomery's pleadings for a single offensive were in vain. Eisenhower was either too stubborn to study alternatives, or was simply totally unable to understand the advantages of concentrating his armies for one strong offensive, as opposed to mounting several weak attacks. His notion of war was reminiscent of American football which he used to play at West Point — all the players are in action at any time the ball is in play. Bedell Smith decided to find out the opinions of the SHAEF staff officers, so he held a meeting attended by both American and British officers in about equal numbers. They were questioned in turn and their opinions were sought regarding the practicality of Montgomery's plan. Maj. Gen. Humphrey Gale, the British Chief Administrative Officer, expressed the opinion that the supply situation absolutely precluded a single front offensive, but not one of these officers seemed to think it was in any way unreasonable for Eisenhower then to launch an attack on three different fronts simultaneously, which, not unexpectedly, resulted in none receiving adequate administration.

As for Bradley's version of Montgomery's proposal for a concentrated attack in the north, it was a little selective. He omitted reference to everything except the destruction of the V-1 and V-2 launch sites, and from this premise he came to the conclusion that Montgomery was determined to command the Allied ground forces in Europe, and he was convinced the American soldiers should never be placed under the command of a British officer, since it had never worked in North Africa.[16] He forgot that Alexander was not only British but also Deputy Supreme Commander and ground commander in Tunisia and Sicily, and he was Supreme Commander in Italy, having the Eighth Army and also the U.S. Fifth Army under his command after Eisenhower had been assigned to northern Europe. There is no evidence to show the American troops objected to such an arrangement, nor is there anything to show they would have protested at the appointment of a British general to command in northern Europe. Later in the year, Montgomery was given temporary control of American forces; they, not surprisingly, accepted the appointment without incident. In addition, Bedell Smith wrote to Montgomery on 22 June 1944 and quoted friendliness, lack of pomp and genuineness as being characteristics which most impressed the GI's when Montgomery visited them before Normandy. When these troops landed they were under Montgomery's command, and again there was no outcry against this arrangement.

Chapter 10—The Campaign Following Caen

Bradley, together with some other American generals, certainly seemed to possess unusual standards that he would believe an army commander of Montgomery's standing would conduct a campaign placing his own reputation on the list of priorities above that of useful accomplishments.

11

The Problem of Appointing a Ground Commander

Eisenhower and Bradley objected to Montgomery's proposed 40-division strength offensive; in doing so they both ignored the fact that Montgomery, while indeed suggesting himself as the commander of the assault, had nevertheless offered to serve under Bradley should it be more acceptable. Bradley tried to add weight to his objection by quoting the stand made by Gen. John J. Pershing during the First World War, when the American Expeditionary Force commander refused to allow the control of his army to pass to either the British or the French. The fact that the circumstances were different eluded Bradley. Pershing was, with justification, apprehensive lest his army be sent to be slaughtered in one of the many infamous "Big Pushes"; Montgomery's plan was not in the same category and, unlike Bradley, having served in the front line during the First World War, one of his main concerns was to keep his casualties as low as possible. Also overlooked by Bradley was that Pershing had seconded American units to the other Allies as temporary reinforcements, thereby allowing the Americans to gain battle experience which was then passed on to others before they too were committed to the front line. Furthermore, Bradley felt Montgomery was not able to move without a massive build-up of supplies, and in addition to his xenophobic belief that the American public would never accept a British ground commander, he was concerned that Montgomery's plan provided for the bypassing of pockets of resistance which were to be mopped up by perhaps 10 or 12 divisions, dropped off as needed. He believed the northeastern route was unsuitable for armor and erroneously contended the British lacked a vehicle capable of towing artillery pieces.

All these unverified objections were extremely weak. The American public obtained their news directly from reporters, and both Bradley and

Chapter 11—The Problem of Appointing a Ground Commander 119

Eisenhower failed to appreciate that the American press could be discreet when so requested. This was demonstrated when Marshall, some time after the second meeting of Roosevelt and Churchill at Quebec in September 1944, appealed to the press to refrain from reporting items with an anti-British tone, such as Mountbatten's differences with Stillwell. The press collaborated and the stories were dropped. As for his fellow countrymen, Bradley underrated their intelligence. The American public has no unique ability to assess the effectiveness of a military decision prior to its resolution; therefore, as with other countries, it assigns the responsibility of making such decisions to the generals. This public, so potentially vocal in Bradley's opinion, was nevertheless conspicuously silent when Alexander assumed the rôle of ground commander in Tunisia and Italy, and again when Montgomery was appointed temporary ground commander during the Battle of the Ardennes, at which time it was Bradley who raised the loud objections.

Bradley's aversion to bypassing pockets of resistance overlooked his own actions with regard to some of the Brittany ports. These were besieged by his armies who made no attempt to capture them, which seemed quite satisfactory to him. If the northeastern route was unsuitable for Allied armor, it was also unsuitable for German armor, for topography rarely discriminates in favor of one side or the other. Since the Allied tanks were a poor match for the German tanks, especially the Tiger, the absence of enemy armor might well have been an advantage. Furthermore, the Royal Artillery did have a wheeled vehicle designed specially to tow any gun up to the size of a 25-pounder field gun.

Bradley's objections, except for one, were totally unfounded. The one of substance was that Montgomery was unwilling to move without the support of adequate materiel, and indeed he rarely moved unless he was confident about his supply line; that was prudence, for he could not abide a hand-to-mouth existence as could Patton.

The single front assault was raised again, but the theory was nothing new, for Morgan had proposed a 100-division assault on Germany. Montgomery was quite unable to understand why an opportunity, such as he put forward, should be rejected all in the interests of calming public opposition which had never been expressed.

Both Eisenhower and Bradley gave the impression it was politically safer to maintain the command organization of the armies, and by doing so risk suffering increased casualties and perhaps prolonging the conflict, rather than change the command and possibly incur the displeasure of the American electorate. Such thinking leads to the unconvincing conclusion that American voters would have been disappointed in a victory in which, under British direction, American servicemen shared.

With the raising again of the subject of a single front offensive, Eisenhower showed signs of irritation. The campaign to date, he alleged, was a success, and should Montgomery wish to continue the argument, then he, Eisenhower, would submit the matter to the Combined Chiefs of Staff stating incompatible differences existed between the two and of them one must go. Since the Supreme Commander had to be American, the loser would be Montgomery. The subject of a single offensive was again broached two months later by Montgomery, Brooke and Churchill, but Eisenhower was quite adamant that there had to be attacks all along the line.

At the time Montgomery first proposed the concentrated thrust there were only 25 German divisions capable of opposing the attack, and these were below strength and disorganized. By Eisenhower refusing to sanction the 21st Army Group's offensive, the enemy was given the opportunity to recover from his setbacks in Normandy, enabling him to halt the Allied push for the Ruhr. Once again the Supreme Commander's narrow military thinking was prominent. He appeared incapable of using anything but the American Civil War and the First World War as the basis for his decisions; in doing so he ignored the fact in the one case Grant's victory over Lee, and in the other the Allied victory over Germany, were both achieved by the use of superior numbers, and both suffered high casualties. In neither war did the victorious side show itself to be the master of maneuver.

Later in September, the subject of a single ground commander was raised yet again, during a meeting between Alan Brooke and Montgomery. The latter expressed two opinions: (1) there was a need to correct the U.S. strategy of attacking all along the line, and (2) there was a need to create two army groups, one for the north of the Ardennes and one for the south, with Bradley to command the southern group and Montgomery to command the northern group. Montgomery obtained Brooke's acceptance of these suggestions and put them to Eisenhower.

Writing to Brooke, Montgomery summarized his understanding of the agreement reached with the Supreme Commander, which was: (1) the broad front attacks would cease, and Eisenhower would concentrate on one main assault; (2) the front was already naturally divided into two by the Ardennes (in essence Eisenhower refused to make changes in the existing organization); (3) Eisenhower did agree to a strong U.S. Army Corps to be under Bradley's command in the north of the Ardennes, with Bradley under Montgomery's operational control; (4) Eisenhower did not agree to Bradley being ground commander.

The differences between Montgomery and Eisenhower were due mainly to their characters being almost diametrically opposite. Eisenhower was a

Chapter 11—The Problem of Appointing a Ground Commander 121

man of great charm who would not deliberately offend another. He was, nonetheless, very much a conciliator, always trying hard to ensure every army commander was kept satisfied with his latest assignment. However, he was not a strong disciplinarian, and he had no prior experience of battle or of commanding large numbers of men.

While the lack of experience did not prevent Eisenhower from assuming command of ground forces, less than five years later, Bradley, when Chief of Staff in Washington, objected to a French officer being appointed Supreme Commander of the Western Union (the North Atlantic Treaty Organization's predecessor) because the French had no wartime experience of high command.[1]

There was another fault possessed by Eisenhower: he objected to being given suggestions by more experienced officers. By comparison, Montgomery was tactless, stubborn, often thoughtless, giving the impression he rarely believed he was wrong. He did have a much greater sense of discipline than did Eisenhower, and he did have prior experience of battle, in addition to having the advantage over the Supreme Commander in that he had risen in rank more slowly, and was accustomed to commanding large numbers of soldiers. His insistence that it was essential to appoint a single ground commander was neither motivated by nationalism nor by an inflated ego. Indeed, there was a display of selflessness in it, for he had offered on more than one occasion to serve under Bradley. It seems fair to assume his persistence was motivated by an earnest desire to finish the war efficiently and as soon as possible.

The antipathy shown by the Americans toward Montgomery emanated from Washington, specifically from George Marshall (who, at times, displayed rigidity and a lamentable lack of comprehension of military skills), from the U.S. War Department and from Congress, plus Eisenhower's belief that if he appointed a ground commander he would lose prestige in the eyes of the Americans, for Montgomery's appointment to that position had been announced at the outset as being but temporary. The American politicians were convinced the British would never tolerate Montgomery being subordinated to Bradley, therefore it was only right to ensure Montgomery would never command the ground forces. Such thinking showed much pettiness and ignorance of British history; it completely overlooked the fact that only 30 years before, during the First World War, and again during the first few months of the Second World War, British troops in France were under the overall command of a French general, and that Eisenhower had been Commander-in-Chief in Tunisia; it was only toward the end of the campaign that he appointed a British officer as his deputy and ground commander.

At the same time that Montgomery was told to clear the approaches to Antwerp, Bradley was given instructions to join the offensive by building up his forces east of Paris and preparing to strike in an easterly direction toward the Saar Valley. In support of the 21st Army Group's move, Gen. Courtney Hodges crossed the Meuse against little opposition and by 10 September was nearing the Siegfried Line between Aachen and Triers. Because of restricted supplies and the loss of two divisions to Patton's command, he was compelled to stretch his line in order to maintain contact with Patton's left flank, resulting in him being unable to cover Montgomery's right, which was headed for the Ruhr.

Patton was instructed by Bradley to advance to Rheims, although the Third Army was again short of fuel, and to any other commander such an order would have been viewed as impossible to execute; but Patton had the solution. The crews of the mechanized elements were directed to proceed as far as they could in their tanks and other vehicles, and when they ran out of fuel they were to continue on foot. Patton was well aware if this happened he would be given supplies at the expense of others, such as Hodges's First Army, and he demonstrated his concern was for nothing except his own operations.

Again, there was no control at the top. By spreading out his forces and supplies, Eisenhower achieved only one thing—failure to enter the Ruhr in strength. The U.S. forces on Montgomery's right did not receive priority of supplies because the thrusts into the Ruhr and the Saar resulted in the dispersion of effort and maintenance. It would have been more sensible had Eisenhower grounded the Third Army, for by 16 September it had outstripped its supplies.

Blumentritt, post-war, said a concentrated attack in September would have succeeded, for the Germans had nothing to stop it and he felt the result would have been victory for the Allies in 1944.[2]

12
Antwerp

The acute shortage of supplies continued to be a problem throughout the remainder of the war. It had been hoped that the port of Antwerp would soon be captured by the 21st Army Group, and the delay was due in part to Eisenhower giving priority to "Market-Garden" and in part because Horrocks, by his own admission, was too concerned with reaching and crossing the Rhine to order Maj. Gen. G.P.B. Roberts to clear the Scheldt after taking Antwerp. Had he done so, Horrocks believed the 21st Army Group could have prevented the German Fifth Army from evacuating the area. Despite this self-denigration, there can be no disputing that Eisenhower's lack of leadership was quite evident and was mainly responsible for the failure to capture a deep-water port earlier.

Once Antwerp was taken the Germans had to use the radio in lieu of the insecure telephone, but their messages were decoded and the Ultra decrypts sent to the 21st Army Group. Montgomery, therefore, had full information of the German intent to block the port. He failed to appreciate the Germans to the north bank of the Scheldt would create a strong defense of the approaches to Antwerp. In fact, during a two-week period, the commander of the German Fifth Army, Gen. Gustav von Zangen, managed to gather a force of approximately 80,000 men, with artillery and other supporting equipment, on the island of Walcheren. Eisenhower, too, was blind to the situation, assisted no doubt by grossly misleading intelligence reports.

The significance of Antwerp to the Allies cannot be overstated. One year before the outbreak of war it was equal to New York in ranking of ports, and it should have been apparent to Eisenhower it was vitally important that a port of such size should be taken as early as possible in the campaign, so it could be cleared of mines and other obstacles and be put to work unloading the much-needed supplies for the Allied armies. Had there been tighter control exercised by Eisenhower over field operations, had there been better long-range planning by his staff, had he only heeded Montgomery's suggestion of 22 August that Antwerp should be taken, the port could possibly have been in use much earlier.

Eisenhower's omission must rank among the worst blunders he made, and it is hard to excuse him for in discussions in 1942 and 1943, it was he who made it clear Antwerp was of great importance and had to be captured and operating as soon as possible. If this conclusion were accurate then, it was certainly accurate toward the end of 1944, and Eisenhower's attitude can only be described as foolishly inconsistent. Two years before, Eisenhower had prepared a paper on the subject of an invasion of Europe; the plan included the proposed capture of Antwerp. In two reports to Marshall, dated 24 August 1944 and 14 September 1944, Eisenhower stated in the first that it was of prime importance to establish a base at Antwerp, and in the second he admitted that the overall supply situation was unsatisfactory.

Just two weeks after the port was in use, it was handling 30,000 tons a day, more than enough to supply the minimum daily needs of the 21st Army Group alone. Writing to Marshall in October, Eisenhower displayed unwarranted optimism for he expressed the opinion that there was a possibility the war might end by 1 January 1945, and this could be done with the existing forces plus the scheduled reinforcements which were soon to arrive. Suddenly, it seemed a deep sea port was no longer a priority. He passed his conclusion on to the British Chiefs of Staff for comment. Their reply, dated 23 October 1944, expressed the opinion the earliest date for the cessation of hostilities in northern Europe was 31 January 1945; they were cautious, though, showing more pragmatism than the Supreme Commander by adding the proviso that all depended on the date Antwerp was operating. They warned that an all-out offensive launched before the port was opened would be suicide. Their warning was a little late, for such an offensive ought to have begun when the enemy was disorganized and not when he was settled in on the defensive.

In spite of knowing that shortages existed, Eisenhower took no steps to eliminate waste, one such example being the GI's food ration. In northern Europe his food allowance was 6 1/4 lbs. per day of which an average of 4 lbs. was actually consumed by the recipient; the rest was thrown away or given away. The German soldier, by comparison, was given only a little more than 3 lbs. per day[1]; while this was not a luxury diet it proved quite enough to ensure he did not starve, nor did it impair his fighting abilities. Had the ration been reduced to the 4 lbs actually consumed, it would have released valuable space for other much-needed supplies. Montgomery was aware of the supply shortages, as indeed Eisenhower ought to

Chapter 12—Antwerp

have been. There can be little doubt the American insistence on having the best-fed army bordered on selfishness, plus a distorted sense of pride. In 1944, Australia was unable to increase its shipments of beef to Britain, citing the demands made by the U.S. to feed its armed forces in the Pacific for the inability to provide help to improve the scanty British rations.

Bradley went to see Montgomery at his headquarters near Amiens on 3 September. During the discussion it became clear to Montgomery that Bradley was determined to take Metz and Nancy, and from there continue on to Frankfurt. The result of this would mean the U.S. First Army would revert to the 12th U.S. Army Group, making it impossible for Montgomery to execute his planned offensive. Montgomery was convinced Bradley had previously agreed to assist the 21st Army Group in its advance to the Ruhr, an agreement denied by Bradley. Once again, the lack of a firm hand at the top was evident. Eisenhower was not present at the meeting, and in view of its importance the reason for his absence has to be questioned. Each army commander seemed primarily concerned with his own situation and it needed someone at the conference to impose a broader perspective on the discussion.

Only a week after the offensive was launched on a broad front, Bradley became agitated. He had just heard Montgomery was to be given priority over supplies, which he contended would soon lead to "over-riding priority" and he quoted yet again what he believed was the popular opinion of the average American—a factor which seemed to unduly influence so many decisions made by him and Eisenhower—by stating the American public would not tolerate this situation. Eisenhower, showing more concern for Bradley's feelings than good judgment, instructed Patton to conduct an active defense, with the understanding that if engaged he would be resupplied. Because of Patton's impetuosity, the British Chiefs of Staff opposed these instructions and Eisenhower was careful to resupply the Third Army only after it had become thoroughly embroiled in an attempt to take Metz, and only after Alan Brooke had left England to attend the Quebec Conference. Under the circumstances, it is not hard to believe Eisenhower's timing was deliberate.

Patton's attack, the subject of the 3 September meeting, began on 5 September, and two attempts to cross the Moselle failed. Less than two weeks later, Bradley met Patton to report that Montgomery wanted the 12th Army Group to stop further offensives so that it would help his own drive in the north. Patton, not unexpectedly, was opposed to this, and replied that he would become so involved in operations on his front it would be impossible for him to be stopped. He proposed Eddy should begin his attack on 18 September with the purpose of reaching the Siegfried Line.

Bradley gave his tacit consent by stating he would contact Patton for a report but not until after dark on 19 September, by which time he knew very well that Eddy's offensive could not be canceled. The offensive was not successful; fuel was so short that the XX Corps was immobilized for five days.

Eisenhower has alleged that he emphasized to Montgomery the need to clear the approaches to Antwerp and to have the port operating as soon as possible. He pointed out, so he believed, that without the capture of any bridges over the Rhine it would be impossible to maintain any forces in Germany capable of capturing Berlin. If his memory was correct, then it raises the question why, as Supreme Commander and ground commander, did he disperse the strength of his armies, thereby delaying the final assault on the mouth of the Scheldt? The subject of Antwerp's capture had long ago been raised by Montgomery, but at the time Eisenhower did not show much concern for it. He believed Montgomery was acquainted with the situation on his own front, but knew much less about operations on other fronts — a clear suggestion he felt circumstances had changed extremely rapidly since Montgomery had been ground commander, for it was only nine days before the meeting that Eisenhower had taken command of the ground forces. His assessment of Montgomery's ignorance of what was happening on other fronts was completely wrong; of the Allied generals, only he used a system of liaison officers to report to him the daily situation in other sectors.

The following day, Montgomery sent Eisenhower a signal stating that the decision not to give the Ruhr offensive priority would cause the Arnhem operation to be postponed several days, allowing the Germans to better organize their defenses; he needed more supplies. This had the desired effect, for Bedell Smith visited Montgomery to inform him the Saar offensive had been closed down and transport from three U.S. divisions was to be used to supply the 21st Army Group. In addition, most of the supplies for the 12th Army Group were to be given to the U.S. First Army, fighting on Montgomery's right.

Again, Eisenhower appeared to be quite unaware of the supply problems facing the armies under his command. The Normandy beaches in the U.S. sector unloaded a maximum of 35,000 tons daily, and soon use exceeded supply; there were occasions when ammunition and fuel had to be rationed. During the drive across France from the beaches to the Seine, a series of supply dumps had been created, but transportation from these dumps to the front line was time consuming and expensive. By the time the armies reached the Siegfried Line the problem became one of insufficient port facilities. Boulogne had been captured on 23 September but was

Chapter 12—Antwerp

not functioning until 12 October. Calais was taken on 1 October but not opened until the following month. Thus, by 1 October, the only harbors operating north of the Seine were Dieppe and Ostend, and their combined daily tonnage equaled roughly 25% of what Antwerp was capable of handling.[2] It would have been wiser to have bypassed Boulogne and Calais in order to concentrate on the capture and clearing of Antwerp, for those two garrisons would have been no threat to the rear of the advancing the 21st Army Group. So great was the shortage of docking facilities that at one time there were 250 Liberty ships in British harbors waiting for available berths in French ports. Later, in early 1945, the problem of supplies was exacerbated by the fact the United States reduced its war production in the ill-founded belief hostilities would soon cease. Eisenhower's indecision was demonstrated in the general delay of the Allied advance, once the Albert Canal in Belgium had been crossed and the Americans had entered Germany. He failed to produce any specific long-range plans, just as he had failed to pursue relentlessly the retreating enemy. He demonstrated more than once that his lack of talent in commanding a force of notable size proved a great impediment, and he never showed any indication he had studied the German strategy and tactics during his nearly two years of fighting them. One mark of a great general is shown in his willingness to learn not just from his own mistakes but also from his opponent's successes.

Never once did Eisenhower muster large forces on a short front in order to mount a swift and devastating blow against the enemy, thereby failing to observe one of the basic rules of warfare. Such a concentration of forces, and subsequent offensive, should logically have been done on the Belgian front, for there would have been easier lines of communication from the ports to the front, and as the Allied armies advanced, the Dutch and German ports would also have become available.

Eisenhower's failure can only have prolonged the war unnecessarily; instead of concentrating his attack, he wanted to reach the Rhine, cross it on a broad front and then mount a single front offensive. He told Montgomery on 15 September he wanted to advance to Berlin by the most direct and fastest route with a combined U.S.-British force.[3] The omission of any practical plan to end the war was compared by Gen. Speidel, the German Chief of Staff Army Group B, to a repeat of the Miracle of the Marne in the First World War, when the British and French failed to exploit their advantage and allowed the enemy to escape from what should have been certain defeat.

13

"Market-Garden"

Montgomery followed up his proposed airborne attack on the three Rhine bridges, presented to Eisenhower at their 10 September meeting in Brussels. He discussed his ideas in general with Bradley and later gave a more detailed plan for Operation "Market-Garden" to Eisenhower (who contended it was his suggestion at this meeting to mount the Arnhem operation) with the object of providing security to the drive eastward. As a result, Montgomery ordered a temporary delay to the capture and clearance of the approaches to Antwerp, causing Eisenhower to regret his decision later, for now, in the absence of an adequate harbor, the lines of communication extended 500 miles from the ports and beaches to the front, and airborne troops were being used in a static rôle. The ultimate target of the operation was the bridge over the Lower Rhine at Arnhem, and it was to be reached by a series of airborne drops to capture the bridges at Eindhoven, Nijmegen and Arnhem. Because of Patton's 18 September offensive, Supreme Allied Headquarters was unable to reduce supplies to the Third Army and thus was unable to halt that attack. Bradley showed his usual ambivalence, believing at first "Market-Garden" was nothing more than a trick by Montgomery to implement his single thrust to Berlin; later he described it as an imaginative plan. Had it succeeded, the operation would have resulted in 300,000 Germans being trapped in western Holland, and the Siegfried Line would have been outflanked.

The supplies which were diverted to support Patton's offensive could otherwise have been used in the north, and so short of administration was Dempsey that out of six divisions he could field only three offensively. Had Patton shown some generosity and much less selfishness by not proceeding with his offensive, he could possibly have contributed to making "Market-Garden" a success, but again the Supreme Commander showed how little authority he exercised over his subordinate generals.

Before the start of the airborne offensive, Montgomery had informed

Chapter 13—"Market-Garden"

Eisenhower the 21st Army Group would need additional logistical support or else he would be unable to cross the Rhine. Bedell Smith immediately promised extra supplies which were delivered by air and by road. In addition, the U.S. First Army was to receive priority of maintenance in the 12th Army Group, so the operations by the 21st Army Group right could be stepped up. Ultimately the air supply reached 400–500 tons a day, and about 500 tons was transported by road. A minimum of 1,000 tons per day was needed. The lack of administration was so acute that Montgomery was unable to use the VIII Corps, and because the U.S. First Army had become so involved in Aachen, the British XXX Corps' right flank was exposed.

The attack began on 17 September. Eventually the bridges at Nijmegen and Eindhoven were captured, but the British 1st Airborne, after some heavy fighting, failed to take the bridge at Arnhem. The weather was bad and for several days air operations were severely restricted.

In the middle of this massive airborne operation Eisenhower became suddenly aware of the supply shortage, and as though the 21st Army Group had not enough problems to handle, he gave instructions that the opening of the Scheldt be given priority. He appeared to be unable to comprehend that both manpower and supplies were limited, and yet he had approved the Arnhem operation before Antwerp was working. He ought to have been aware of the continuing problem of administration, and at one time the U.S. Third Army had to limit its use of artillery to the firing of small-caliber guns due to ammunition shortages. Despite some successes, the overall situation was not good, and the withdrawal from Arnhem commenced on the night of 25/26 September.

There is the question of why Montgomery mounted "Market-Garden" before clearing the Scheldt. The excuse that Eisenhower specifically authorized him to delay that project until "Market-Garden" was finished does not absolve him from blame. "Ultra" signals clearly showed Hitler intended to deny the use of the Scheldt to the Allies for as long as possible, thereby making Antwerp unusable. Even though Horrocks admitted he failed to instruct the XXX Corps to clear the approaches to Antwerp, there seems to be no reason why Montgomery could not have issued orders to that effect prior to the airborne assault on the Rhine bridges.

The behavior of Patton, with Bradley's approval, before and after "Market-Garden" showed either a surprising lack of strategic knowledge, a reprehensible lack of discipline, a streak of unforgivable selfishness in his character or a combination of all three. He was determined he would not suffer from a lack of supplies, and yet his military experience was great enough he should have appreciated that an attack all along the line was not a practicable option before the supply problem had been resolved. There is no record he ever suggested to Eisenhower there was a need to capture and open ports along the north coast of Europe, but there is plenty of evidence to show he flouted orders, and his actions assured him of full administrative support.

During the entire "Market-Garden" operation Patton was trying to capture Metz, notwithstanding the fact Eisenhower had instructed Bradley to stop that attack. There was nothing so vital about the city that it was essential to take it while another big offensive was in progress, but consideration for others was not one of Patton's outstanding qualities, especially if the other commander happened to be Montgomery.

It was while the attempt to take Arnhem was in process that Patton showed an unjustified anxiety to join forces with "Dragoon" again dragging Hodges's army too far to the south, resulting in the U.S. First Army being unable to concentrate in order to pierce the Siegfried Line. Because of this, the First Army was incapable of maintaining pressure against the enemy as it had been instructed to do in support of "Market-Garden." Throughout the planning of the assault on the bridges, Eisenhower could not rid himself of the desire to ensure U.S. soldiers shared the credit for the anticipated victory, again showing how quickly and easily he forgot his idealism. This, and his nationalism, did not help the progress of the battle.

The main objective of "Market-Garden" was not achieved, but with the capture of valuable ground and a series of bridges, it did result in an improvement in the Allied position, although the cost was expensive and gains could have been obtained more economically without the use of airborne troops. Nevertheless, it is undeniable this operation was Montgomery's biggest failure, and it is notable that during the planning stage of the operation his Chief of Staff, de Guingand, was in England on sick leave.

At the beginning of September, Eisenhower instructed Hodges to prepare for an attack on Aachen. His orders were to mount a two-pronged assault, one from the north through the Aachen Gap and the other through the Metz Gap in the south. The Supreme Commander was convinced it would result in the destruction of substantial numbers of Germans, leaving the way open for a rapid advance to the Rhine. He believed this despite the fact the plan totally lacked originality, for the Gap is the traditional route for armies invading Germany from France, and the Germans had therefore prepared strong defenses. When he gave these orders, Eisenhower was well behind the front line at Granville.

The area around Aachen is hilly and wooded, which favored the defenders and made Hodges's task far from easy. Nevertheless, a total of 17 divisions was committed to the attack, and Gen. J. Lawton Collins's VII Corps was instructed that if stiff resistance prevented quick penetration of German defenses, it was to halt and await more supplies. The Germans soon became aware of the American intentions and dispatched a division to reinforce the town. The cost of the offensive was high, and it was closed down because Montgomery was receiving priority of supplies for "Market-Garden." In the course of one week the Americans had advanced just 12 miles into Germany, had achieved little else, and suffered 20,000 casualties. The U.S. First Army took a much-needed rest and on 2 October 1944 the attack recommenced. Three hundred planes dropped their bombs but not one of them hit any concrete fortifications, and the ground attack went in without the benefit of an effective air strike. The artillery support included 6 mm mortars, but their shells made no impression on the concrete pill-boxes.

With the capture of Alsdorf, northeast of Aachen, the Americans managed to isolate their objective, and the town was bombarded by air attacks and nearly 5,000 rounds of artillery shells. Final victory was achieved after six weeks of bitter fighting, but the U.S. First Army was exhausted; they had lost 8,000 killed, wounded and missing, and 200 tanks, which did not help them when they were attacked later during the Battle of the Ardennes. The only accomplishment was that a town of some importance to the Nazi Party was in Allied hands—a wasteland, strategically of little value.

Marshall was aware of the plans to take Aachen and also aware that the venture would strain the Allied supply lines, which would in turn encourage the Germans to attack. His answer to this problem was that Eisenhower should keep the enemy stretched everywhere,[1] thus showing he had failed to appreciate the result—the Allied lines of communication, too, would be extended almost to the breaking point. One result of the offensive was that it left the Allied forces in the center very weak, and the Germans made good use of this defect during their assault in the Ardennes just two months later.

14

West of the Rhine

A conference was held on 18 October 1944 at Montgomery's headquarters in Brussels to discuss the winter strategy. Eisenhower proposed his usual unimaginative plan to mount twin offensives, but before they could take place he felt it was essential to clear the entire west bank of the Rhine. To accomplish this, the U.S. First, Ninth and Third armies were to advance to the Rhine and cross it if possible. Montgomery was to clear the area to the west which he had bypassed during the "Market-Garden" offensive; he was then to turn south from Nijmegen to the Ruhr, between the Rhine and the Meuse. The U.S. First and Ninth armies were to start their advance on 5 November 1944, and the Third Army was to start on 10 November. Eisenhower issued his final orders for the offensive on 28 October, showing once more his inability to realize there was no indication why this broad front attack should succeed where others had not. His plan did include instructions to the 21st Army Group to open Antwerp (the approaches to which were taken in early November, allowing the first convoy to enter the port on 28 November) and in addition the British Second Army was to prepare for a drive southeast between the Meuse and the Rhine in order to give support to the U.S. advance across the Rhine. The U.S. First Army was to cross the Rhine in the area of Cologne between 1 and 5 November; the U.S. Ninth and First Armies were then to encircle and clear the Ruhr.

The offensive commenced and the three American armies prepared for a drive to the Rhine while the British Second Army attacked to clear the area west of the Maas, which was reached on 5 November. The clearing of the west bank of the river was undertaken with the help of U.S. 84th Division; this unit was in need of battle experience and suffered heavy casualties attempting to advance west of the Wurm.

Patton's attack opened with only artillery preparation. His progress was hampered by the Moselle being at its highest level in half a century.

Chapter 14—West of the Rhine

In the north conditions were no better and an apparently impatient Bradley, only five days after the attack had begun, gave 17 November as the deadline for specified objectives to be attained. These were that Hodges was to breach the Siegfried Line and continue to Düren. The Roer was to be crossed 15 miles east of Aachen, and Hodges was then to press on to Cologne, 25 miles away.

The weather cleared enough for the Allied air force to bomb some of the Rhine bridges to prevent the enemy from moving reinforcements to the front. For all Bradley's optimism, the Americans made slow progress. They advanced only 17 miles in two weeks, with Hodges failing to capture the Roer Dams, and after being repelled at Schmidt due to supply problems, he unwisely turned his attention to the Huertgen Forest, where the First Army suffered heavily. Hodges demonstrated he had failed to appreciate that by controlling the Roer Dams, the Germans could prevent the Americans from crossing downstream simply by opening the floodgates. It would have been far more sensible had he attempted to take the dams, which would then have placed him in a better position to inconvenience the enemy. His failure to do so and his attack on the forest are difficult to justify. The weather was appalling and German resistance was so stubborn that the village of Huertgen changed hands 14 times. The American losses were extremely heavy, and in one battalion morale broke.

Late in November 1944, Eisenhower and Montgomery had a discussion on the situation. Despite some successes, the fighting had proved costly to the Allies and had not achieved the hoped-for results. Montgomery was concerned that Bradley's 12th Army Group seemed unbalanced. He suggested the situation could be corrected if Patton's offensive were halted and some Third Army divisions moved north. When he learned of this, Bradley wrote a letter to Montgomery, contending Patton's offensive was producing results as evidenced by the capture of 25,000 prisoners. He expressed the belief the Seventh and Third Armies should continue the attack, which he felt was most important. Montgomery disagreed, pointing out the Allies had failed to reach their objectives as set forth in Eisenhower's directive dated 28 October. This was due to Eisenhower's failure to implement Montgomery's strategy of defeating the Germans west of the Rhine, establishing bridgeheads over that river and the Ijssel, and then deploying in strength east of the Rhine in preparation for taking the Ruhr. Montgomery felt a new plan was needed. Churchill, too, became concerned and in a message to Roosevelt blamed the removal of forces from Italy, which was certainly a contributing factor.

The Americans failed to heed Montgomery's warning, and they paid for their omission. By 2 December, Patton had reached the Saar at Saarlautern. At heavy cost very little of strategic value was achieved; once more it showed the difference between the U.S. military thinking and that of the Germans. The Americans believed it was essential to capture territory, including towns and cities of little or no strategic value. The Germans, by contrast, believed in the destruction of enemy forces, which was the essence of their blitzkrieg tactics.

As a result of the differences of opinion between the two army commanders there was a conference at Maastricht on 7 December 1944, attended by Eisenhower, Tedder, Bradley and Montgomery. The meeting opened by Eisenhower giving an optimistic review of events since September. Montgomery was asked for his opinions and he presented his solutions to the problem. The Ruhr, he claimed, was the only objective of immediate value because it was the heart of German industry. It was essential to force the enemy into conducting a mobile defense since he was short of fuel, and this would immobilize his transportation and tanks. With these points in mind, the Ruhr should be the prime target and the route to that area should be in the north, where there was suitable country for mobile warfare. He was opposed to simultaneous attacks from the north and south, contending neither would succeed.

Again Montgomery put forward his plan for an offensive on the 21st Army Group's front, with the U.S. Ninth Army under his command, and supported by the balance of the U.S. 12th Army Group. The object was to capture or surround the Ruhr. Montgomery emphasized the importance of forcing the enemy into conducting the type of campaign which would drain his fuel supplies and which, if successful, would greatly hinder his war production. He stated there should be one army commander, who should be either Bradley or himself. In all discussions regarding a single ground commander Montgomery always offered to serve under Bradley should he be an unacceptable candidate.

Eisenhower disagreed not only with Montgomery's assessment of the situation, but also with his plan for a narrow front offensive. He felt his own plan, which he believed did not differ much from Montgomery's, was better. It was for a major attack on the Ruhr in 1945, with a secondary assault from the south. He did agree the Ruhr should be isolated, but as usual was opposed to a concentrated attack. He thought such an offensive would not result in the destruction of large numbers of Germans. Thereby he seemed to agree with Clausewitz (who stated the destruction of the enemy's armed forces is the first aim of generalship), but then he ignored the likelihood that the enemy would fight strongly for the Ruhr and in doing so would cause the weak Allied force to suffer heavy losses.

His plan was for a subsidiary attack along the Frankfurt-Kassel line,

Chapter 14—West of the Rhine

thus assaulting from two directions, north and south. Not content with that, he decided Patton's operations were to continue, all of which provoked Montgomery to write to Brooke telling him that he should remove Eisenhower from command of the Allied armies because he did not know what he was doing. He was convinced Eisenhower's plan would divide the Allied force and prevent it from concentrating for a single thrust, in evident contradiction to what had been agreed to earlier.

It was not the first time Montgomery had complained about Eisenhower's shortcomings. In September he had written to the Supreme Commander in reply to the latter's agreement to allow Patton's army to advance at the same time as the 21st Army Group's offensive was in progress. Montgomery stated, frankly but accurately, there were insufficient supplies for two simultaneous full-scale attacks. He pleaded for only one offensive, aimed at Berlin, to end the war in the West sooner than could be accomplished by two concurrent operations. Montgomery was convinced Eisenhower had no intention of mounting a narrow front offensive. The Supreme Commander was certain his broad front strategy was wearing down the enemy resistance and since the killing of Germans was the prime objective of the Allies, it was immaterial where the offensive was mounted.[1] He was totally unable to appreciate two important factors: (1) the British had limited resources both natural and human, and (2) after five years of war they were very tired. For these reasons, Montgomery felt it was essential to finish hostilities as quickly as possible.

Eisenhower ignored Clausewitz's dictum that if the purpose is to overcome the enemy by a lengthy campaign, then only small objectives should be the target, since large objectives require a greater expenditure of force. He also appeared to be oblivious to the fact the American system was producing insufficient replacements for the armies in northern Europe. This shortage was not due to a lack of manpower, but to inefficiency. For every 100,000 men in the U.S. Army only 23,000 were front line troops, which compared unfavorably with the Russian army, of which 80% were sent into battle, and with the British, who fielded a minimum of 62% and a maximum of 89% front-line troops. The abundance of ancillary troops was noticed and commented upon by Churchill soon after the American forces began to arrive in Britain, and he observed in one instance such troops outnumbered the infantry by 43,000.[2]

In addition to waste in the army, the United States never accepted the need to switch its economy to a full war-time basis, for its industry was producing, even to the final days of the war, luxury items and its manpower was inefficiently used in war production. It resulted, during the Ardennes offensive, in the U.S. armies on the Belgian Front not receiving thoroughly trained reinforcements. Instead, the best the Americans could do was to use men who were below the minimum level of physical requirements and who had received less than the standard length of training. Later, between February and June 1945, all the country could do was to send to Europe 56,000 third-class replacements.

So lacking in enthusiasm for supporting the war against the Axis was the American government that as late as April 1944 men over the age of 26 were not conscripted into the armed forces, and some American politicians in 1943, just two years after the Japanese attack on Pearl Harbor, seemed not to appreciate the severity of the situation. Sen. Burton K. Wheeler introduced a bill, which did not pass, excluding fathers from the draft.[3]

Montgomery's doubts about the Supreme Commander's ability were understandable for, in direct contradiction of his 26 October directive, Eisenhower continued to assert too much emphasis must not be placed on the Ruhr because it was merely a geographical location — the same description he had used before in North Africa and was to use again in reference to Berlin; his judgment was just as poor then as it was in regard to the Ruhr. His assessment of the importance of the Ruhr showed how little he understood the significance of that area in relation to Germany's production capacity.

Despite Montgomery's attempts to compromise by suggesting the 21st Army Group and the 12th Army Group should attack the Ruhr and the mobile campaign in the north should be postponed until spring, no agreement was reached. It left Bradley's 12th Army Group divided into two concentrations, with four divisions spread over a distance of nearly 100 miles, and both Bradley and Eisenhower had apparently forgotten that at West Point they had been taught a U.S. division should hold a front of not more than five miles in length.[4]

In the event, it was not the Allies who struck first but the Germans, and only six days before the offensive opened Roosevelt had relayed to Churchill the information that Eisenhower had estimated on the Western Front the armies under his command were inflicting losses in excess of the enemy's ability to form new units.

To Marshall, Eisenhower gave his opinion that the enemy might be able to maintain a strong defense, but only with the help of the weather. His optimism may have been fed by Bradley's conversation with him during which he stated that if the Germans attacked in the Ardennes area they would be caught in a vise between Hodges's First Army and Patton's Third Army, a clear example of Bradley's tendency to overestimate the capabilities of the armies under his command and of underestimating the determination of the Germans.

Chapter 14—West of the Rhine

Five days after the Maastricht meeting, Eisenhower was in London to confer with Alan Brooke and Churchill; also present was the Deputy Supreme Commander, Air Chief Marshal Sir Arthur Tedder. Eisenhower opened the conference by restating his stale plan for a broadfront attack all along the line, which caused Brooke to point out the shortcomings of such a strategy. He further made it clear if Eisenhower was determined to proceed with his plan then he should wait until the new year, for it was estimated that by March 1945, he would have under his command a total of 80 divisions. This came as a surprise to Eisenhower, despite his position, which showed the lack of attention he paid to his future situation.

After Brooke explained how the assault in the Frankfurt area would involve 25 divisions, thus making it stronger than the northern offensive, in contradiction to Eisenhower's assurances, the Supreme Commander made the excuse he was going to create a general reserve,[5] something he had never before contemplated. When questioned about the positioning of this reserve, he admitted he had given it no consideration. He was soon to have his attention focused on problems more immediate than the location of a figment. Four days later, the Germans struck.

15

The Germans Strike in the Ardennes

The German offensive began in the early morning of 16 December 1944, at the time when the Americans were engaged in trying to take Aachen and Metz. In total 250,000 Germans, commanded by von Rundstedt, with five divisions in reserve (between 60,000 and 70,000 men), were opposed by 50,000 Americans. This attack should have been no surprise to Eisenhower. Aside from the concerns expressed by Montgomery on 28 November at Zonhoven that Bradley's armies were unbalanced, only 12 days before the assault started Patton's G-2, Col. Koch, reported a number of enemy units opposing the U.S. Third Army had been withdrawn. Extremely heavy traffic had been observed moving toward the Eifel region in the area north of the Saar and a little to the east of the Ardennes. Koch concluded it was all part of a large build-up of troops opposite the south flank of the U.S. First Army. The report was forwarded to Supreme Headquarters where it was evidently given no attention, for by now the pessimism which had prevailed in the G-2 section of SHAEF had given way to extreme optimism.

Two months before, SHAEF G-2 noted that armor was being withdrawn from the German Seventh Army front, and it was believed this was intended to reinforce Army Group B in the Aachen area. By the end of October, SHAEF thought the enemy would soon be able to field Panzer and parachute units for an attack in the north. Bradley's 12th Army Group felt if the Germans were left undisturbed until the beginning of December, they would be able to accumulate a strong force for an offensive. SHAEF was of the opinion the offensive would come earlier, in November, and the question was whether it would be a spoiling attack or an attack in earnest.

SHAEF was well aware the Fifth Panzer Army had withdrawn from

Chapter 15—The Germans Strike in the Ardennes

the line and had not been heard of for some time. By mid-November there was evidence that enemy activity in Westphalia coincided with troop movements east of the area from Ruhr to Luxembourg. SHAEF intelligence concluded this formation of ten divisions would lead to an offensive sometime before winter. These new forces, it was assumed, were to be used against the forthcoming Allied attacks in the Eifel, northeast of the Ardennes. The U.S. First Army G-2 was convinced the Germans intended to launch a major offensive, but he mistakenly believed the attackers had insufficient fuel to reach both banks of the Meuse.

As a result of these reports, SHAEF decided the enemy was aware of the pending Allied attack toward the Ruhr and had built up an armored force to resist this assault. The Allied G-2s by November believed the German Sixth Panzer Army to be west of the Rhine, with the purpose of defending the line of the River Roer and halting the Allied attempt to reach the Rhine. The G-2s were fully aware that three out of five of the Fifth Panzer Army's divisions were in the area of the Aachen Front and they interpreted this to be von Rundstedt's defense against an attack on the Ruhr. The G-2s also believed the Germans would have to wait for a weakness to appear in the Allied defenses before they would attack.

During the first week in December, German hospital trains were spotted on rail sidings on the west bank of the Rhine, Tiger tanks transported on flatcars were seen heading for the front and on 6 December Allied fighters located 50 searchlights,[1] later used by the German Fifth Army to create artificial moonlight during their attack. Again, five days before the offensive began, Koch reported the enemy had created a large reserve of armored forces, giving them the capability of launching a spoiling attack. No attention was paid to this report either. Koch was not the only G-2 to produce reports showing the possibility of an enemy offensive. Brig. Gen. Edwin L. Sibert, G-2 in the 12th Army Group, reported to Bradley at the end of November that the Germans were capable of mounting an assault in the Ardennes.

In the first week of November, a German deserter told his captors about Panzer units, part of Sixth Panzer Army, re-forming in Westphalia. A German general, captured by the French on 20 November, under interrogation told of the existence of the Sixth Panzer Army, as yet uncommitted to battle, which was under the command of S.S. Gen. Josef "Sepp" Dietrich. The prisoner stated this army was to be used in a single large-scale attack commencing at the end of December. In early December, a copy of a letter, signed by the Chief of Staff of the German LXXXVI Corps, fell into Allied hands. It gave details of a special unit of men who spoke the American dialect[2]; the unit was to be equipped with U.S. uniforms, weapons and vehicles, all previously taken from Americans. About this time prisoners of war were reporting alterations to army boundaries, especially in the areas of the 15th Army and 5th Panzer Army.

By December, the G-2s were becoming a little concerned because the enemy was shifting divisions between the north and the south parts of the front. They concluded the Germans were planning an attack to commence before Christmas, but they could not agree that the Ardennes would be the main target. During the week of 3 December, the Germans were observed moving tanks from the Rhine to Bitburg in the Eifel; this appeared to be offset by the departure of other units. The 12th Army Group's G-2 thought the enemy was rotating experienced troops out of the line to be replaced by raw recruits, and the First Army's G-2 felt this was to provide fresh troops with battle experience before they moved to a more active sector. The U.S. VIII Corps concluded, six days before the German offensive opened, this movement was indicative that the enemy wanted the sector to remain quiet, and the day before the offensive began, issued a report stating the enemy capability showed no change.

A fortnight before the German attack, SHAEF G-2 Kenneth Strong, at a chiefs of staff conference, warned there could be only three possible uses for the newly formed Panzer units: they could be sent to Russia, they could be used to counter an Allied offensive, or they could be used to mount an attack through the Ardennes. Eisenhower stated he had discussed the situation with Bradley and had decided rather than build up defenses in the Ardennes he would keep up his offensive actions. The commander of the First Allied Airborne Army maintained his G-2's assessment of the potential enemy action was the most accurate, but it was ignored because no Allied airborne forces were in action.

Eisenhower was unimpressed by the SHAEF G-2 reports, so he concentrated on the elimination of the Colmar Pocket, which was occupying eight Allied divisions. Despite the obvious indications of enemy intentions, the Supreme Commander showed he was lacking in versatility, unwilling to amend his plans to check a very likely enemy attack.

On 10 December, the First Army's G-2 announced that since the previous report, dated 20 November, enemy resistance had increased and he was improving his defenses behind the Roer and along the Erft. The object of this, the report continued, was to exhaust the Allied offensive and follow up this success with a powerful counterattack between the two rivers. After reading this account, the commander of the First Army, Courtney Hodges, asked Bradley for the transfer of two divisions to his command, but the request was refused. Just before they began their offensive in the Ardennes, the Germans moved three divisions to an area north of 's Her-

Chapter 15—The Germans Strike in the Ardennes 141

togenbosch, and intelligence summaries concluded it was intended to mount a simultaneous attack with that in the Ardennes. To forestall such intentions, the Canadians moved the 4th Armoured Division from Nijmegen to bolster their position around 's Hertogenbosch.

There can be no reasonable excuse for Eisenhower, and most of SHAEF staff, ignoring the obvious warnings. The Ardennes had been used before by the Germans. Between the 16th and 18th centuries the Ardennes had been the route chosen by the invaders no fewer than 10 times, something which Eisenhower and his G-2 staff should have known and noted. There was no reason why this direction should not have been used again to invade France.

The critical situation in December was not helped by the U.S. War Department diverting to the Far East reinforcements originally destined for northern Europe, contrary to the agreement giving priority to Europe. Nor was the situation helped by Eisenhower's wildly optimistic report to the President at the beginning of December, expressing the opinion regarding the enemy's inability to form new units.

Both Bradley and Eisenhower were obviously well aware of the fact the American front in the Ardennes sector had been thinned to provide support for a broad front offensive. The two generals, on a tour of the area only a day before the Germans attacked, decided the risk was worth taking, thereby ignoring the study made by the French in the spring of 1938. This study assumed the Germans had attacked with armor and motorized columns. Gen. André-Gaston Pretelat, in charge of the exercise, showed by using one infantry, four armored and three motorized divisions, the area could be penetrated.[3] His estimate of the time it would take the Germans to reach the Meuse during this hypothetical assault was exactly the time it took when they attacked through the area in 1940.

Patton was certain a German attack had a good chance of breaking through the American lines, but his Commander-in-Chief was so full of confidence he told Butcher the Germans could "swing a push" through the Ardennes if they wished,[4] in the mistaken belief the U.S. armies would have little difficulty in defeating the assault. Not even in Supreme Allied Headquarters was this confidence shared by all the staff; there was at least one officer who showed concern. The Intelligence Officer (G-2) Kenneth Strong had already noted in one of his options that there was a threat to the Ardennes, and he felt if the offensive did occur it would endanger Liège. Bradley believed it would be nothing but a spoiling attack[5] designed to delay his own offensive, and he told Eisenhower it would be impossible for him to reinforce the area without withdrawing men from both Patton's and Hodges's armies, which he objected to doing.

Following a discussion of the situation, Bedell Smith sent Strong to confer with Bradley. When Bradley was told by Strong of the possibility of a German strike in the Ardennes, he again displayed unjustified self-confidence by replying: "Let them come."[6] He had, he assured Strong, certain divisions which were ready to respond should the Germans attack, a reply which was all too similar to the one given by French Gen. Maurice Gamelin who said a breakthrough, such as Pretelat envisaged, could never occur in a real war for the defenders would commit their reserves. The French had no reserves in 1940 and Bradley had none in 1944. This blunder was half-heartedly admitted on 16 December at a meeting in Eisenhower's Paris headquarters. After Bradley had telephoned Patton to give him instructions to move the 7th Armored Division southward, Bedell Smith told Bradley he now had the counterattack he had been wanting. Bradley's reply was to the effect he had indeed wanted an attack but not such a big one. Following the end of the war, Bradley asserted nobody had told him about the possibility of an impending enemy offensive. A feeble excuse, for Bedell Smith was not in the habit of sending the SHAEF G-2 on social visits to the various Army Group commanders; if Bradley felt Strong's visit was not to draw his attention to a possible German attack then it is reasonable to question what purpose he thought the meeting did serve.

It was in November that Alan Brooke and Churchill visited Eisenhower. Brooke left with the definite impression the Supreme Commander had no clear idea of what was happening at the front, and he believed Eisenhower's strategy was foolish. After the fact, the Supreme Commander alleged he had been certain from the beginning the Germans had launched a major assault and there are many who support his assertion. Unfortunately, his reactions at the time do not uphold his contention. Not only had he, as ground commander, failed to issue any directives to his army commanders for eight weeks,[7] but his staff was just as lax for only five days before the attack, ignoring reports by SHAEF and the 12th Army Group G-2s regarding the whereabouts of the German 6th Panzer Army, SHAEF reported nothing was known of this army's position apart from vague rumors.

On 10 December, the First Army's G-2, Col. Benjamin A. Dickson, predicted an all-out German offensive, but he was mistaken with regard to its location, although four days later, at a meeting with Hodges and the General Staff of First Army, he correctly stated the Ardennes would be the location for the offensive. About this time, a couple of German civilians crossed into the American lines and under interrogation revealed they had seen signs of a build-up of German troops across the Our River. There was

Chapter 15—The Germans Strike in the Ardennes

no excuse for being taken by surprise on the basis of the intelligence reports available to both Eisenhower and Bradley, but this is exactly what happened. SHAEF intelligence officers seemed inclined to heed the wildly optimistic evaluations of the U.S. First Army's G-2, who reported on 1 August 1944 that within the next four to eight weeks Germany would be reduced to a state of chaos. However, Dickson had obviously modified his conclusion four months later.

Toward the end of November, the German general Manteuffel toured the German positions in the Eifel area to observe the situation at the front. One thing he learned was the Americans would stand guard until sundown and not resume their watch until one hour before dawn[8]; as they had demonstrated in North Africa, they seemed unable to appreciate the value of intense patrolling. During the time the Americans were not on the alert, the Germans would send out patrols with nearly total immunity, proof the American command was unprepared for an attack in the Ardennes sector.

The build-up of the Nazi forces was done with great skill. Control over radio transmissions was imposed, giving no indication to the eavesdropping Allies anything unusual was in progress. The enemy managed to conceal ten divisions in the forest, an accumulation skillfully done since secrecy demanded all movements take place at night to avoid being spotted and attacked by Allied planes. The enemy was helped by the fact that, due to lack of patrolling, the local American commanders were unaware of the German disposition on their fronts. Taking advantage of this slackness, the German intelligence officers were able to assess the American strength with great accuracy.

Opposite the Germans were only three U.S. divisions. Of these, the 99th had been in Europe only a month and the 106th was untried, having landed at Le Havre just six days before the offensive began; it was transported by road to the Ardennes to gain battle experience in what was confidently believed to be a quiet sector of the front. Finally, there was 28th Division, which had been moved to the Ardennes to rest and refit after being badly mauled in the brutal and bloody fiasco of the Huertgen Forest, for which Eisenhower must share the blame; it resulted in the Americans losing 27,000 killed, wounded, sick and missing. In addition to this light force of infantry, there was a screen of armor including the 9th Armored Division, which had been in the area for two months, but apart from occasional patrols it had seen no action. There was also the 14th Cavalry Regiment with halftracks and reconnaissance vehicles, none of which was a match for the German tanks.

The offensive opened with an artillery bombardment which did little damage, either material or human, but did succeed in cutting telephone communications. The result was commanders of anything bigger than a brigade were unable to keep in contact with their units. Three German armies mounted a concentrated attack on a 75-mile front. The consequence was predictable. Under cover of very bad weather, resulting in the absence of Allied air cover, German storm troopers infiltrated the loosely held American line. English-speaking Germans dressed in American uniforms succeeded in creating havoc behind the American positions. These infiltrators were to be launched in two waves, the first of which was to create as much confusion as possible among the Americans, while the second was to capture bridges across the Meuse.

In the event, the second wave was stalled because it lacked American transportation, and it was forced to make do with its own vehicles disguised as American equipment. This resulted in them moving with extreme caution. They failed to achieve a clean breakthrough and did not link up with the first wave waiting for them to attack the bridges. The operation of the second wave was eventually canceled. The balance of the attackers were very successful, losing only eight jeeps out of forty-two, and those men who were captured managed to convince their captors of the existence of a large force behind the U.S. front. Adding to the confusion, the American press initially reported the enemy attacks had been either stopped or repulsed; this misinformation passed the censor, which reflects adversely on the control exercised by SHAEF's public relations section. It was not until the battle had been in progress for two days that the reports began to describe German successes, and it took Bradley the same length of time to appreciate that the U.S. armies under attack lacked the mobility he had not long before asserted they possessed. He ordered Patton to stop his offensive. On the same day a SHAEF intelligence summary stated, a trifle optimistically, the situation in the Ardennes was under control, and there was no reason why the planned Allied offensive should not start on time.

The confusion caused by the Germans was briefly successful. Middleton's VIII Corps was attacked by twenty German divisions, of which seven were armored, including tanks supported by armored assault guns. Hodges remained doubtful with regard to the German intentions, and delayed reporting the attack to SHAEF for ten hours. It was not until 18 December, when the enemy had captured Stavelot and was threatening his headquarters at Spa, that he evacuated his position to safety after becoming convinced this was not a mere spoiling attack. The Americans had neither a plan of defense nor units in the immediate area capable of resisting the skillful enemy attack. Their predicament was not helped by a communications system based not on radio but telephone, a dangerous choice as Bradley was soon to discover. As for any plans to counter the German attack, the only one they had was propounded by Troy Middleton, which was to fight all the way back to the Meuse if necessary.

The German objectives were Liège, Namur, and Antwerp; had they been successful they would have captured American supply dumps and divided the U.S. and British forces. With that accomplished they had hopes of reaching the coast to cut off the British supplies, forcing another Dunkirk-type evacuation. The assault did not go as smoothly as it appeared to from the Allies' perspective. Part of the problem was the need for secrecy, resulting in only a few officers being informed of the proposed operation. Manteuffel was given such short notice of his part in the attack he had to move his 5th Panzer Division from the area around Hanover to the front in just three nights. There was a shortage of reinforcements and many divisions existed in theory only. Hitler was eventually persuaded to make an amendment so that the attack commenced at 5:50 A.M., instead of the artillery starting its barrage at 7:30 A.M. with a delay of three hours before the infantry began its assault.

Against weak and surprised troops there was generally little opposition; it was only beyond Stavelot that the Americans were able to put up a strong fight. The enemy's main problem was that their movements were held up by poor weather and a shortage of fuel, which was not helped by the planners having made a careful calculation of how much fuel an armored division used to move 100 kilometers. The result was a totally inadequate allowance, and the situation was not improved by the supplies being kept too far to the rear to be of much use to the advancing tanks and motorized units.

The loss of Liège and Namur would have created a grave situation for the Allies, and it was clear they would have to act quickly in order to stabilize the situation. Bradley's headquarters were in Luxembourg, where he was isolated from the northern sector of the front, and his communications with his commanders in the area soon became difficult and threatened. The U.S. First Army had paid little attention to radio communications during the course of its training and consequently had to rely almost exclusively on the use of the telephone. Contact with Bradley's armies was so poor that Churchill depended on nightly situation reports from the 21st Army Group headquarters, even though it was SHAEF's responsibility to provide such information.[9]

Bradley's communications had a repeater station located at Jemelle, which was in the direct path of the advancing German 5th Panzer, and to add to his troubles it soon became impossible for him to visit his army commanders in the north because of the danger involved in traveling; bad weather made flying impossible or at least extremely hazardous, and by road it was equally dangerous due to icy conditions and the unknown whereabouts in some areas of German infiltrators. It reached the point where Bradley could not control operations in both the north and south sectors, and Eisenhower was forced into the realization that the command of the U.S. First and Ninth Armies would have to be transferred to Montgomery. For reasons lacking logical explanation, he delayed making this transfer, waiting for the British to request the change, which provoked Brooke to write in his diary he regretted the U.S. leadership and its lack of a plan to restore order to Hodges's chaotic sector.[10]

As Eisenhower recalled the events, far from being caught by surprise, the day the attack began he was immediately convinced it was to be no local offensive, and he declared he had always been certain that before the enemy was finally defeated he would launch a desperate counteroffensive. He further asserted that, although surprised by the timing of the attack, he and his staff were not surprised by the enemy's choice of location. That claim, however, was written in his official diary some seven days after the offensive began, giving him ample time to modify his original reaction. If he expected an enemy attack in the Ardennes, he certainly showed a very unusual and extremely unsuccessful method of preparing for it. Such was his appreciation of the seriousness of the situation that on 18 December he expressed the belief that part of the 12th Army Group could hold the Germans while the remainder of the Army Group joined the 21st Army Group in mounting an offensive. His plan was to have entailed an attack by Montgomery southeast from the area of Nijmegen between the Rhine and the Meuse while the portion of Bradley's 12th Army Group secured the lines of communications along the line Namur-Liège-Aachen. They were then to relieve the 21st Army Group east of the Meuse and launch an offensive to converge on the area between Bonn and Cologne. This was to be followed by the 6th Army Group, plus six divisions from the 12th Army Group, taking over part of the 12th Army Group's sector in the area of St. Dizier to Thionville, and from there along the Meuse. Fortunately, at a later conference held at Verdun, he changed his mind and instead stressed the need to stop the German advance.

Two days after the Battle of the Bulge began, Eisenhower still had made no change in the command organization; eventually two British generals on the staff of SHAEF, Strong and Whiteley, told Bedell Smith they had received a suggestion that Montgomery should be placed in command of the Allied defense of the Ardennes. Apparently Eisenhower had forgotten it was he who was in command of the Allied forces in northern Europe — a strange lapse of memory in view of his previously

Chapter 15—The Germans Strike in the Ardennes 147

displayed anxiety to keep the armies under his direct control. Eisenhower had ignored the obvious threat in the Ardennes even as late as 15 December, and he aggravated the problem by delaying any reorganization of command until the last minute. Whether his tardiness was a case of military ignorance, nationalism, or a fear his reputation would be injured by Montgomery's appointment is now a matter for speculation. Nevertheless, Eisenhower and Bradley were evidently incapable of arriving at a reasonably accurate assessment of German capabilities and intentions, and this failure was to prove costly in American lives in the Battle of the Ardennes.

The information from Strong and Whiteley was passed to Eisenhower, who postponed any action until a staff meeting was held the following morning; only then did he instruct Bedell Smith to telephone Bradley and inform him of the change of command. The Supreme Commander's recollection of this entire incident was that it was his decision and his alone; in his memoirs he makes no mention of the events which preceded Smith's telephone call to Bradley. In fact, on 19 December 1944, three days after the German offensive began, in a report to the Combined Chiefs of Staff, he stated he realized it would be impractical for Bradley to continue in command of both the north and south fronts, and he had therefore redrawn the boundary, giving Montgomery command of the north.

If this "realization" is accurate he was extremely slow in arriving at it, and his recollection does not appear to agree with the fact he had to be prodded into making the decision. It needed no military genius to appreciate the longer the Allied command in the Ardennes remained divided, the greater the chance of a German victory. When Bedell Smith telephoned to give him the news, Bradley protested the situation did not warrant what he called "a fundamental change."[11] His objection was quiet unreasonable, for he was well aware the road to Spa had been cut by the 2nd Panzer Division, making command of his troops in the north even more tenuous. Bedell Smith asked him if the change would have made sense had Montgomery been an American. Bradley replied in that case he would have agreed entirely with the change of command. It is an indication of Bradley's character, and his failure to understand military needs, that he was so reluctant to temporarily yield command of some of his forces to one of another nationality, albeit for a very good reason.

It appears two things ruled his thinking at the time, neither of them in the best interests of making a quick end to the war. The first was, again, nationalism, and the second was an inordinate concern that Montgomery's appointment might discredit the U.S. Army in the eyes of the American public, although it might not have been the reputation of the U.S. Army which concerned him so much as his own. If only Bradley had considered the situation with more objectivity he might possibly have realized if von Rundstedt had succeeded in advancing to the Meuse this would have threatened the rear of the U.S. 12th Army Group. The result would have made Bradley's strategic position uncomfortable and would have done little to enhance his military reputation. Had that threat materialized, a reasonable reaction would have been to blame the generals, not the soldiers. Bradley would have been held accountable for Montgomery not being given the temporary command. He failed to understand that in order to counter any threat to the U.S. 12th Army Group's rear, Montgomery, to support the U.S. front, would have had to use the reserves he had created, and the commitment of these British forces would have done nothing to bolster Bradley's standing in the opinion of the U.S. public.

Bradley not only refused to move his headquarters from Luxembourg but, making the same mistake as Eisenhower, he also waited too long to visit Hodges to offer assistance, and was finally prevented from doing so by enemy action. So out of touch with events on his front was Bradley that he was unaware Hodges had moved his headquarters from Spa. Montgomery, too, was kept uninformed by Eisenhower and Bradley, but his liaison officers ensured he had a fairly good picture of what was happening on other fronts; Bradley's communications were so weak it was not until 25 December that he was able to meet Montgomery.

Once his appointment was made on 20 December, four days after the offensive began, Montgomery set to work immediately, unlike Eisenhower. He began to "tidy up" the battlefield, which provoked Bradley to criticism because he felt Montgomery was simply wasting time, but Bradley never did show much appreciation for the finer points of military thinking, least of all Montgomery's. The British Field Marshal was firmly convinced a commander whose army was unbalanced would lose the battle, and therefore he always prepared his positions in such a way he would have minimum difficulty in countering an unexpected enemy move.

It was in the Ardennes that Montgomery's system of liaison officers proved invaluable. Having a clear idea of the situation on the entire front enabled Montgomery to organize the two American armies in preparation for a counterattack. He canceled his plans to cross the Rhine and had already created a reserve consisting of the British XXX Corps under Horrocks, a display of forethought and the need to be balanced. This reserve was eventually committed to the U.S. Third Army's left flank, taking over from the U.S. First Army the Givet-Hooton sector. The move completed, it allowed the U.S. VII Corps the freedom to push forward to Houffalize on 3 January 1945.

Chapter 15—The Germans Strike in the Ardennes

The Allied defense of the Ardennes was based on two towns— St. Vith, near the German border, and Bastogne. The selection of Bastogne was made by Whiteley; he put the suggestion to Bedell Smith, who in turn agreed and gave the orders for it to be defended. The U.S. 101st Airborne was resting at Rheims and, together with the 282nd Airborne, it was instructed to go to Bastogne, where the number of defenders totaled about 18,000. Bastogne was a major target which the German generals fully appreciated, for it controlled the junction of seven roads. Patton offered to move the axis of his attack through an angle of 45 degrees in order to relieve Bastogne. It proved a brilliant example of maneuvering, the sort of thing he had practiced frequently during military exercises before the war, but the skill of the change of direction bore no comparison with the execution of the advance. It was badly planned and used poorly trained troops, many of whom had no previous experience of battle.

Patton's network of telephones and radios was not secure, and the Germans were able to take note of the Third Army's moves. A stubborn defense of the town was made by the Americans under very hard conditions; they were short of supplies, the weather was extremely cold, and no air support was possible for some time, but when a demand for them to surrender was sent in by the Germans it was curtly rejected. The besieged town was eventually relieved by the Third Army, which met the U.S. First Army at Houffalize on 16 January 1945, thereby eliminating most of the bulge. At Bastogne, after the war, the Americans erected a monument; inscribed on its walls is a narrative of the battle.

In the north, the Germans made a quick advance to the region around St. Vith and two days after the offensive began were astride the road leading to the town. Thereafter they advanced so rapidly in some parts of the front that the American defenders fled, some continuing for many miles, others surrendering as soon as they were surrounded, making little attempt to fight their way out. The resulting confusion behind the American lines was so great that U.S. 7th Armored Division, ordered to St. Vith from Vielsalm, had to push past vehicles and men of the 14th and 106th divisions who were fleeing from the front. To add to the state of disorder, the American radio system here was also insecure. The Germans were therefore well aware of the total chaos existing behind the American lines and also knew of the American intentions, such as the order given to Gavin to move the 82nd Airborne to provide back-up for the defenders of St. Vith. The situation was not helped by the surrender of over 8,000 U.S. soldiers in the Schnee Eifel, releasing German forces for the attack on St. Vith.

By the fifth day of the German offensive, Montgomery decided the

Americans should withdraw from St. Vith, but so strong were Hodges's objections that the order was rescinded, with the proviso that Gen. Matthew Ridgway's forces must halt at Vielsalm in their attempt to relieve St. Vith. Ridgway's corps was given the task of re-establishing a line which ran from Malmedy to St. Vith and Houffalize, but he had too few men to do this, and therefore he was halted and instructed to hold open a corridor to be used as a possible escape route. When the American position at St. Vith became untenable after four German divisions began closing in on the town, the defenders, thanks to Montgomery's foresight, were given a means of escape which they may not have had if Hodges's myopia and unimaginative stubbornness had prevailed in total. The German infantry was supported by Tiger and Panther tanks and a mixed force of Americans put up a stubborn defense; in the end, however, they had to withdraw under Gen. Robert Hasbrouk's leadership.

The evacuation of St. Vith was completed on 28 December, but despite the momentary setback the defenders, in and around the town, had succeeded in delaying the enemy for five days when in fact he had not expected the town to be defended at all.

Gradually the Allied position was brought under control due to several factors, including the improvement in weather which allowed the Allied air forces to operate regularly, and also to the worsening fuel situation experienced by the German mechanized units. The Germans under Manteuffel suffered another blow which impeded their plans; after his failure to capture Bastogne, the 2nd Panzer Division was hit by an Allied force consisting of the Guards Armoured Division and the U.S. Second Armored Division, which prevented an advance to Dinant or the Meuse.

During this crisis, the Supreme Commander, paying too much heed to his security advisors, was playing the recluse in a hotel room at Versailles because of the rumors that German assassination squads were hunting for him. As a result he knew little, if anything, of what was happening at the fronts and he was resorting to using the telephone to conduct operations, in much the same way that Fredendall had commanded the II Corps during the Battle of Kasserine Pass. Bradley, too, was infected by the rumors of death squads searching for high-ranking Allied officers, for when he went to see Montgomery on 25 December he had hidden the insignia of rank on his uniform with white tape and, perhaps due to these rumors or to unusable roads and air facilities, he had visited neither Hodges nor Simpson. By contrast, Montgomery did go to see the U.S. troops under his command as well as Hodges. At this meeting between Bradley and Montgomery, relations between the two dropped to the lowest point during all the fighting in northern Europe. The cause could have been Mont-

Chapter 15—The Germans Strike in the Ardennes

gomery telling Bradley, bluntly but quite accurately, that he had made a mess of operations on the Ardennes Front.

For the first ten days of the battle, Montgomery had received no messages or instructions from Eisenhower; he was therefore unaware if the Supreme Commander had any future plans. Eisenhower had failed to keep in touch with Bradley, too, for by Christmas Day it was six days since they had conferred. Although at times tactless, Montgomery was never hesitant to express his appreciation of having commanded American troops. Upon returning the command of the U.S. First Army to Bradley, he stated in a letter that it had been an honor for him to command such fine troops, and stressed how important it was that Bradley had accomplished so much in the south, especially by holding Bastogne. Nine days earlier on 5 January 1945, in a postscript to a letter from Hodges to Harmon, he added his congratulations to the U.S. 2nd Armored Division for the work it had done in defeating the Germans in the Ardennes.

Despite this, there was no real accord in the Allied camp. Patton had visited Bradley's headquarters and, while having Christmas dinner together, Bradley said Montgomery's attack across the Rhine would not be ready for another three months; they agreed this was fortunate because otherwise they might be instructed to withdraw to the Saar-Vosges area or even to the Moselle, which they considered to be a loathsome prospect. This conclusion reflected an unfortunate belief that to retreat was unthinkable, and this included a strategic withdrawal made in order to shorten the line, create reserves and, if possible, to rest some of the men. At St. Vith, Hodges's strenuous objections to his orders to withdraw were based on nothing more than a local withdrawal to shorten the line; it was to have been simply a move designed to improve his position. Regrettably, as they demonstrated more than once, these generals were averse to such a move. To the British a strategic withdrawal was a matter of necessity dictated by the circumstances of battle, intended to strengthen their position. The Americans, not having had the exposure to wars the British have had, considered such a move tantamount to treachery and Hodges was not alone among the American generals in the way he thought on the matter. The U.S. XVIII Airborne Corps paid heavily for Hodges's decision.

Bradley was another one who could not tolerate a planned withdrawal. At one time during the Battle of the Ardennes, Montgomery had believed the enemy would stage a second large attack, and if this should have happened he would have considered retreating further west. In a letter to Hodges, Bradley stated he would be alarmed at any plan carried out under British orders which resulted in the ceding of territory which could be used by the U.S. First Army as a base for a counterattack. This was an unwarranted and unprofessional interference on Bradley's part. Hodges was under Montgomery's command, but Bradley was potentially placing him in an uncomfortable position in his relationship with Montgomery. This letter once more showed indications of Bradley's Anglophobia, extreme tactlessness, and a lamentable lack of sound professional judgment.

With the exception of Patton and Montgomery, the Allied generals were initially unable to appreciate that the German offensive was anything but a minor spoiling attack. There was no excuse for SHAEF failing to foresee the possibility of an offensive, in view of what had happened before in the area and, of greater importance, from the information gathered from prisoners, civilians and captured documents. Even the date of the start of the attack was known. SHAEF was also well aware that, since October, Panzer divisions were being withdrawn to refit, with some of these units being used to create the Sixth S.S. Panzer Army. Despite enemy precautions, elements of his tank units were spotted moving toward the Ardennes, where some newly formed infantry divisions were also noticed. With all this information at his disposal, Eisenhower was still caught by surprise, and it was a surprise which could have been far more disruptive, dangerous and costly than it proved to be. The Germans were, on balance, better positioned than were the Allies; they were not overextended like the Americans, they did have some reserves in position, and they had thoroughly prepared for the assault.

The Battle of the Bulge need never have happened, according to Montgomery; undoubtedly Eisenhower and Bradley dismissed the possibility of an attack in a very casual manner, and they showed that they were dangerously overconfident in the ability of just four depleted U.S. divisions to repel a major assault in this area. There was evidence Eisenhower lacked firmness in managing the situation (a deficiency noted before by Tedder in Tunisia), and he was wanting in essential authority in his dealings with his subordinate commanders.

It is difficult to understand what Eisenhower thought he was gaining by delaying the appointment of Montgomery to command the defense of the Ardennes. His lack of control over Bradley and Patton was quite evident, and had he been a stricter disciplinarian he would not have tolerated such a negative attitude from these two generals. He had stressed before the Anglo-American force was to be an allied one and not one composed of a variety of nations. He failed to live up to this standard; it cost the Allies six weeks of valuable time and the Americans incurred heavy casualties in an operation which could have been avoided. By slowing the Allied advance on the Western Front, the Germans had clearly demon-

Chapter 15—The Germans Strike in the Ardennes

strated they were far from finished, despite the assessment by SHAEF, Bradley and Eisenhower to the contrary. Eisenhower's misplaced confidence was evidenced by the bet he made with Montgomery the day after the Germans opened their offensive. His wager was the war would be over by Christmas of 1944.[11]

During the Ardennes battle, Eisenhower again displayed his inadequacy as a field commander. He wrote to Stalin seeking to send to Russia a senior officer from SHAEF with the purpose of discussing Russian plans for the future. The result was his deputy, Sir Arthur Tedder, his Chief of Operations Staff, Maj. Gen. Harold Bull, and a senior officer from SHAEF Intelligence section were sent to confer with the Russians. Such hasty action, giving preference to co-operating with a far from co-operative ally and ignoring the more pressing need to finish the Battle of the Bulge, demonstrated indisputably Eisenhower's inability to appreciate the relative importance of matters of urgency. As for Hitler, so optimistic was he that the Ardennes offensive, plus the attack on Britain using "doodlebugs" (the flying bombs) and rockets, had drained the Allied resources and spirit, that he stripped the Western Front of men and materiel in order to hold the Russians at the river Oder. The Battle of the Bulge had been costly to both the Germans and Americans. The enemy had lost 1,400 tanks and assault guns, which they could ill-afford to do, and their casualties were reasonably estimated to equal the American losses.

Eisenhower, having learned nothing from past events, issued his orders for a counteroffensive, stating there was to be another aggressively conducted offensive on a broad front. The more things changed, the more they stayed the same, for variety was not one of the Supreme Commander's notable assets. He did not understand the Battle of the Ardennes resulted from the failure of his broad front strategy.

16

The Final Assault Against Germany

Montgomery was correct about "Dragoon"; it had resulted in the 15th Army Group in Italy being greatly delayed in achieving its objectives. Churchill could not resist the opportunity, on 6 December, of bringing this to Roosevelt's attention. The Rhine had not yet been reached, which had resulted in heavy fighting. Within the short time of two weeks the situation, far from improving, had become considerably worse. Manteuffel believed that, following the failure of the Ardennes offensive, Hitler indulged in a multitude of disconnected actions; he was undoubtedly assisted by Eisenhower, who also failed to produce one big plan for a final offensive aimed at the destruction of the enemy.

Once the situation in the Ardennes was under control, Eisenhower managed to visit the northern flank of the Allied line, and while there he had a meeting on 28 December with Montgomery in a train at Hasselt. It was here Montgomery propounded his plan for an attack on the Ruhr, emphasizing the need to use concentrated forces under a separate ground commander. He followed this with a letter of confirmation the next day, in which he restated the points he had made the previous day. He appreciated that Bradley would not agree to being subordinated to him, so someone else should be appointed ground commander, since it was too much for the Supreme Commander to handle. The Ruhr, Montgomery wrote, should be given priority handling by assigning all available forces for the offensive, and if this were not accompanied by the establishment of a single ground commander for the assault the result would inevitably be failure. He did not propose he should be that given the assignment, making it clear in item three of his letter that he was fully aware Bradley would object.

The importance Montgomery attached to the Ruhr was shared by oth-

Chapter 16—The Final Assault Against Germany 155

ers; on 1 January 1942 the Chiefs of Staff had considered a landing on the north coast of Europe on the assumption German morale would collapse. The object of that 15-division invasion force was to capture the Ruhr, thus striking a severe blow to enemy war production. Upon his return to his headquarters in Versailles, Eisenhower discussed the Montgomery plan with his three confidants, Bedell Smith, Kenneth Strong, and J.F.M. Whiteley. Of these three only Whiteley had ever before served on a headquarters staff. The plan devised by these four was essentially Whiteley's, which entailed a drive across the middle of the Bulge, followed by a drive eastward, using the same routes as had the Germans in their offensive. Whiteley's plan, eagerly accepted by Eisenhower, had none of the merits of a well-conceived idea but all the indications of an amateur strategist. It displayed a lack of imagination and to a great extent duplicated the enemy's line of advance. The Germans had taken three months to plan their offensive, yet Eisenhower believed the Allies needed neither a period in which to recover from a major reverse nor any detailed preparation in order to mount a major offensive. Such a plan was in direct contradiction to the one he had given Montgomery to believe he had accepted. Eisenhower made but one alteration—he added the condition that when Patton's advance from Bastogne had joined forces with Collins's attack from the north, Bradley would resume control of the U.S. First Army.

Once again the important differences between Montgomery's methods of planning a battle and those of Eisenhower and his staff were brought to light. Montgomery based his concepts of battle on sound military principles, coupled with a fairly accurate appraisal of the enemy's capabilities. Eisenhower's approach lacked the finesse of a competent field commander and displayed far too much of an attempt to recover lost prestige, besides being a result of a planning committee, the very thing he allegedly abhorred. At the same time he received Montgomery's letter, there arrived a telegram from Marshall stating the British press was critical of Eisenhower, but he assured the Supreme Commander he had the complete support of both Roosevelt and himself, and the appointment of a British officer to command above Bradley would be objectionable to the American public. Marshall was apparently expressing his personal reservations, for there is no evidence the American public had voiced any objections to the possibility of Montgomery taking charge of ground operations with Bradley as his subordinate. Lt. Gen. William H. Simpson, commander of the U.S. Ninth Army, stated his relationship with Montgomery was very good and he made it plain that once Montgomery had assumed command of the Ninth Army during the Ardennes battle, the orders given were clear and precise, unlike those Simpson had previously received from Bradley.

Marshall's reaction to this British press criticism was very slanted, for when the American press was criticizing Montgomery's handling of operations around Caen support from Marshall was noticeably absent. Since Marshall seemed to have such fear of American public opinion in matters not of a civil nature, one is led to believe he felt the Americans generally were as capable as he of assessing the effectiveness of a military decision.

Montgomery's message caused Eisenhower a great deal of annoyance, and it was fortunate Montgomery's Chief of Staff was able to use his charm on the Supreme Commander, thereby gaining a little time. De Guingand explained to Montgomery that Eisenhower was very perturbed by the situation, and told him of a draft telegram from the Supreme Commander to Marshall, threatening to resign should Montgomery be appointed ground commander. Persuaded by de Guingand, Montgomery wired Eisenhower regretting his letter of 28 December had caused distress, and explained he was only expressing his opinions, as Eisenhower appeared to appreciate frankness. Evidently Eisenhower did not value such outspokenness on Montgomery's part, nor did he appreciate the advantages of an assault to take the Ruhr being placed under a single commander, quite possibly because he viewed such a change as one which would reflect upon his own abilities as a ground commander.

A little more than a week later, Montgomery was again demonstrating his propensity for tactlessness. He held a press conference, and it was one which he later admitted should never have taken place. The text of the press release had been cleared with both Churchill and Eisenhower. Reading the notes of the statement can easily lead to the conclusion that he meant to stress the Ardennes counteroffensive had been a good example of Allied co-operation. Unfortunately these notes were also interpreted to mean it was the British who saved the day for the Americans. It is extremely unlikely this is what Montgomery intended; he simply related the facts as he saw them. This conclusion is supported by an editorial in the *New York Times* dated 9 January 1945, which gave credit to Montgomery's appreciation of the performance of U.S. soldiers in battle. The uproar was caused by some American newspapers quoting Montgomery out of context. Bradley did nothing to help by complaining to Eisenhower about the revelation that command of the U.S. First Army had been transferred to Montgomery and, furthermore, he disliked what he felt was the pro–Montgomery bias shown by the B.B.C. and the British press.

The root of the protests was undoubtedly the American generals' sensitivity, for they could neither accept the fact their army had been routed nor that the British had assisted them in recovering from a dangerous situation, both of which were the result of their generals' dereliction. Two

Chapter 16—The Final Assault Against Germany 157

days later on 9 January, Bradley, in an apparent display of childish pique, issued his own statement. He stressed, among other things, Montgomery's appointment had only been temporary and the entire problem could have been avoided had only SHAEF made that fact clear. This was yet more confirmation of how sensitive and insecure he felt. With his incomparable insight, he declared U.S. public opinion would not tolerate neglect of the battle south of the Ardennes, and he accentuated his belief that for political reasons it was vital an American should command the next offensive. In addition, he suggested the German massing of a large force in the Cologne area had been noticed weeks before the attack began and the possibility of an assault through the Ardennes had been taken into account, following a study of the subject by himself and his staff. Their conclusion was they could afford to take a risk by leaving the Ardennes lightly defended, using the bulk of their forces to attack other areas.

Bradley's assertion is not convincing. The attacks he referred to were achieving nothing. They failed to compel the Germans to reinforce the areas subjected to American pressure, thereby leaving the Ardennes exposed and inviting a German offensive. The U.S. assaults had all been halted by the first week in December, freeing German units to be moved to the Ardennes. Offering no account for the greater importance of other areas, both Bradley and Eisenhower maintained that to have defended the Ardennes more strongly would have impeded both Patton's and Bradley's offensives. An accurate excuse for Patton but not for Bradley, for he was not scheduled to go onto the offensive until January. Therefore the U.S. concentration around Aachen served no immediate purpose, and on 16 December there were four divisions in that vicinity which were in reserve; some of these divisions could have been sent to the Ardennes to rest, where their presence would have been very useful. If it is accurate to say Eisenhower and Bradley took a calculated risk, it is certainly strange they did not confide their decision in Montgomery, whose the 21st Army Group would have been threatened by any attack through the Ardennes.

Even four days after the German offensive began, it was quite evident from Bradley's behavior he had no idea at all how to control the situation. He was an indifferent strategist and he proved he was better at following another's directions than he was at acting on his own initiative when under heavy pressure from the enemy. He, like Eisenhower, was an ardent believer in the broad front assault.

A contributing cause of the tension between Montgomery and Eisenhower was the public relations system used by the American armies. The U.S. commanders would willingly give reporters an account of the operations in their own command and, understandably, make it appear their operations were of major importance, while SHAEF gave only sketchy reports. The result of the two systems was the broadcast or printed news was often slanted. By contrast, the 21st Army Group operated a tighter system by which all press releases went out from its headquarters where all the briefings of the news media took place. It would have been much better if all statements for publication had been subjected to careful approval by the public relations department of SHAEF.

The Allies suffered as a result of the Ardennes assault. The British, with their severely strained resources, promised to raise 250,000 men. By comparison, the United States had not maintained an adequate rate of conscription because it felt hostilities would soon come to an end. This unwarranted optimism resulted in Marshall having to obtain replacements by creaming off excess personnel from defense commands and other military installations in the United States, Panama and Alaska, but it reflects poorly on the U.S. military that it made such a miserable effort to use its human resources more effectively when it was the more lavish in manpower. Not only on the American continent was there wastage; Bradley's headquarters at Namur consisted of 15,000 men, about equal to a division, and SHAEF had a staff of 100,000.

The last few months of the war in Western Europe were not marked by any spectacular victories by the Allies. In January 1945, the British Second Army mounted an offensive which resulted in it gaining the Roer Valley after two weeks of fighting. The advance, which ended in the British obtaining a modest 10-mile foothold into Germany, was halted along with the rest of the Allied armies so that the entire force could regroup. Eisenhower gave Montgomery orders to return the U.S. First Army to Bradley's command effective 17 January, and the British in the area of the Ardennes were withdrawn to begin preparations for Eisenhower's plan to cross the Rhine, which was given the code name Operation "Veritable." The plan was discussed in SHAEF on 16 January and it was agreed that the U.S. First Army should take over part of the 2nd Army Group's line. Bradley gave the impression he had acceded to the arrangement, but two days later Montgomery received a directive informing him, upon Eisenhower's orders, Bradley was to continue his attacks in the Ardennes which were not to be closed down in order to assist Montgomery. Both Bradley and Eisenhower were quite adamant there must be no crossing of the Rhine until all the Allied armies were lined up from Nijmegen to Switzerland. To accomplish this, Bradley was instructed to exploit the enemy's weakness in the Ardennes. He was to attempt to breach the Siegfried Line, following which he was to advance in a northeasterly direction along an axis from Prum to Eustkirchen. The offensive failed. Far from bringing to bat-

Chapter 16—The Final Assault Against Germany 159

tle the hoped-for large numbers of Germans, Strong reported in late January the enemy had actually been able to move his Sixth Panzer Army from Cologne, the ultimate target of Bradley's attack, to the Russian front.

Eisenhower's plan was another of his misguided attempts to try to please both Bradley and Montgomery. He succeeded in pleasing one but not the other. He left Montgomery uncertain about his proposed offensive between the Maas and the Rhine, which was to be mounted by the Canadians, together with a northeasterly thrust by the U.S. Ninth Army aimed at linking up with the Canadians on the Rhine; the Ninth Army, however, had been reduced to two corps and five divisions to provide reinforcements for the Ardennes counteroffensive. Montgomery had asked the Supreme Commander to reinforce the U.S. Ninth Army with 16 extra divisions, but Eisenhower would agree to only 12 being transferred to Simpson's command. Nonetheless, the 12 divisions could not be moved because they were involved in Bradley's operations in the south, which were costing the U.S. First Army about 800 casualties a day and achieving nothing.

Up to the end of January, Montgomery was placed in the unenviable position of being the recipient of promises which could not be kept; as a consequence he never knew if the link-up between the Canadians and the Americans was to be effected. To add to the confusion, Eisenhower gave instructions to Montgomery and Bradley that they were to prepare plans for an offensive north of Düsseldorf, which was to begin as soon as Eisenhower had closed down the U.S. First Army's offensive. The lack of progress made by Bradley in this operation caused rumblings of discontent in SHAEF. Even the ardent anti-Montgomery faction began expressing criticism of the handling of the battle in the south.

Eisenhower held a conference in the Trianon Palace Hotel on 31 January to try to rectify his strategy. He decided Operations "Veritable" and "Grenade" were to be mounted by Montgomery who was instructed to commence his attack on 8 February. Bradley's pride, deeply hurt by the change of command during the Ardennes offensive, suffered more as the result of the Supreme Commander's latest decision. It meant he had to shut down his operations in the Ardennes and attack Düren in order to capture the Roer Dams; that offensive was aimed at outflanking the dams by straightening the remaining bulge in the line. Again Eisenhower had indulged in his weakness. He had given Montgomery to understand that "Veritable" and "Grenade" were to be the main operations. A day later, on 25 January, he agreed to permit Bradley to continue his Ardennes offensive, but on 1 February he authorized the mounting of Montgomery's operations.

Decisiveness on the part of Eisenhower was not in evidence. He had sacrificed a possible success by insisting on a broad front offensive, and it cannot be overlooked that he was hoping for a victory by an American army under an American commander. There certainly appears to have been no justification for the assault by Bradley, other than to make sure he was kept fully occupied, and there is a reasonable suspicion his other motive was to ensure that Montgomery was deprived of reinforcements for Simpson's Ninth Army. Eisenhower succeeded in only wasting time; he showed misguided patriotism which played an all-too-important part in his military decisions, for after the offensive was halted he ordered some of Bradley's forces to be sent to Simpson. By delaying Montgomery's offensive Eisenhower gave the Germans the much-needed time to reorganize, which they did with speed and efficiency.

To add to Montgomery's problems, SHAEF was in favor of sending reinforcements to clear the enemy still holding out in the area around Colmar and Strasbourg; the resulting drain on resources available for Veritable led Montgomery to the conclusion there was no proper control over the three army groups since each appeared intent on going its own way. As though to cock a snook at Montgomery, Patton started an offensive and issued orders to the Third Army that the next objective was Cologne. His action meant supplies intended for other areas would be restricted; one of those to suffer was Montgomery. Such action by Patton again revealed Eisenhower's lack of control over his subordinates.

Operation Veritable was meant to capture the west bank of the Rhine, and the main effort was to be in the north of the Ruhr. With the U.S. Ninth Army and a total of 35 divisions under his command, Montgomery was to cross the lower Rhine and enter the plains of Germany; a supporting attack was to be made by the 12th Army Group with such strength as it could muster. The U.S. First Army was to attack in a southeasterly direction across the Erft River toward Cologne, while the U.S. Third Army headed northeast to the Siegfried Line. To the south, the U.S. Third and U.S. Seventh armies were to mount two converging attacks in a southeasterly direction toward the Rhine. With this operation, Eisenhower had created his favorite broad front offensive, which appeared to be the only type of offensive he knew. Alan Brooke opposed this plan, for he felt clearing the west bank of the Rhine would entail the use of too many divisions and would place the northern attack in peril.

The British had little faith in Eisenhower's strategy, which lack of confidence did not result in him considering the criticism to be in the least constructive. Bedell Smith managed a compromise whereby the northern attack by the 21st Army Group would proceed without waiting for the Americans to reach the Rhine throughout its length, and the U.S. Ninth Army was to stay under Montgomery's control. Despite Montgomery's

Chapter 16—The Final Assault Against Germany 161

poor standing in the opinion of many American commanders, Simpson reported Montgomery issued orders which were precise and clear, in contrast with Bradley's ambiguity.[1]

Operation "Veritable" closed down a month later, with the 21st Army Group established on the west bank of the Rhine and lined up from Nijmegen to a point opposite Düsseldorf. During this month of fighting, the Germans suffered heavily; about 90,000 of them had been killed, wounded, were missing or taken prisoner and the enemy had lost most of his artillery and mortars. These losses considerably reduced Hitler's ability to risk a strong stand on the far side of the Rhine.

"Veritable" was slower in achieving its objectives than the planners had anticipated, due to the ground being unsuitable for armored units and also to the unexpectedly stiff resistance from the enemy. Nevertheless, the attack in the north helped the Americans in their assault, which opened on 23 February, against the Roer River line. The American offensive, using four of their ten divisions, encountered little opposition for the Germans had switched their troops to oppose the British attack. The U.S. losses amounted to fewer than 100. The British and the Americans eventually joined forces on 2 March. Three weeks later, as part of Operation "Plunder," elements of the Black Watch landed on the German-held Rhine bank, and by dawn of the following day the 21st Army Group had established three bridgeheads, all of them securely held.

Prior to the Rhine crossing, the British Chiefs of Staff had suggested the Supreme Commander be requested to submit, on or before 31 January 1945, a written review of his operational progress, together with his plans for his winter campaign. Eisenhower replied explaining how a broad front assault was essential. Until the offensive was started, it was vital to have a defense line which could be held with minimum strength, and the Allies would then be in a good position to threaten the enemy in a variety of locations. It was also imperative for the Allies to hold the Rhine in reasonable strength to deter the Germans from attacking the Allied lines of communications. He admitted differences existed between himself and Montgomery; however, he contended the Field Marshal's plan for a thrust into Germany had been exposed as dangerous by the enemy offensive in the Ardennes. He stated he would abide by any orders given him by Marshall or by the Combined Chiefs of Staff regarding the place of the proposed offensive. Nevertheless, he felt he had to secure a long flank line which could be easily defended. If this were not done then he would be forced to immobilize more troops than he felt was prudent. The British Chiefs of Staff were unmoved by these arguments. The poorest of Eisenhower's contentions was that the Ardennes had proved Montgomery's single thrust into Germany would have been a mistake. Had the British plan been put into effect, it would have done two things: first, it would have provided a strong U.S. force to hold the line of the Loire to Orléans and from there to Troyes, Chalons and Rheims, and it would have required the U.S. Seventh Army to have advanced to Nancy and the Saar, thus placing the Allies in a good position to resist any Ardennes-type of attack by the enemy, assuming they would have been capable of mounting such an assault; second, it would have tied up German forces in the north to such an extent the chances of Hitler being able to muster a new army for an offensive in another part of the line would have been far too remote to warrant serious consideration.

Once again Eisenhower had revealed his lack of aptitude for war, and Marshall can have known no better, demonstrated by his failure to see the weakness in the Supreme Commander's assessment of the situation. The British Chiefs of Staff were concerned that Patton would employ his "rock soup" tactic, causing Eisenhower to divert maintenance from its intended destination to support the U.S. Third Army. In essence, the difference of opinion between the British and the Americans was whether, by mounting subsidiary attacks, Eisenhower's accumulation of supplies would be wasted and that Patton would be weakening the main offensive. Not surprisingly, the army commanders could not agree, or more accurately, Montgomery dissented from the majority opinion. He declared that the German offensive in the Ardennes clearly showed the dangers of a broad front offensive; the opposing view was that American public opinion demanded a major thrust south of the Ardennes by American forces.

The military astuteness of the U.S. service commanders has to be questioned. One is led to believe that the U.S. army was the only one at war in which the field officers had to obtain the direct or indirect approval of the civilian population before implementing a strategic or tactical decision. A more inefficient and dangerous way to conduct military operations is difficult to imagine. What was far more plausible was that Eisenhower, supported by Bradley, was seeking to substantiate his strategy and was unwilling to admit he might be wrong. An additional problem facing the Supreme Commander was to assess the strength required to defeat Germany. His conclusion in January 1945 was that the latest Russian offensive had been ineffective; this led him to believe the Germans now had the opportunity to move troops from Italy and Norway, resulting in 100 enemy divisions facing the Western Allies. Of these, Eisenhower estimated the Germans would be able to field 80 divisions, which he thought would be understrength. He calculated the Allies would have 85 divisions and in addition there were between 5 and 8 new French divisions to be

Chapter 16—The Final Assault Against Germany 163

brought up to strength. To add to his concern was the Siegfried Line. As a result, he was adamant that it was essential for his armies to have a strong natural defense line, and the Rhine, in his opinion, fulfilled the requirement.

In a message to Montgomery, dated 17 January 1945, Eisenhower presented a menu of possibilities. If the Germans concentrated north of the Ruhr, the Allies might not be able to break through in that area. Whether the Germans could assemble sufficient forces for a Ruhr assault would depend on the Allies. If the Allied Army Groups were on the Rhine when the Germans attacked, Eisenhower felt they could be held with a total of 25 divisions, leaving 55 for a counteroffensive. If the Colmar Pocket could be reduced, it would release ten divisions for the Ruhr offensive, but at least 35 divisions would be needed for a major attack in the north. Therefore, any line west of the Rhine would result in the Allies having sufficient forces for a main attack, but none for a secondary assault in the area of Frankfurt. What was required, he concluded, was the defeat of the Germans west of the Rhine, and then an advance to the river on a broad front. He proposed a series of attacks north of the Moselle, in an attempt to inflict a major defeat upon the enemy. Afterward the armies would try to gain the western bank of the Rhine north of Düsseldorf. With that completed, the main effort would be launched to destroy the enemy on the remainder of the front west of the Rhine.

The second phase of the offensive would be an attack to establish bridgeheads across the Rhine between Emmerich and Wesel in the north, and between Maintz and Karlsruhe in the south; the Allies would be then be in a position to advance from the lower Rhine into the plains of Germany.

This proposal was not original. It was Eisenhower's solitary strategy — the broad front offensive. He was scared Montgomery's plan would be met by a major concentration of Germans, ignoring the fact that Germany had just suffered a major setback in the Ardennes, where it had lost the equivalent of five divisions or more, and had suffered heavy losses in valuable armor and artillery. The creation by the enemy of sufficient forces to severely hamper a narrow front offensive could only have been done by weakening other fronts, to the advantage of the Allies. Marshall, on his way to the Yalta Conference, met Eisenhower to discuss the situation on the Western Front, and especially the subject of command. He assured Eisenhower that he had his full support, and if a ground commander were appointed he would resign his post as Chief of Staff. In this, three American generals had something in common, for Eisenhower previously, and Patton subsequently, also used the threat of resignation when faced with an unacceptable situation.

Three days later, Eisenhower received a directive that he should immediately begin operations north of the Moselle aimed at destroying the enemy in the area, go on to the Rhine north of Düsseldorf, and make every effort to eliminate other German forces which were still west of the Rhine. By doing this it would help the Allies in their attempt to cross the river. Eisenhower replied he would not wait to proceed to the Rhine along its entire length before establishing bridgeheads over the river. He also promised to advance across the Rhine in the north and south as soon as it was possible to switch forces from south to north. He was careful not to be too specific regarding the future operations in the areas south of the Ruhr and south of the Moselle; the continuation of operations in these regions was the basis of Montgomery's objections. The problem, as usual, was Eisenhower's lack of precision in his orders. He did not explain what the situation would have to be to allow the transfer of men and materiel from the south to the north, nor did he give a time limit by which Allied forces would have to be assembled in the south.

Four days after the crossing of the Rhine by British forces, Montgomery heard that Eisenhower had broken his promise to allow him to drive on to Berlin. The 21st Army Group commander had sent Eisenhower a signal on 27 March stating his intention of going for the river Elbe, using the British Second Army and the U.S. Ninth Army, and he hoped to reach Berlin by autobahn.[2] One day later, Eisenhower informed Montgomery that the U.S. Ninth Army would remain under the 21st Army Group command only until the Ruhr was encircled, which was done on 21 April; at that time the Ninth Army was to revert to Bradley. Eisenhower's behavior was reprehensible. He had written to Montgomery on 15 September 1944 stating indisputably the objective of the Anglo-American armies was Berlin.

On 25 March 1945, Montgomery had given both Eisenhower and Bradley details of his future plans, using a map to ensure there was no misunderstanding. He had drawn a boundary on his right flank and Eisenhower had gone as far as to suggest Magdeburg should be in Bradley's zone, to which both Montgomery and Bradley agreed.[3] There was no further comment from Eisenhower, yet he must have been aware at the time that he was going to change the main attack to the southeast of Dresden in order to make contact with the Russians.

Given the circumstances, the 21st Army Group's progress had been quite rapid. Not only was there flooding, which hampered the Canadians, but the Germans were adept at forming ad hoc battle groups to fight delaying actions. The enemy was very skilled in the use of demolitions and booby traps, all of which impeded Allied progress. During this operation,

Chapter 16—The Final Assault Against Germany 165

Bradley telephoned Patton and asked if it was possible for him to halt the Third Army's advance due to the supply problem. Patton became very upset and threatened to resign his command if forced to go onto the defensive.

At the end of January 1945 there had been a meeting between the British and the Americans at Malta. In the course of discussions the subject of operations in the west was raised; the Americans fallaciously contended that the British plan for a main thrust in the north was not in conflict with Eisenhower's broad front policy. They assured the British Chiefs of Staff that the Supreme Commander's operations, both past and present, were designed to accomplish the same objectives as Montgomery's, that the operations in the south of France were meant to draw off German forces in order to protect Frankfurt and at the same time provide an alternative operation in case the battle in the north failed.

The U.S. Chief of Staff stated the northern sector offensive needed 36 divisions with 10 in reserve, leaving 12 divisions which could be used in the south to support Patton's drive for the middle Rhine. This did not please his British counterparts, who believed such an operation would result in no decisive action. For his part, Eisenhower accepted the need for urgency, in view of the rapidity of the Russian advance on the Eastern Front. Despite the assurance of the U.S. army chiefs that the Western Front could be kept on the offensive along its entire length from north to south, they again ignored the still-unsolved problem of supply distribution and the basic lesson taught at all good military academies— the need to concentrate forces in an offensive.

This meeting gave Marshall another opportunity to express his feelings about Montgomery. He felt the "insufferable British commander" was trying to gain all the publicity in the fight against the Nazis.[4] Marshall appeared to have forgotten the object of the war was to defeat the enemy as soon as possible, and as economically as possible in lives; this was not the time to turn down another's ideas solely on the grounds that he might be trying to obtain all the credit for fighting the Germans. He also seemed to have overlooked the fact it was a war which was being waged, not a popularity contest.

The subject of a single ground commander had again been raised, this time by Churchill, and as a result there was a meeting between Montgomery, Churchill and Brooke to discuss the issue. The British Chiefs of Staff believed the Supreme Commander was too involved with problems of supplies and politics to be an effective ground commander. Eisenhower strongly denied this, contending the Ruhr was the logical dividing line between the 21st and 12th Army Groups and it would be impossible for a separate ground commander to obtain better co-ordination and control of operations than the Supreme Commander. He maintained that a ground commander would only complicate the situation because he would become involved in such matters as supplies, the allocation of troops and the creation of communications. While denying any expression of nationalism, Eisenhower emphasized if two ground commands were established, one on either side of Luxembourg, it would result in the 21st Army Group having under its command 14 British divisions, including the Canadians, and between 45 and 50 U.S. divisions. The other army commander, presumably Bradley, would have to be satisfied with a purely defensive operation. This, Eisenhower submitted — without substantiation — was illogical and would not work. He conceded it might be more appropriate if the deputy commander were an army officer instead of an air force officer. For all Eisenhower's protestations one must ask the same question as did Bedell Smith: "Would it have made any difference had Montgomery been an American?" The fact that Eisenhower was conscious of the Americans outnumbering the British and had used it to support his contention the ground commander had to be American was in contrast to something noted by Churchill. The Prime Minister wrote, but did not send, a memo to Eisenhower pointing out in North Africa Alexander was subordinate to him, and yet the British had four times as many troops in the area than did the Americans. Again, in Italy, an American, Mark Clark was in command of the Fifteenth Army Group where the majority of the troops were British, Commonwealth, Indians and Gurkhas.[5] Churchill felt Alexander would make a good ground commander, which would entail a change of command in Italy. Montgomery expressed the practical opinion that neither the American press nor the American generals would ever agree to such an arrangement. As a result, Montgomery met Eisenhower at Zonhoven on 14 February 1945; when the suggestion was put to him, the Supreme Commander agreed that because he did not want a ground commander the existing arrangements were quite satisfactory.

Eisenhower wrote to Brooke stating on no condition would he agree to have anyone between him and the Army Commanders. If such a change were made, the U.S. generals would think the British were trying to exert pressure in order to get their strategic plan adopted, forgetting on this basis the British generals, in turn, might think the Americans were trying to enforce their strategy over the wishes of their ally. He was of the opinion the front was far too long to be handled by one commander efficiently. His solution was, of course, to contradict himself by continuing to hold two commands, namely Supreme Commander and ground commander. He felt the creation of a separate ground command would be "futile and clumsy" and would interfere with, rather than assist, his own plans. There can be few better examples of "L'état, c'est moi." He failed to explain what the difference was in Tunisia, Sicily and Italy by comparison with that in northern Europe, and in reply to Churchill he wrote his sole object was to "exercise the authority of his office" to maintain a partnership essential to win the war.

In the absence of any evidence to the contrary, one is left to speculate if Eisenhower's decision was influenced by the fact that the campaign in northern Europe was the one given the most publicity, and was also the most important of all Western Allied operations. It is evident he found support from Marshall, who told him he would never allow him to be saddled with the "burden" of an overall ground commander.[6] The division of labor, so much in evidence in American industry, did not seem to have been adopted by the American armed forces, giving the impression that Marshall's decision was tainted with chauvinism.

17

The End of the War in Europe

The Russian advance on the Eastern Front had been very rapid; with the threat to Berlin and the loss of the Silesian coalfields, the Germans transferred two Panzer armies from the Western Front to the Russian Front. Soon after the Allies had crossed the Rhine, the position in Germany began to deteriorate even further. At Montgomery's Venlo headquarters, Eisenhower asked Brooke if he now agreed the push for Frankfurt had been right. Under the circumstances, Brooke's reply was extremely tactful. He answered that since the Germans were obviously crumbling, the situation had changed. He was quite convinced he had never told Eisenhower, as the latter alleged, "You were completely right."[1] He was convinced Eisenhower was completely wrong, and it was his opinion the Americans subconsciously resented the greater military experience of the British.

The Allies now had an opportunity to carry out a double envelopment strategy which, Brooke believed, had not been the case when the enemy had been able to resist more strongly. Having fumbled his way from the Seine toward victory, helped by both the Russians and Hitler, Eisenhower now sought praise for his indifferent efforts. As Dr. Samuel Johnson observed: "It is not done well, but you are surprised to find it done at all."

The American First Army, in a commendable show of initiative, captured the Ludendorf Bridge at Remagen on 7 March and upon hearing this Eisenhower promised Bradley full support, adding one more division to Bradley's estimated needs. Soon after, Eisenhower had second thoughts, limiting the Remagen reinforcements to five divisions because he had promised Montgomery ten divisions for his offensive. Hodges was thus hampered in his advance over the bridge and was given orders to hold the

Bonn-Frankfurt Autobahn when he reached it and advance no further without Eisenhower's instructions. Had the entire front not been on the offensive, it is possible Hodges's success could have been exploited to a more profitable extent.

The surrounding of the Ruhr was belatedly completed on 1 April, the Allies had air superiority and the Germans in the west were collapsing; however, in the east they were holding firmly to the Oder-Neisse Line and also held the Bratislau Gap which led to Vienna. Under these circumstances the British felt it was essential to attempt the capture of Berlin, but the U.S. leaders, political and military, were quite unable to appreciate the British reasoning. Even Bradley, albeit post-war, stated the skeptical attitude of Marshall and Eisenhower toward the British was naïve; nevertheless, he had done nothing to support the British position and was guilty of impeding Montgomery's operations.

Jan Smuts had a clear understanding of the politics of war and he questioned where the British and Americans would be upon the cessation of hostilities, showing concern the Russians might easily appear to have won the war. Lacking the political and military acuity of the South African leader, the Supreme Commander seemed to have an almost morbid fear that if the U.S. armies did not halt at a prearranged line there would be a risk of tangling with the Russians, a fear he did not express regarding the meeting of the II Corps and the Eighth Army in Tunisia, nor when the 6th Army Group met Patton's Third Army.

He gave orders to the U.S. forces they were to halt at the Elbe, despite the fact that the road between Berlin and the First and Ninth Armies was open, with only a few scattered and disorganized German units capable of resistance. He then wired Stalin directly, informing him of his decision to halt his advance[2]; he had no authority whatsoever to make such a direct contact. Churchill, when he heard of such blatant interference in political affairs, expressed the opinion it was unfortunate Eisenhower had sent the telegram to Stalin on 28 March. He made the point that no British commander had been consulted, whereupon Eisenhower tried to defend himself by saying Stalin was the Commander-in-Chief of the Russian armed forces and it was simply a case of one commander consulting another — a very weak excuse indeed. The Chiefs of Staff had not been consulted about this communication despite being responsible for not only ground strategy, but also for issuing directives to the Allied commanders in chief. Clearly, then, Eisenhower had ignored his superior officers in taking this course of action. He, as Supreme Commander of the Allied forces in Europe, was not on a par with Stalin. Roosevelt was Commander-in-Chief of the U.S. armed forces, but Eisenhower used Marshall as the intermediary to contact the President.

The problem of the Western Allies possibly ending up in the Russian zone was of Eisenhower's own creation. It was not his responsibility to interpret political decisions, and Churchill's concern at his action in making direct contact with Stalin was understandable. On 7 April, Churchill had sent a minute to Gen. Ismay, a member of the Chiefs of Staff Committee, stating if the Russians, or the Americans and British, should find themselves in the other's "zone," no withdrawal should be made on military grounds. In keeping with the Yalta agreement, which stated the drawing up of occupation zones was not to hinder operations of the armies, any such withdrawal was to be a political decision.[3] Berlin, Prague and Vienna could be captured by whoever arrived first. This information was reiterated by Ismay seven days later, after the death of Roosevelt. Truman, having become President, told Churchill the Western Allies' forces should be withdrawn to their own boundaries as the military situation allowed, obviously expecting that Eisenhower's armies could easily take territory which was within the Russian zone.

Marshall sent Eisenhower a copy of Churchill's message and asked if Tedder had been informed before the offending wire had been sent to Stalin. Eisenhower said he had, but Tedder denied ever seeing it. It was seen by Strong; nevertheless, a copy was not sent to Montgomery, Brooke or Churchill, all of which leads to the conclusion that Eisenhower had been less than frank with his British allies. By contrast with the orders given to the Americans, Montgomery, acting on Churchill's instructions, had the 21st Army Group continue its advance to halt only when it met the Russians coming from the east; this occurred on 2 May and, despite Eisenhower's fears, no clash occurred.

Some Eisenhower adherents believe that the halt on the Elbe was wise because the Russians had taken so much of Germany while the Western Allies were still struggling to cross the Rhine. Consequently, the Russians were in a better position to capture Berlin. Their reasoning ignores the terms of the Yalta agreement and overlooks the fact that had Eisenhower only possessed the competence to appreciate the value of Montgomery's concentrated offensive, the crossing of the Rhine and the capture of the Ruhr could have been done earlier. This would have freed Allied forces to make quicker progress into Germany, thereby negating the stop on the Elbe. Eisenhower's reason for his action was that Berlin was nothing but another geographic location, and he assured Montgomery he had never been interested in such things. His inconsistency did not end there. Montgomery sent him a message on 6 April explaining his final strategy for the 21st Army Group. He would cut off the Schleswig Peninsula, take Kiel and clear Denmark of enemy forces. Since Berlin was of great importance, the

Chapter 17—The End of the War in Europe 171

21st Army Group would then head southeast toward the capital; for this he would require the help of ten U.S. divisions. At the time, both Marshall and Churchill were expressing the need to take Berlin, but Bradley was making heavy weather of clearing the Ruhr. Although now under Bradley's control, Simpson's Ninth Army was idle and could have been used to assist Montgomery, but its lack of involvement merely helped the Germans, giving them time to prepare for their next attack.

Eisenhower, in a letter to Marshall dated 6 April, expressed his doubts regarding the ability of the Germans to break out of the Ruhr pocket, but he was still unable to make up his mind what to do, so he sent a cable to Marshall stating he would change his plans and head for Berlin if he were so instructed. Gen. Alexander Bolling, commanding the U.S. 84th Division, when asked by Eisenhower on 8 April for his immediate plans, answered his division was going to Berlin "... and nothing can stop us." To which Eisenhower replied: "... keep going — and don't let anything stop you,"[4] thereby contradicting the terms of his wire to Stalin.

Furthermore, in his book *At Ease*, he rejects any suggestion that he ought to have taken the capital, contending that it was of no use to the Western Allies since it was in the future Russian zone of occupation. In the same book he asserts that he was so enthralled by Clausewitz's *On War* that he read it three times. Unfortunately, his tactics and strategy showed little indication of this.

Again Eisenhower displayed his inconsistency, for on 9 April he instructed Montgomery to guard Bradley's flank while Bradley advanced to take Dresden. What use that city was to either the Allies or the Germans is difficult to conceive for it had been flattened by R.A.F. bombing. It transpired that there was to be an advance by Bradley on a three-army front, something quite incomprehensible to Montgomery, and Berlin was not the ultimate objective. Bradley, not usually one to hold an isolated opinion among his fellow Americans, went so far as to say the contention that Berlin was of no military or political significance may have been wrong. This post-war opinion did not agree with his telephone call to Eisenhower on 15 April, when he estimated it would cost the Americans 100,000 casualties to take the capital, and the prize was not worth the cost. It was a conclusion which ignored the fact that if the enemy was willing to suffer high casualties defending it, then the city must have been of great importance. Under those circumstances its loss would have been demoralizing to them, as indeed it proved to be. Bradley, again postwar, modified his telephone conversation with Eisenhower, contending he intended to mean most of the 100,000 losses would have been incurred fighting inside Berlin, not in the course of the advance to the capital. Bradley, so reluctant to incur 100,000 casualties in capturing an objective as vital as the enemy's capital, displayed no such reservations in three other battles, including the Ardennes, all unnecessary, in which he incurred a total of more than 130,000 casualties.

Simpson, also after the war, stated it would have been possible for his Ninth Army to have reached Berlin.[5] He had adequate supplies; enough transportation, including 10-ton trucks; a couple of bridges across the Elbe and sufficient men to do the task. The capital was 53 miles from his front line and he estimated it would have taken no more than two days to reach it. He was astonished when he was instructed to stop his advance. Once Berlin was no longer the target of the Western Allies, it was a simple matter to justify the switch of emphasis from Montgomery's Army Group in the north to Bradley's in the center. Eisenhower broke the news on 12 April to Patton. The U.S. armies would not attempt the capture of Berlin because it would only burden the U.S. forces with the feeding, clothing and sheltering of thousands of Germans, an argument lacking in a display of humanity and one he had never used with regard to other areas liberated by the American armies. Furthermore, each prisoner who had to be clothed, fed and housed was one German less to fight the Allies. Not surprisingly, Patton urged Eisenhower to press forward and establish a line on the Oder River as quickly as possible. He pleaded in vain.

Consistency was again absent from Eisenhower's thinking. Having suggested to the Russians that the Elbe should be the limit of the U.S. advance into Germany, suddenly and inexplicably Berlin became important to him, for he later held some U.S. forces in readiness to go to Berlin because he felt the Russians seemed slow in capturing the city.

Eisenhower lacked decisiveness in handling the final advance, a shortcoming evident during his entire command of Allied troops. Had he possessed any strategic skills he could possibly have shortened the war by several weeks and saved many hundreds of lives, for von Rundstedt was of the opinion that a concentrated attack by the Allies would have resulted in the thorough defeat of the Germans. It was unfortunate the concept of a concentrated attack was not part of Eisenhower's recollection of his training as an officer, and he failed to appreciate what succeeded for Gen Ulysses S. Grant in the American Civil War was not necessarily appropriate for a modern and more fluid type of warfare.

With the death of Franklin D. Roosevelt on 12 April 1945, it was soon evident his successor, Harry Truman, was lacking in foreign affairs experience, for Roosevelt had not kept his Vice-President informed on the subject. It resulted in Marshall assuming too much responsibility for the conduct of the war, leading to a complete misinterpretation of the terms

Chapter 17—The End of the War in Europe

of the Yalta agreement, which not only did not preclude the Western or Eastern allied armies from pursuing the enemy into the other's zone, but provided for the division of Germany into zones of occupation only after the defeat.

The end of the war was but two months away, and in late March the final assault on the usual broad front began in the West. When Patton heard of this plan he gave orders to the 80th Division to join the XX Corps and 90th Division because he felt it essential for the U.S. First and Third armies to become so involved in battle as to thwart Montgomery's plan to use them in an attack on the Ruhr plains. During the course of this operation, Patton instructed Gen. William Hoge, whose troops had captured the bridge at Remagen, to send an expedition 60 miles behind the enemy lines to free some 900 American prisoners of war, among whom was Patton's son-in-law, Capt. John Waters.[6] The camp was at Hammelburg, about 55 miles from Frankfurt. Commanding the expedition was Lt. Col. Creighton Adams, who believed the reinforced company he was given was inadequate for the task. He was overruled and under the direct command of Capt. Abraham Baum, "Baum Force" set off on 26 March. It consisted of about 300 men and an assortment of vehicles. Waters, due to his wounds, was left behind; those who were fit enough were transported to freedom. Rejoining the main force were only 35 men of the original total. Later Patton strenuously denied he had known his son-in-law was held at Hammelburg. He alleged he was afraid the Germans would slaughter the prisoners before retreating, but he provided no support for his assertion. When Waters was finally released on 6 April, Patton again denied he was aware his son-in-law was a prisoner at Hammelburg. Both denials contradicted what others recall being told by Patton at the time the operation was ordered. Eisenhower ought to have been aware of this raid, and it was another demonstration that he had very poor control over his subordinates. There is no indication the Supreme Commander, once he learned the particulars of the raid, ever asked Patton for an explanation nor did he ever reprimand him for incurring unnecessary casualties. Bradley, also, must be held accountable. He, too, omitted to express disapproval of Patton's actions.

In the meantime, Montgomery was preparing to cross the Rhine, building up a force of 25 divisions and a quarter of a million tons of supplies on the west bank in the area of Wesel; opposing him were 25 weak German divisions. Despite criticism, especially from Americans, of the size of the buildup, Montgomery was expecting to be able to head for Berlin and would therefore need the support of a large base. Five days before the offensive opened, Eisenhower sent a message to Montgomery informing him it was quite likely that the U.S. Third and Seventh Armies would be committed to battle north of the Ruhr. Montgomery thought this inadvisable, but it did conform to the Supreme Commander's desire for a broad front assault.

Montgomery's attack of 23 March was preceded by heavy air and artillery bombardments, and at dawn the next day Allied airborne troops were dropped north and northwest of Wesel, joining forces with the ground units. The U.S. Ninth Army crossed the Rhine between Duisberg and Wesel and met only light resistance. After only two days a bridgehead across the Rhine had been established, which was 25 miles long and six miles deep. The U.S. First Army under Hodges began its race for Frankfurt on 26 March, and at the same time some of its armored units headed northward to the west of Kassel. The U.S. Third Army crossed the Rhine at Maintz, and some units also went in support of the First Army's attack. In the north, Montgomery's forces advanced into the northwest sector of the Ruhr, finding the worst impediment to their advance to be the rubble created by the bombardments, while on their left flank Holland was invaded on a 30-mile front.

The first contact between the Western and Eastern allies was made on 25 April, when patrols of the U.S. First Army met the Russians at Torgau, followed five days later by a meeting of U.S. and Russians at Dessau. By the middle of April, the British Second Army was on the outskirts of Bremen, and it then struck north toward Hamburg. On the left, the Canadian First Army liberated areas of east and north Holland, while in the south the U.S. Third Army headed for Czechoslovakia, and some U.S. detachments were 20 miles inside Austria. The U.S. Seventh Army captured Nuremberg and Munich, and moved south toward the Inn River. The First French Army had taken Karlsruhe and Stuttgart and proceeded to mop up the Germans in the Black Forest; by 1 May they had advanced along the Swiss border to the west of Lake Constance, and were moving into Austria with the U.S. Seventh Army.

At the other end of the line, the British Second Army, with the U.S. XVIII Airborne Corps under its command, cut off the Danish peninsula by reaching the Baltic on 2 May, and joined forces with the Russians. By this time, the German position was untenable, and the enemy forces in the northwest of Germany, Holland and Denmark surrendered on 4 May; the total surrender of Germany was signed by Hitler's successor, Adm. Karl Doenitz, on 7 May 1945.

The reaching of the Baltic was not achieved without a revealing exchange of messages between Montgomery and the Supreme Commander. Eisenhower again showed his ignorance of the simple elements of strategy. He suddenly became concerned that the 21st Army Group was not moving quickly enough to capture Lüebeck, thereby allowing the Russians to take Denmark and from there threaten Norway. He therefore sent Montgomery a message dated 8 April asking if he needed further logistical support. Montgomery answered in the negative; dissatisfied with this, Eisenhower visited the 21st Army Group headquarters 12 days later. The result was that Ridgway's airborne corps was attached to Montgomery's command, which did nothing to please Bradley who continued to be responsible for supplying these troops. Still unhappy with Montgomery's progress, Eisenhower instructed one of his staff on 26 April to telephone Montgomery and stress the need to enter Lüebeck ahead of the Russians. The message irritated Montgomery and he directed de Guingand to telephone Whiteley at SHAEF and point out that he, Montgomery, had always been aware of Lüebeck's importance, as substantiated by his signal of 28 March. Far from Montgomery lacking appreciation of this matter, it was Eisenhower, de Guingand pointed out, who had prevented the speedier advance of the 21st Army Group by depriving Montgomery of the U.S. Ninth Army. De Guingand continued by making it quite clear should this vital port fall to the Russians, only Eisenhower could be blamed for its loss. Eisenhower failed to understand Montgomery's point, and wired him again emphasizing the need to take Lüebeck as quickly as possible. Once more, in his reply, Montgomery stressed that the 21st Army Group had been severely weakened by the transfer of the U.S. Ninth Army. However, he assured the Supreme Commander he had every intention of advancing on the port with all possible speed. In a log entry dated 27 April 1945, Montgomery expressed the wish that Eisenhower should realize wars are not won by public opinion.

Bradley criticized Montgomery's final campaign, asserting it was the most cautious and uninspired of the war. Never once did Bradley advocate the taking of Berlin, Prague or Vienna by the Allies, but he suddenly became engrossed in what was happening in an area which was not within his command. To what extent his interest was generated by the fact it was Montgomery who was responsible for the liberation of Denmark and Norway is now open to conjecture. He was certainly not tardy in finding excuses when his own advance slowed down in the Cherbourg Peninsula, describing it as being "unavoidably delayed." The fact that the 21st Army Group had been given a task which was, for its size, a difficult one, and that he, Bradley, had not seen fit to make better use of an uncommitted Ninth Army, were considerations which were noticeably overlooked in his assessment of the British commander.

Churchill was concerned about the situation in Czechoslovakia and

Allied Headquarters 7 May 1945, Rheims, France, following the signing of German surrender. Left to right: Soviet Gen. Susloparoff, F. E. Morgan, Walter B. Smith, Harry Butcher, DDE, Arthur Tedder, Harold Burrough. U.S. Army photograph. (Courtesy Dwight D. Eisenhower Library.)

on 30 April 1945, he sent a message to Truman urging him to stress to Eisenhower the importance of capturing Prague. In this he was supported by the British Chiefs of Staff. Patton had already crossed the border and would have willingly headed for the capital. Marshall equivocated and finally left it to Eisenhower to decide. In reply to Churchill, Truman stated Eisenhower intended to head for Pilsen and Karlsbad, but was not going to take purely political action which would be "militarily unwise." The reason for the Supreme Commander's refusal to relieve the Czechoslovakian capital was because by giving too much attention to politics and insufficient attention to the battle, he had put himself in the position of being caught between the Devil and the deep blue sea. He had told Gen. A.I. Antonov (Chief of Soviet Gen. Staff) of his intention to advance to Vltava and then to continue on to Prague.[7] The Russian replied by asking him not to cross the previously approved demarcation line, pointing out to Eisenhower that he, Antonov, had agreed to halt on the lower Elbe at the Supreme Commander's request; therefore he expected the Americans to co-operate with him.

Chapter 17—The End of the War in Europe

It was obvious to the British that the Americans would leave Czechoslovakia for the Russians to capture. They suggested the Western Allies should at least take Prague, but Marshall replied he was reluctant to risk American lives solely for political reasons, apparently forgetting it is virtually impossible to divorce politics from war, and further forgetting the pointless losses the Americans had incurred in the Huertgen Forest, the Ardennes, at Metz and at Aachen. After the surrender of all German forces in northern Europe, Churchill cabled Eisenhower expressing the hope that he intended to capture Prague. His hope was not realized. Eisenhower was determined that neither Vienna, Berlin nor Prague would be taken by troops under his command, even where there would be no opposition worthy of note. His decision cost the lives of about 8,000 Czechs who rose against the occupying Germans, anticipating help from the U.S. Third Army, which was already in the suburbs. The radio station was in the hands of the Czech partisans, but the Germans disbelieved their reports of the signing of the surrender document. The result was the Russians entered the capital on 12 May and refused to allow the Czech Brigade of the U.S. Third Army to enter until the end of the month.

Although not in the original plan, Eisenhower had diverted units to liberate Paris earlier than had been intended, due to the French Resistance rising in anticipation of American assistance. The Supreme Commander's motives in refusing to liberate three other capitals must be suspect. These omissions, together with involving himself in politics by proposing to the Russians that upon meeting, either side was to have the right to request the other to withdraw to the zone boundaries, give rise to the possibility Eisenhower had already decided to make an attempt for the Presidency. He never once suggested that Paris, Brussels or The Hague should not be captured by his armies, and yet three other capitals were left to the Russians to occupy, with no involvement from the Anglo-American force which could easily have reached them. On humanitarian grounds alone he could have sent in the Third Army to save the insurgents from slaughter, as he had done in Paris.

Toward the end of the war in Europe, it became evident Eisenhower was giving more credence than it deserved to the possibility of an attempted stand by the Germans in the Southern Redoubt. Although believing the rumors, he ordered no investigation by patrols to authenticate the presence of a stronghold, and ignored intelligence reports which doubted its existence. It seems reasonable to assume that before Eisenhower came to his conclusion he would have based it upon fairly solid evidence. In fact, not only had he ordered no reconnaissance of the area,[8] but he had given no consideration to the absence of natural resources with which to support such a stand.

Churchill had also heard the rumors but, by contrast with Eisenhower, he had instructed the British Chiefs of Staff to do some research and report their findings. The answer was that final resistance in the area was unlikely. Their conclusion was based on the fact the area was self-supporting in neither agriculture nor industry; this would therefore have entailed creating an enormous stockpile of food, fuel and armaments, quite beyond the capability of the shrunken Third Reich. Eisenhower was not persuaded; he ordered two U.S. armies, the Third and the Seventh, to be diverted to capture this mirage.

Eisenhower either failed to understand the reports he read or disbelieved them because they contradicted his preconceived conclusions; he seems to have been the victim of his own fuzzy thinking and the Nazi propaganda minister's bombast. Not only did the SHAEF Intelligence Committee disbelieve the existence of the Redoubt but a report issued by Eisenhower's G-2, dated 10 March 1945, gave details of a buildup in progress in the area, but expressed skepticism that a final stand could be made there. These reports, negative though they were, did not prevent Bradley from supporting his chief, for he had told reporters in early April that the war might easily continue into the following year. He felt the Redoubt was capable of supporting at least 20 S.S. divisions which would be supplied by a series of underground factories. What he omitted to disclose was the source of fuel and raw materials for these production lines; south Germany was not a highly industrialized area and from intelligence reports he should have been fully aware the Germans, in the Ruhr, had insufficient fuel and ammunition to break through the Allied cordon. He also failed to account for Hitler's alleged ability to increase his army from a corporal's guard to one of 20 divisions or more in a period of about six months. He became so obsessed with a possible German stand in the Redoubt that

Eisenhower and Churchill in Northern France, March 1945. U.S. Army photograph. (Courtesy Dwight D. Eisenhower Library.)

Chapter 17—The End of the War in Europe

he refused to send help to Montgomery, believing such action would lessen the pressure on the enemy in the south, allowing him to reinforce the Redoubt.

Two months after hostilities ended, Churchill and Montgomery were discussing the war. They agreed that the Americans had made five big errors:

1. They prevented the initial attempt by the British to capture Tunis.

2. By clinging to the beaches at Anzio, they failed to establish better positions inland.

3. They insisted upon "Dragoon," thereby preventing Alexander from taking Trieste and Vienna.

4. Eisenhower had refused to mount a concentrated attack against the Ruhr, preferring a broad front offensive which could not logically be supported; he allowed von Rundstedt to attack in the Ardennes, prolonging the war by several weeks.

5. Eisenhower refused to capture Berlin, Vienna or Prague.

18

Eisenhower's Errors

To the extent that the Nazis were defeated, the campaign in the west was a success. Examined in detail, it was flawed. Some points in the list of enumerated errors need to be examined in detail, and to that list can be added seven more items. Most of the errors were made by the American generals, not surprisingly since they were more in number than any other nationality and in many cases their errors were due to their reluctance, or inability, to admit that while they were numerically the superior partner in the Anglo-American alliance, they were lacking in essential experience. One indication of this was the haphazard method of selecting military commanders. Too often did they appoint an officer to a position which was above his capabilities, and Roosevelt at one time was considering Marshall for the position of Supreme Commander in northern Europe. The appointment would not have been made on the basis of Marshall's proven war record, not on the basis of his strategic astuteness, not on the basis of having commanded at least an army during peacetime, but solely on the basis the President felt a Chief of Staff was rarely remembered by history, while a field commander receives most of the acclaim for victories; a strange method of selecting an officer to fill such an important position.

The first error was made by Marshall, who was answerable for the appointment of Eisenhower as the Commander-in-Chief of the Allied armies in North Africa; in view of the fact he had neither experience of commanding large units nor experience of battle, it is not surprising Eisenhower's abilities have been compared with those of a co-ordinator.[1]

The second error was Eisenhower's failure to appoint a ground commander in northern Europe, which must rank as one of the worst mistakes he ever made. That this decision was partly political is well supported by an officer in the Operations Divisions of the U.S. War Department. He stated the predominating factor in the determination of the ground commander's nationality would be the availability of a qualified person for the

Chapter 18—Eisenhower's Errors

position. He continued by admitting there was no American commander with the equivalent experience of Montgomery or Alexander. It would therefore be injudicious for the Americans to propose the creation of a separate ground command, because that would likely lead to the appointment of a British officer to the position. For all Montgomery's faults, when he suggested the appointment of such a commander he clearly expressed his willingness to serve under Bradley, reaffirmed in a letter to the British minister of War, John Grigg, in which he stated he would be proud to serve under Bradley.

The appointment of a ground commander would have left Eisenhower free to concentrate on the administrative duties of his command, for which he was better suited, and it has been suggested the difference between command organizations in North Africa and Northern Europe was that in Africa there was only one Army Group, whereas in Europe there were three. Therefore, the argument goes, the situation was more complex because of U.S. numerical superiority, and a British ground commander could not be considered. Since the appointee had to be American, who could equal Eisenhower as the Supreme Commander?

This reasoning, if such it can be called, is based on the false assumption that the more men under command, the greater the need for one man to be both Supreme Commander and ground commander, which is as logical as contending a division should have only one officer — its commanding officer.

The argument omits two important points: first, it must be devoutly hoped that West Point had produced more than one officer capable of commanding three army groups, and second, the entire line of argument is tainted with xenophobia, which was the very thing Eisenhower claimed was an anathema to him and would not be tolerated in armies under his control. Having selected the Supreme Commander exclusively on the basis of nationality, the ground commander, because of the indisputable importance of that position, should have been selected on no basis other than experience and competence. Despite this, Eisenhower appeared obsessed with the possibility of his reputation suffering should he yield direct control of the Allied armies, for he clung to his two positions with obvious relish and failed to halt the internecine bickering conducted by some of his commanders. If Montgomery's failing was he knew only one plan of attack, a left and right hook, then Eisenhower's was he, too, knew only one form of attack, and one which was far less effective, the broad front offensive. He was too timid to face the possibility that had he ordered a single front offensive it would have meant he would have had to inform Bradley that one or more of his armies would have a static rôle. He obdurately refused to appreciate supplies were a vital consideration for any offensive operation, especially in regard to the Allied situation existing before Antwerp was fully operative.

Despite the objections raised to Montgomery's plan of an assault on a 40-division front, it was more sensible than Eisenhower's insistence on the entire front being in motion at all times, for no better reason than he could not abide the thought that the two American army groups would not participate as entities in the anticipated victory. Not only did Eisenhower fail to heed Montgomery's suggestions, but also he never seemed to understand the possible benefits of letting Patton loose at the right moment. He failed to take advantage of the fact that Patton and Montgomery were diametrically opposite in their styles of fighting, and yet, under the right conditions, this could have been used to the benefit of the Allies. Eisenhower's appointment as Supreme Commander in northern Europe raises the question of why the British did not ask for a list of more suitable American officers. It appeared American national pride required the position be filled by one of their own choosing, but already Brooke realized Eisenhower was not qualified for the post. There is no evidence to suggest Churchill had discussed the proposed appointment with Brooke before consenting to it. If there was no more talented general than Eisenhower in the U.S. army at the time, then in the interests of achieving the common cause of Hitler's defeat as quickly and economically as possible, a qualified general of some other nationality should have been chosen. The selection of the overall commander did not conform to the rule that a general should be appointed to the post on the basis of superior abilities and his capability as a leader of large numbers of troops. Had Eisenhower been less a student of the American West, as depicted in fiction, had he shown but the slightest evidence that he had understood Clausewitz's *On War*, then his conduct of operations would undoubtedly have been different. He violated many of the principles enumerated by Clausewitz, and from his reading he failed to learn anything which could have helped him in planning his campaign in France and Germany.

If Eisenhower's objectives in Europe had been to keep the enemy off balance by attacking all along the line, then it should not have been beyond his abilities to appreciate that he would be unable to accomplish this successfully because of the problem of administration. He failed to comply with the directive given to him, which in part read that he would be responsible for co-ordination of logistical arrangements on the continent. He was evidently unable to understand that to supply 40 divisions attacking on one front would have been an easier task than to supply first one army and then another as each in turn went over to the offensive. His strategy

Chapter 18—Eisenhower's Errors

was similar to the German blitzkrieg attacks inasmuch as the Germans usually opened their assaults on a broad front, intending initially to do nothing more than distract the defenders' attention. The difference was, with this accomplished, one or two concentrated attacks were then developed to crush the opposition; it was this concentration of effort which Eisenhower failed to understand and implement.

From the Seine to the Rhine and beyond, the Supreme Commander lurched forward with all the skill and refinement of a novice car driver unable to co-ordinate the engagement of the clutch with the necessary amount of throttle. He failed to force the enemy to comply with his will in battle, mainly because his plans were ill-formed and imprecise. He neglected to concentrate his forces at a point on the front where a decisive assault was to be mounted, because he failed to comprehend this was one of the four elements needed for a favorable decision, and because he was more concerned in making sure the American armies were always fully involved in battle.

In total, Eisenhower commanded the more powerful army, but he never understood the important requirement was to be strong at the point of the decisive attack. He had no superior abilities as an army commander, a total absence of experience in leading large numbers of troops, and he had been given no careful probation before being elevated to command international armies, the three qualifications which Clausewitz gives for the selection of a general. The third error was Eisenhower's failure to order the speedy capture of Antwerp. He had been given definite instructions to this effect, for the directive issued to him as Supreme Commander Allied Expeditionary Force ordered him to capture adequate channel ports, following which an area was to be secured to be used in air and ground operations against the enemy. He reported to the Chiefs of Staff in Washington that Allied prospects were dependent upon the capture and clearing of the Scheldt. He admitted the supply situation all along the line was poor, but he felt certain the capture of Antwerp would be a big boost to the Allies' situation. Had he taken steps to capture the port sooner, the position may not have been so critical for so long. His dilatoriness is inexcusable, for in 1944 he made no fewer than 10 mentions, oral and written, of the importance of the port to the Allies and the need to have it fully operating as quickly as possible.

The fourth error was the attitude of the Pentagon toward the armed forces. Marshall, while adept at creating large forces, failed to understand numbers alone are no guarantee of success. An army has to be highly trained before it can be of much use in the field, yet there were Americans who landed in French Morocco who had not even finished their basic training. Marshall ignored the fact that the Allies would be very likely opposed by battle-hardened Germans, and there was therefore the need to use experienced troops and not green, poorly trained men, which were the only forces then available to the United States. He acted like an amateur chess player who moves his pieces across the board with little understanding of what he is doing, and even less understanding of the consequences, other than knowing the worst that can happen is that he will lose the game. The results of losing a war, though, are a little more serious than those of losing a chess game.

Marshall's record must be compared with Pershing's in the First World War. The circumstances were similar, for each of them found the Americans under his command to be ill-prepared for combat, and in both wars there was a large influx of raw recruits. Pershing was determined that his army would not be used purely for cannon fodder. He therefore ensured the recruits were given proper training in trench warfare and were slowly introduced to actual combat. Pershing then agreed to provide the British and French with reinforcements for particular operations, but only for a specified period, after which they were withdrawn and used to teach newcomers the art of trench warfare. Thus, by the time the American Expeditionary Force went into action as an independent army, it was well trained and much of it had had actual battle experience.

The fifth error was ignoring the situation in the Ardennes. To have acknowledged the weakness of the U.S. position and done nothing to correct it must have broken every rule of sound military teachings. The error was unforgivable. The battle was costly to the Americans in both men and materiel, and it delayed the Allied victory by at least six weeks. In addition, Anglo-American relations were hardly improved by Montgomery having to take over temporary command of the battle.

The problem, from Eisenhower's viewpoint, was that had the Ardennes been reinforced as a preventive measure it would have resulted in one or more offensives having to be closed in order to provide the men and supplies. His reluctance to take this essential action contradicted his diary entry of 27 January, 1942. He ignored Clausewitz's dictum for attaining a favorable decision in battle, which is always be strong, first generally, then at the decisive point. Despite the area's history, Eisenhower failed to take heed of how vulnerable the Ardennes was. He appeared to be far too anxious to involve the U.S. armies in battle, not primarily to attain final victory, but to try to ensure these forces were remembered in the annals of military history. He possibly succeeded, but not in the way he intended.

The sixth error was Eisenhower's inability to understand the significance of his stripping the 15th Army Group to create the "Dragoon" inva-

Chapter 18—Eisenhower's Errors

sion force, a failing made obvious by his letter to Marshall of 31 August 1944. He felt Alexander should be prepared to send forces into the Austrian Alps in order to suppress any move by the Germans to continue the war by guerrilla action. Having denuded the armies in Italy of so much of their strength he then expected of them the impossible. If Marshall and Eisenhower were blind to the obvious, Hitler was not, for as early as 30 September 1943 he told a conference of officers that if the Germans contained the enemy in southern Italy for even the shortest period it would prove invaluable to the Nazi cause.

Hitler, not Eisenhower and not Marshall, appreciated the connection between northern Europe and Italy. The Germans were forced to maintain in Italy 45 German divisions, 4 Italian divisions and various other units made up of nationals from German-occupied Europe. These divisions were mostly first-class troops, but they suffered the same disadvantages, as did the Allies; they too were short of replacements.

The seventh error was the failure to attempt the capture of Berlin despite the fact U.S. forces were so near to the capital, and it was known there would be little opposition to any advance on Berlin from the west. Certainly, on the basis of his own statements, Eisenhower seemed quite unable to make up his mind as to the importance of the city to the Western Allies, and in this he was at odds with Roosevelt's opinion, given to Churchill at the 1943 Quebec meeting, which was that the Western Allies should reach Berlin simultaneously with the Russians. At about the same time, an American staff officer wrote an assessment of the Russians, and he concluded it would be to the advantage of the Western Allies if they reached Berlin first. By 14 April, Simpson's Ninth Army had an open road to the capital, but due to the unauthorized agreement made by Eisenhower with the Russians, the Americans halted their advance. It is doubtful if the Russians would have been so accommodating that they would have refrained from advancing across Europe to the Franco-German border if the Americans had become stuck there, and it is equally unlikely they would have agreed to wait at some predetermined position for the arrival of the Western Allies.

One argument for the halt on the Elbe is that the American public would not have tolerated an advance on Berlin because it would have better served the interests of the French and British than those of the United States. The Americans, so the argument goes, were far more desirous of returning to normal than they were to take action requiring a commitment to Europe east of the Elbe. This contention has all the indications of one propounded by politicians too concerned to assure their reelection, and one which gives little consideration to the future of Europe for which many

U.S. servicemen had given their lives. If these politicians believed the United States could once again retreat into comfortable isolation then they were too easily misled, and with no difficulty one can conclude they were less anxious to free Eastern Europe than they were to liberate Western Europe.

What significance the Elbe was to him Eisenhower never revealed. In fact, it was nothing more than a geographical location, the very feature which he asserted on more than occasion was useless—consistency was not one of the Supreme Commander's notable characteristics.

By stopping on the Elbe, Eisenhower ignored the principle that one cause for the enemy's defeat is the capture of his capital city. He ignored the principle of war which states that the major decisions of war are always made by politicians and not by the military. He failed to decide on the location of the most important point in Germany, whether of military, social, economic or political significance, which, if captured or destroyed, would have caused the collapse of Nazi Germany. He again showed his lack of consistency, for in a cable dated 24 October 1943, addressed to the Combined Chiefs of Staff, he declared it was important to capture Rome because its fall would be a symbol of victory in Italy. Unfortunately, he soon forgot the importance of a capital city once the Allies crossed the Rhine into Germany.

Berlin was the political center of Germany, as was the Ruhr the industrial and economic center of the country; Eisenhower never grasped the significance of the former and was slow to appreciate the latter. Indeed, in his "Supreme Commander's Report" he wrote Berlin was no longer an important military objective, and to him military matters were more important than political ones. Once more he failed to give any explanation not only for his change of mind regarding the German capital, but also for its diminished importance as a military target. He stressed in an interview with Alastair Cooke, nearly a quarter of a century after the German surrender, that the capture of Berlin had never been in his plans. Time had proved to be the thief of his memory.

The mistakes made by Eisenhower were sufficiently numerous to question his ability as a ground commander, and Horrocks, commander of the British XXX Corps, upon first meeting him, could not refrain from wondering why he had been selected as Supreme Commander, for whatever other qualities he possessed it was clear Eisenhower was no military prodigy; he was a co-ordinator, not a commander. Eisenhower had started the Normandy campaign, as he had the North African landings, filled with idealism, which soon gave way to chauvinism. He was not helped by Marshall who, being in Washington, was a few thousand miles from the scene

Chapter 18—Eisenhower's Errors

of the conflict and was prone to interfere in operations, although having little or no idea of the detailed conditions existing at any given time. This happened in August 1944 when he instructed Eisenhower to assume direct command of the armies in northern Europe. He was the one who insisted upon launching Operation "Dragoon." Marshall, like Eisenhower, appeared to know only one method of attack, which was to lower the head and charge like an enraged bull tormented by a waving cape. There was no finesse in his thinking, and in his dealings with Eisenhower he never once advocated an attempt to outmaneuver or deceive the enemy. They each believed in weight of numbers to achieve victory.

Eisenhower had demonstrated on more than one occasion his memory was unreliable. In addition, he was inconsistent to the point where one can question if he really understood the full significance of what he had ordered. On 8 October 1944, he sent a message to Montgomery, the first paragraph of which stated that due to diminished strength on the northern flank, the plan for a co-ordinated attack on the Rhine would have to be postponed. The second paragraph stressed both army groups, the 21st and 12th, must keep in mind their main objective, which would be the gaining of the line of the Rhine north of Bonn as quickly as possible. Montgomery replied that he had stopped the Second Army's operations against the Ruhr and was concentrating on opening the approaches to Antwerp in order to have the port operational as soon as possible. Eisenhower's answer showed he had suddenly appreciated that problems of administration existed, and ignoring his previous message, he replied that unless Antwerp was operating by the middle of November, all offensives would come to a halt. He assured Montgomery that the clearing of the Scheldt was of prime importance. Again, in July 1944, he gave another example of self-contradiction. In his diary he complained the Far East was being supplied excessively to the detriment of the European theater of operations. He continued by saying it was a mistake to fight two wars simultaneously, yet he had previously advocated that supplies to the Pacific should be given priority over those to the European theater, although that was before he was appointed Supreme Commander.

He had no hesitation in mounting offensives on two or more fronts at the same time when he should have been fully aware adequate support could not be given to all those operations. He was never conscious of his own inconsistency, for even 25 years after the end of the war he paid Churchill a compliment by stating the wartime Prime Minister understood one of the basic rules of warfare, a lack of dispersion. Dispersion — the very blunder which Eisenhower made on more than one occasion.

The Americans gave the impression that following their experiences in the First World War they would never again subordinate their army to one of their allies. This display of xenophobia led them to ignore the obvious—the prime objective of the fighting was to win the war as quickly as possible with the fewest number of casualties, and it ought to have been clear to them the best commander should have been selected to lead the armies regardless of his nationality. Both Marshall and Eisenhower, together with Patton and Bradley, demonstrated on several occasions that they were far too interested in trying to achieve results, more spectacular than useful, which they hoped would redound to the credit of the American armies. The four generals, especially Bradley and Patton, were often very quick to criticize the British, but failed to appreciate their own shortcomings.

Eisenhower showed how vulnerable he was to criticism, for on 28 April 1959 Montgomery gave a television interview for the United States. He expressed the opinion soldiers should not enter politics. The Prime Minister, Harold Macmillan, apparently felt this could be interpreted as reflecting the opinion of the British government, despite the fact Montgomery was not then, nor ever had been, a government spokesman; he sent Eisenhower a letter disassociating himself from Montgomery's comment. Eisenhower, in a caustic reply, revealed the extent of his sensitivity, for he protested far too much by making the discourteous comment that neither of them was likely to be affected by what he termed "the chattering of a small magpie."

Eisenhower proved to be a poor selector of army commanders. Bradley had no battle experience prior to the invasion of Africa; he was a flexible character, too flexible at times, and dismissed by Patton in unflattering terms. He wanted to make the army his career since his teens, and after he graduated from West Point he served in the American Expeditionary Force in France during the First World War. Twenty-six years later in France, Bradley demonstrated that he seemed neither able nor willing to exercise control over Patton, and Bradley all too often, together with Patton, indulged in what seemed to be a private war to undermine Montgomery's operations. Bradley would have accomplished far more had he taken a positive approach and given full co-operation to the conduct of operations in northern Europe; while at first he admired some of Montgomery's attributes, he soon became disillusioned with him when Montgomery requested the U.S. II Corps be placed under his command to take part in the proposed 40-division attack on the 21st Army Group's front. Bradley was suspicious of Montgomery's motives, feeling his request for these reinforcements was for self-aggrandizement; furthermore Bradley, having a strong sense of his own importance, felt any transfer of American units to British command would adversely affect his reputation. Thereafter, he sided with Patton whenever the latter made a derogatory remark about Montgomery, or whenever Patton proposed a course of action which would potentially interfere with Montgomery's plans.

Bradley failed to appreciate the gravity of the situation and his reluctance to hand over temporary command to Montgomery was not based on sound military judgment, but has all the attributes of being due to either personal animosity toward Montgomery or outright Anglophobia; it seems the latter is more likely from his reply to Bedell Smith at the beginning of the Ardennes offensive. His contention that he was still able to control events in the battle area is hard to support. It was eventually clear, even to Eisenhower, that communications between Bradley and the forces in the Ardennes were most unsatisfactory, and it does Bradley's reputation no good that he was unwilling to surrender command to a person who was in a much better position to co-ordinate control of the defense, and the later counterattack, against the enemy. Bradley's Anglophobia was demonstrated again in his letter of 23 January 1945 to Eisenhower, in which he commented on Montgomery's proposed Operation "Grenade." His opinion was that since the United States was providing about 79% of all the Allied troops in northern Europe, there was no reason for the Americans to agree to strategy formulated by a British commander. He believed American interests should come first. To what extent British and American interests differed in this case he did not explain, but this showed how narrow-minded and self-centered he was, for the objective of both allies was the speedy defeat of the Germans, and it should have mattered little if the master plan for that was originally British or American.

As for Patton, he disliked the British in general and Montgomery in particular, and on more than one occasion attempted to thwart the British commander's plans. Such behavior was very unfortunate for it did nothing to help in the defeat of the enemy, and it negated Patton's talent as a military leader. From an early age he had shown obvious signs that he would make the army his career, and he had a great admiration for his ancestors, some of whom had seen active service in the army. He soon gained the reputation for being a braggart, but much of that was a façade to hide his fear of being thought a coward. His many escapades on horseback, stemming from his desire to prove he was fearless, resulted in several injuries, including two kicks to the head after falling from his horse. His tempers and his tears may have resulted from these injuries.

The main asset Patton had as an army commander was his ability to move with speed. He rarely needed much time to accumulate supplies, feeling confident any problem of administration would be resolved in his favor, albeit at the expense of others. Rundstedt gave his opinion that of the two best generals he had encountered, Patton was one and the other was Montgomery. Despite this praise from the enemy, Patton lacked an important quality — he was unable to make a clear distinction between objectives of purely military importance and those of purely personal significance. Eisenhower showed no ability to deal firmly with him, nor was he helped by Bradley, who too often condoned his deviations from orders. Had strong supervision been exercised over him and had Eisenhower only been a more shrewd soldier, it is likely Patton and Montgomery could have been made to operate in conjunction with each other, to the Germans' disadvantage.

19

Montgomery

Of the four generals who established a reputation in North Africa and Europe, Montgomery was indisputably the one with the most qualifications. He had entered Sandhurst at the age of 19 and passed out 13th out of 150; his first posting was to India in December 1908, returning to England in 1913, and by the August following the outbreak of the First World War he was a lieutenant, aged 26. He saw two months of action in France before being wounded in the chest and knee. He was invalided to England to recover, and returned to the Western Front in 1916 as a brigade major. At the termination of hostilities he was Chief of Staff, 47th (London) Division and while holding this position he did much to improve the standard of communications between the men at the front and headquarters in the rear, which included his system of liaison officers.

Following the war, Montgomery served in southern Ireland during the Sinn Fein uprising, which ended in 1922. He was later appointed to Staff College, Camberley, as an instructor, where he was in good company, for among other lecturers was Alan Brooke, later to be Chief of the Imperial General Staff. In January 1931, he was stationed in Palestine and then spent three years in southern India, after which he returned to England to take command of an infantry brigade in Portsmouth. A year before the declaration of war on Germany, Montgomery was again sent to Palestine to command army units fighting an Arab revolt. Here he was responsible for raising the 8th Division, returning to England in August 1939 to command the 3rd Division, headquartered on Salisbury Plain in the south of England. The division was to form part of the British Expeditionary Force to be sent to France in the event of war with Germany, and he eventually took command of it a few days before the outbreak of hostilities.

After the evacuation of Dunkirk, he was ordered to take his division to the south coast and there prepare defensive positions against a possible invasion. He turned the 3rd Division into a well-trained fighting unit, and barely a month after he had returned to England from France he was promoted to command the V Corps, whereupon he immediately instituted a training program which emphasized physical fitness.

Montgomery was given command of the Eighth Army in August 1942 and while on the way from Gibraltar to Cairo he began to think of the problems facing him. After considering the physical geography of Libya and the make-up of the Axis forces opposing the British, he concluded that he needed to create a corps similar to the German Panzer Grenadier Division, which consisted of motorized infantry and armor, to act as a spearhead for his as-yet unplanned offensive. Within one day of receiving instructions, the Deputy Chief of General Staff produced what was to be the X Corps, consisting of three armored divisions, which included a New Zealand Division of one armored and two infantry brigades. After making other changes, Montgomery began preparing for what he was certain would be Rommel's attempt to break through to Alexandria and Cairo. The fighting withdrawal of the Germans and Italians, and the subsequent union of the American II Corps and the Eighth Army in Tunisia, followed his successes at Alam Halfa and El Alamein.

Such was the man so often denigrated by the Americans and some British; those who did so seemed to place an inordinate emphasis on his personal character and gave him insufficient credit for his military skills. It is indisputable he sometimes appeared pompous and intolerant of those who disagreed with him; in addition, he was accused of being tactless by one of his superior officers. Brooke felt that Montgomery was brilliant in action and superb as a trainer of men, but he was apt to make many errors due to lack of tact and an inability to understand the other person's point of view. Brooke also regretted the Americans did not like Montgomery and felt difficulties arose when Montgomery was fighting close to them. Another assessment of him was given by an American, who felt Montgomery was flamboyant, strident, demanding and a glory hound.

Eisenhower, in one of his more perceptive moods, stated that Montgomery's outstanding characteristic was his tactical ability to prepare for, and fight, a planned battle, in which he was both careful and meticulous. Montgomery's opponent, Erwin Rommel, thought him to be a cautious general who was not willing to take risks, but at the same time he gave credit for his astuteness. He wrote that during the Battle of Alam Halfa the Germans were left in possession of the original British minefields and some excellent points from which the Eighth Army could be observed. The British made no effort to recapture the ground; Rommel believed this was wise from Montgomery's viewpoint because any such attempt would have been soundly defeated. As for Rundstedt, he considered Montgomery to be very systematic.

Some of the antipathy to Montgomery is understandable, but some can be refuted. He was the outstanding British general when it came to pride and loyalty displayed by the troops under his command. In part, the reason for this was certain aspects of his character. He was not a physically imposing person; perhaps for this reason he became the only staff officer in the British army to wear two cap badges on the front of his Tank Corps beret. This was the only indication in his dress of flamboyancy and otherwise he could be a little untidy when he was in the field. So far as his speech was concerned he made promises to the Eighth Army before the Battle of El Alamein, one of which was "... together we will hit the enemy for six right out of Africa." To some, the use of this cricket term may have sounded like an exaggeration, but Montgomery was always sure his plans would succeed and it was only at Arnhem that he failed.

The Americans were quite unable to understand that Montgomery's plans were thoroughly thought out and he was always prepared to alter them to fit the enemy's reaction. He had the commendable ability to be single-minded, which was another attribute the Americans found hard to accept. Unfortunately for the Anglo-American alliance Marshall, Eisenhower, Bradley and Patton failed to appreciate that many of Montgomery's decisions were based not only on the writings of experts such as Clausewitz, but also on experience, which they lacked, for of the four only Patton had been in action during the First World War.

Montgomery believed in concentrating his forces and reinforcing success. To most American officers these principles seemed distasteful, and if they had read about them they did not believe them.

Eisenhower was quite unable to comprehend the advantages of Montgomery's proposed single thrust into northern Germany. Part of this was due to his absence of battle experience, much was due to chauvinism, and part was due to Montgomery's paucity of communication with Eisenhower. The problems between them began in Normandy, where too often Montgomery gave the impression that a forthcoming attack by the 21st Army Group was intended to achieve a breakout. When this did not occur it was not surprising Eisenhower and the American press began to have doubts about Montgomery's capabilities to command not only the 21st Army Group but also the 12th Army Group, since he was ground commander. The trouble was rooted in the fact that Montgomery, having obtained Eisenhower's approval for an assault, did not feel it necessary to explain to him in fine detail what he expected to accomplish, and when subsequently the attack appeared to have failed, he did not explain any advantages which had been gained, such as causing the Germans to move armor from the American to the British sector.

If Montgomery was a glory hound, then it was a quality which was always modified by the desire to end the war as soon as possible while incurring minimum casualties. By comparison, the Supreme Commander at times gave but slight attention to the need to maintain low casualty lists, preferring to see the U.S. armies in action as often as possible, regardless of the need for any particular operation.

Another factor in the differences which existed between the two nations can be attributed, in part, to the failure of many Americans to understand what hardships the British population had undergone (one group of American officers suggested to a British mission to Washington that the British were using too many ships for the purpose of importing food — had only those Americans been forced to live on the meager British rations they would not have been so crass as to make such an allegation), nor did they appear to fully understand the difficulties in preparing and executing a cross-Channel invasion. They were inclined to use the Pacific as the basis for comparison; to them the hundreds of miles a task force had to sail to attack a Japanese-held island obviously resulted in a far more complex operation than the crossing of a few miles of English Channel. Such simplicity could have done nothing to convince the British that their ally was fully aware of the war conditions which prevailed in the Western Hemisphere.

The poor relationship which existed between Montgomery and some of the American officers was regrettable, but not surprising. Had each side made a greater effort to understand the other perhaps the broad conduct of the war, and particularly the campaign in Europe, could have been conducted with less friction.

Eisenhower had grand ideas as to how perfect unity could be achieved, but failed to implement any one of them. Montgomery, for his part, seemed incapable of contributing to the smooth operating of SHAEF, for he was undoubtedly as conscious of the American lack of war experience as was Brooke. If the Supreme Commander had been a man of greater ability, then Montgomery's relationship with him would almost certainly have been more productive. Churchill gave a succinct assessment of Montgomery: "... indomitable in defeat, invincible in retreat, and insufferable in victory."

20
U.S. Chief of Staff George C. Marshall

The United States had not been involved in any major conflict since the end of the First World War in 1918, and had no widespread empire needing to be garrisoned, as did the British. The American involvement in the First World War had been of far shorter duration than that of the British or French, resulting in their casualties being extremely low by comparison with those of the other two Allies. Upon the outbreak of war in Europe in 1939, the American armed forces were not only totally inadequate in the event the country was involved in the conflict, but were led by officers many of whom had no recent experience of warfare. The strength of the military was easy to rectify, but this was not accompanied by the equivalent improvement in the quality of the officer corps, especially the graduates of West Point, who had been trained at best by instructors with only a few months' exposure to fighting between 1917 and November 1918, and who therefore tended to use the American Civil War as the basis for their teaching.

One product of the First World War was George C. Marshall, who had served in the U.S. Army as a staff officer, but had no experience of commanding men in action. When he became Chief of Staff he gave he gave the impression that because an officer was promoted on his recommendation that made the man automatically competent to hold that position. One of his major failings was that he believed because he had decided something was a practical possibility, therefore it was. He ignored the difficulties of transporting troops and supporting equipment to France without the availability of landing craft. He shared a characteristic with some of his fellow officers—impatient for results, he could not appreciate that a head-on attack ran the risk of being very expensive in casualties, ignoring Napoleon's contention: "Never attack a position in front which you can gain by turning." Like Eisenhower, he was blind to the fact that the Russian tactics resulted in heavy losses. The lack of simple ingenuity displayed by the United States military was again evident when it later became involved in the Bay of Pigs, Vietnam and Grenada, in addition to their inept attempt to rescue the Tehran hostages.

The contrast in patience between the British and Americans is reminiscent of the two bulls, a young one and an old one. These two bulls were grazing in a field, next to another containing a herd of nubile cows. The gate between the two fields was always kept closed, except on one occasion when it was accidentally left open by the farmer's son, who had returned the herd to the field after it had been milked. The young bull raised his head while chewing on a mouthful of grass and spotted the open gate. He turned excitedly to the old bull and exclaimed: "Oh look! The farmer's boy has left the gate open! Let's run over there and make love to a couple of those luscious cows before we're caught!" The old bull slowly looked up, shook his head, and replied: "No! Let's walk over there ... then we can woo the whole damned lot!"

Too often Marshall and Eisenhower failed to appreciate the potential advantages of indirect attack. "Dragoon" was an exercise in futility, a fact which ought to have been obvious to them before it was launched; it resulted in reinforcements being added to the armies in northern France which could more profitably and speedily have been landed nearer the main action. In mounting "Dragoon," the 15th Army Group was stripped of men who could easily have been of more value in the fight for Italy. This revealed another side of the American military and political character. Not only did the Americans misinterpret Churchill's intentions in the Mediterranean, they displayed misguided impatience by refusing to finish the campaign in Italy before starting another in the same area.

The Americans by 1945 had raised an army of eight million, of which fewer than three million were in Europe on VE-Day. Indeed, throughout the war, blatantly disregarding prior agreements, the U.S. gave preference to the war in the Pacific, and Marshall failed to act on his own conclusion that the major consideration in the defeat of Germany was the employment of huge forces to invade Europe. While the raising of such a large army was a commendable achievement, even if smaller than had been projected, Marshall seemed unable to comprehend that numbers, and numbers alone, would not win the war but they could be the cause of high casualties. He proved himself too anxious to commit these forces to battle, even though they were not immediately needed. This low standard of training and discipline, which was too common, especially in the early months of the American involvement, appeared not to register with him,

Chapter 20—U.S. Chief of Staff George C. Marshall

for he pressed for operations against the French north coast when the U.S. army was incapable of providing not only enough troops who had received a reasonable level of basic training, but any at all who had received advanced training of any kind. None of the forces Marshall proposed using had any training in amphibious landings. Had his impatience and shortsightedness been ignored, a premature assault on France would have been made with consequences which would likely have been disastrous, but neither he nor Eisenhower seemed able to learn from their errors, believing the size of their armed forces was an adequate substitute for prudence.

21

Eisenhower's Qualifications

Much has been written about Eisenhower's war service and, in his own country at least, he is looked upon by many as a war hero. A little of this adulation may be deserved while much is not. He has been described by Field-Marshal Sir Alan Brooke as a man who made up for his lack of military skills by his charming personality, but such compensation was totally insufficient to make him a general of note. Even the Germans initially misjudged him, for in a lecture given on 7 February 1944 at the Luftwaffe Academy, it was stated Eisenhower was an expert in the use of armor, and inclined to leave the endeavor to his subordinates whom he inspired to great effort. In fact he was no tank expert, for his knowledge of its use in battle was based purely upon theory, and there was at least one Allied army commander who would have disagreed with the second evaluation.

Eisenhower did not apply for a vacancy at West Point because he had a strong desire to make the army his career; he wanted an education, which his parents could not afford. His application was accepted, and in his senior year at West Point he was ranked sixty-first out of 164, indicative of nothing but an average student. Toward the end of 1918 he was ordered to France as an instructor in tank warfare, but he arrived in New York on the day the Armistice went into effect, and was thus unable to participate in the conflict on the Western Front, thereby being deprived of the opportunity to gain essential experience so lamentably lacking 24 years later.

He subsequently held various posts in the United States, the Philippines and the Panama Canal Zone where he served on the staff of Gen. Fox Connor, whose large library on military history was at his disposal, but he appears to have remembered little, if anything, of what he read. His other assignments included that of commander of the Second Battalion 24th Regiment in Fort Bennington and before assuming the post of Allied

Chapter 21—Eisenhower's Qualifications

Commander-in-Chief of the North African invasion forces he had commanded not even a division.

Three months after the Japanese attack on Pearl Harbor, he was an assistant to George C. Marshall, the U.S. Chief of Staff. He became a good staff officer and was responsible for organizing the command system in southeast Asia, where the armed forces were of various nationalities. His appointments to command Anglo-American forces in North Africa, Sicily, Italy and then in northern Europe, were not made on the basis of proven military abilities as a field commander. Not only had he no prior experience of commanding large forces but he had no experience of combat whatsoever. It does Marshall no credit that he could find nobody better qualified to assume that post. Clausewitz wrote: "A general is chosen for his reputation for superior abilities, and leaders of large bodies of troops after careful probation...."[1] Eisenhower had no reputation for superior abilities as a field officer and he had been given no period of probation before being appointed Supreme Commander. Had he but been a little self-critical he would have realized he knew little about tactics and strategy; he might then have appointed a ground commander with the experience and knowledge he himself lacked.

Eisenhower was promoted above his abilities. He was undoubtedly a man of great personal charm but, as Alan Brooke wrote in his diary, it was in Africa that Eisenhower showed his lacking in essential war experience; this evaluation can justifiably be extended to include Europe. He showed a complete lack of imagination in his strategic thinking, he was dilatory in expressing a final decision and he learned nothing from either his mistakes or his opponent's successes. He owed his rapid promotion to Marshall, who kept a list of officers whom he felt were good potential material for advancement. Eisenhower was one of the names on that list. From being a lieutenant colonel in September 1939 he rose to the rank of brigadier general, a promotion earned following a 1941 exercise in which there was such a shortage of armor that some trucks were labeled "Tank." In the summer of 1941, one officer gave his opinion of Eisenhower that he was a good plodding student. By the following year, he was a lieutenant general, later to command two armies, the British First and Eighth, plus the U.S. II Corps.

Eisenhower clearly displayed his inabilities as a field officer while in command in North Africa. He lacked the capability to recognize and solve problems, a fact made evident not only by his behavior but also by his correspondence. In December 1942, he wrote to Butcher expressing his confidence in the present prospects, and to the Combined Chiefs of Staff in Washington to assure them he would make every effort to capture the "critical area"[2]; he was so transported by his own verbosity he forgot to explain what he meant by his vague phraseology. His uncertainty in his own judgment is clearly illustrated in a letter to his West Point roommate, P.A. Hodgson, executive officer at Fort Sam Houston, San Antonio. He told his friend that he often wished the two of them could meet in order to discuss the numerous problems, big and small, which daily confronted him as Commander-in-Chief. A further example of his indetermination was shown after he took up a position in the War Department in 1940. Having considered the options open to the United States in the event of war with Japan, he came to the conclusion the Pacific should have priority over any conflict in Europe. He gradually changed his mind and became convinced that Germany should be dealt with first, then Japan. On 22 January 1941, he wrote it would not be possible to win a war sitting down and handing out limited supplies all over the world, with no theater of operations receiving sufficient materiel. With the passing of time he soon forgot this, as demonstrated by his strategy in Europe. His rapid promotion owed everything to the fact that he had caught Marshall's attention and nothing to his possessing any experience or proven talent in strategy, tactics, or the command of large forces.

Eisenhower was not above indulging in a little inaccuracy. Writing to Marshall on 15 February 1943, he said he felt sure Marshall would be impressed by the magnificent spirit shown by the GIs[3]—the same men who, because of inadequate training, poor discipline and indifferent leadership, were demoralized and routed at Kasserine. Of Fredendall, he wrote in the same letter he was impressed by the II Corps commander's thorough knowledge of the battle front and disposition of his troops[4]—the same man, just two months previously, who had surprised Eisenhower by having his headquarters some 80 miles behind the front line—the same man who was so knowledgeable of the battlefront that he was later relieved of his command by Eisenhower—the same man who, not long before, had refused to give up his troglodyte existence to visit the front and make a personal assessment of the situation.

Eisenhower, the general, not only lacked the vital experience of commanding large forces but he was completely lacking in imaginative strategy. His decisions were rarely based on sound military principles, but too often in the hope of gaining kudos for the American armies. Rommel believed a man was usually aware of his own limitations; despite his unassuming character, Eisenhower was unable to accept the fact that he was deficient in essential qualifications and in April 1942 he made a diary entry complaining about the number of amateur strategists in Washington, as though he were more competent than those he criticized.

Chapter 21—Eisenhower's Qualifications

Churchill's approval of Eisenhower as Allied Commander-in-Chief and later as Supreme Commander, contrasts with the British government's reaction to the appointment of a successor to Eisenhower as Supreme Commander of SHAPE (Supreme Headquarters Allied Powers in Europe). After Eisenhower retired to run for the Presidency of the United States in 1952, U.S. Gen. Al Gruenther was proposed as his replacement. The British Chiefs of Staff, supported by the government, objected on the grounds he had never commanded anything in his entire career — had the British only been as particular ten years before.

The choice of Eisenhower, although flawed, was not without a redeeming feature. He was a competent administrator and there were few others who, under the same circumstances, could have accomplished so much to make the Allied command work as smoothly as it did. He did his best to ensure those who showed dislike for anyone of the opposite nationality were quickly returned home. Nevertheless, it cannot be overlooked that SHAEF was principally an American operation. Had he only limited his involvement to being a co-ordinator it is doubtful if many could have had justification for criticizing him. Unfortunately, he was determined also to hold the position of ground commander, for which he had neither the aptitude nor the qualifications. With no experience of commanding an army, let alone three army groups, in peace or war, and no battle experience whatsoever, he took control of the entire European operation, succeeding only in stumbling to victory, supported by Marshall more than 3,000 miles away, who was equally unsuitable as a field commander.

Eisenhower, like Ulysses S. Grant of the American Civil War, could think of no method of attack other than the direct assault; perhaps this was due to lack of imagination or a misguided desire to ensure all American armies participated in the advance. Nonetheless, the main objection to his moving the entire front moving forward at the same time was the problem of supplies. The Allied Air Forces and the Maquis had effectively put the French rail system out of action, a great benefit to the invaders initially, but no advantage to them once their armies broke out of Normandy and headed for the Seine and Germany. On occasions, the allied forces on the offensive had to suffer supply lines which were between 250 and 400 miles long. Not until the end of August did the first train from the beachhead arrive in Paris via a circuitous route, and about nine days later the port of Dieppe was in operation. The answer to the problem of moving supplies from the beach to the front was a system of road transportation, but this had the disadvantage of being inefficient. It was wasteful in vehicles, fuel and men, and at one time 48% of the U.S. supplies were stalled in Normandy, with long delays before they were moved to the front line.

The situation was not eased by large-scale pilfering, the products of which found their way onto the black market. The sensible solution was to capture a large deep sea port quickly and as far to the east as possible.

Surprisingly, Eisenhower at one time fully appreciated the need for Antwerp. He wrote to George Marshall on 24 March 1944 detailing plans for an invasion of Europe. It provided for a landing between Le Havre and Boulogne, and the subsequent capture of Antwerp, emphasizing a large port was essential to the continuation of the invasion. Again, on 24 August 1944, he wrote to Marshall saying it was vital to establish a depot at Antwerp, which agreed with the planners of Operation "Overlord" who had clearly stated the necessity for taking Antwerp as soon as possible. One can only assume Eisenhower was so entranced with the prospect of crossing the Rhine that he overlooked the need to secure his administration. He was certainly reminded of that need, directly and indirectly, on more than one occasion by Montgomery and Patton.

If Eisenhower believed by attacking on different parts of the front simultaneously he was seriously inconveniencing the enemy he was mistaken, for these all-too-often unconnected attacks were nothing but a nuisance to the Germans, who at worst never knew where the next assault would be launched. What the Allies gained by his strategy was minimal; it did nothing to assist in the grouping of their forces for a concentrated attack against Germany; it did nothing to destroy the coherence of the enemy forces; it did nothing to threaten the German lines of communications. More than anything else, Eisenhower's strategy lacked directness, for he showed no signs of having a focal point as his ultimate target in any of his offensives. Once again, it would not have been difficult for him to have learned from recent events. In 1942, the Germans mounted simultaneous operations against the Russians. Both offensives were too weak to achieve their goals, and Hitler in the east, like Eisenhower in the west, succeeded in conquering territory but not the enemy.

The capture of land, the loss of which would have no adverse effect on the enemy, and the failure to defeat the opposing armies, directly contradict the basic principles of war. Not only was Eisenhower apparently obsessed with capturing territory of no particular value, he never once concentrated his armies for a major offensive against the enemy. The Supreme Commander displayed an inexcusable lack of simple caution when he allowed the line at the Kasserine Pass to be thinly held by inexperienced troops, repeating the same error in the Ardennes, where once more he showed he had he failed to learn not only from his own mistakes but also from the mistakes of others; the French in 1940 had covered that area with their Ninth Army, which was the weakest of all their forces. At

Chapter 21—Eisenhower's Qualifications

Kasserine, he had contradicted his own conclusion which was that an essential of a good army was ample training; he was very upset by published reports, passed by the censor, criticizing the indifferent performance of some U.S. units. In Belgium, he was fully aware of the low density of the defending Americans, as well as the fact the defenders were either understrength or inexperienced. Once more he took no steps to remedy the situation, refusing to reduce the buildup of men and supplies for a planned offensive, which could achieve very little, in order to strengthen a weak and vulnerable section of the front.

Like the French in 1940, Eisenhower failed to learn anything from the German campaign in Poland. The immediate objective of the Nazis was not the capture of territory but the destruction of the Polish armed forces. After the limited success of Falaise, the Supreme Commander made no attempt to destroy the German army by outright defeat in battle, and he seemed far too concerned about how his handling of the northern Europe campaign would be assessed by the American public and from the political point of view. It was no advantage to the Allies that he was reluctant to assign command of the ground forces, in North Africa and northern Europe, to a more qualified officer. His attitude toward appointing a ground commander was even more apparent in northern Europe, when he delayed appointing Montgomery to command the Battle of the Ardennes, and earlier when he used as his excuse for his obstinacy the incorrect assertion that Montgomery had suggested only himself for the post of ground commander. This allegation is so obviously wrong it can only be assumed that both rapid promotion and nationalism had clouded his judgment and he could no longer tolerate the thought of relieving himself of certain responsibilities, especially to a more qualified foreigner. He illogically argued in favor of retaining control of the ground forces by reasoning a major operation required a single ground commander. When the line was extended from the North Sea to Switzerland, he then contended it became too much for one man to control and direct operations intelligently; he therefore assumed the task himself and proved his conclusion to be correct, at the expense of a speedier victory.

There is a strong possibility that the justification for Eisenhower and Marshall being reluctant to see a British officer in command of Allied armies was that, to them, politics and national egos were much more important than military successes. If Montgomery had been made ground commander and deputy to Eisenhower and had met with even the slightest failure, it was felt this would jeopardize the chances of Roosevelt being reelected in 1945; as soldiers, they should have concentrated on the war, not on domestic politics. Montgomery's suggestion for a narrow front offensive was also repugnant to the Americans; it would have entailed stopping Patton's Third Army, which the U.S. generals believed would have been totally unacceptable to the American press, which on more than one occasion showed its real or imagined powers in the minds of those generals.

Anglophobia, too, was widespread in the American army, with Patton being the most obvious perpetrator and Bradley a close second; Mark Clark was so determined to have Americans, rather than British, capture Rome it became almost an obsession, resulting in the unauthorized switching of his line of attack at Anzio to give the Americans the chance of taking the capital. His action resulted in delaying the breakout from the beachhead and a tragic increase in casualties. He, too, had an eye for history. He stated the Americans intended to be the first army in 15 centuries to capture Rome by an attack from the south — his knowledge of history was faulty.

Soon after the landings in Normandy, the Supreme Commander showed how poor a field officer he was. Had he taken the time to study Montgomery's plan at Caen he would not have derogated the accomplishments of the 21st Army Group. In one message to Montgomery he wrote it was unfortunate Bradley's attack to the south was not fully developed before some Panzer units had time to switch to his front. It was a totally inaccurate statement, clearly demonstrating he had not understood what was happening. By 9 July 1944, the British and Canadians had drawn 610 enemy tanks onto their front whereas Bradley's army group was faced with 190. Eisenhower should not have been ignorant of this vital statistic.

If Eisenhower's understanding of tactics was questionable, so was his evaluation of an officer's ability. In an interview with a magazine reporter, he stated Bradley was the greatest field officer of World War II, substantiating this sweeping assertion by stating Bradley was in command of all U.S. armies participating in the assault on Germany. Had the Supreme Commander only resorted to a little self-examination before expressing this opinion, he might have concluded the holding of high office is not in itself indicative of ability.

Politics and the execution of war are closely connected, but in a democracy the two are operated separately, and it is generally accepted that the armed forces follow instructions from the politicians. Nevertheless, Eisenhower made the purely political decision to halt on the Elbe, contradicting a statement made to the press prior to his appointment as Supreme Commander, in which he asserted his new job would be to smash Germany. There was no military reason why he should not have attempted

Chapter 21—Eisenhower's Qualifications 205

the advance to Berlin, Prague and Vienna, but he chose not to do so, leaving the citizens of Prague to suffer heavy casualties. The Supreme Commander, having deliberately become involved in politics by obtaining the Russian approval to halt on the Elbe, showed his political acuity was on a par with his comprehension of strategy. He, and others, paid for his impropriety by having to agree to the Russian request not to advance on to Prague.

Eisenhower was quick to criticize Montgomery, contradicting his favorable first impression of the British commander, but not all his reproofs were valid. He failed to understand that by advocating a single thrust in the north with the object of taking Berlin, Montgomery was proposing a type of action which ran counter to his own reputation as a conservative general. His single offensive was to have been a hard and speedy drive through the north German plain. On two previous occasions, in Libya and in northern Europe after the closing of the Falaise Gap, he demonstrated he was capable of just such an advance.

The Supreme Commander also showed evidence of an inferiority complex. In talking to journalist Cornelius Ryan, he alleged Montgomery had become so personal in his efforts to ensure the Americans in general, and Eisenhower specifically, received no credit for their successes that he and Montgomery ceased talking to each other. Considering Montgomery always gave credit to the American soldier this accusation was quite unwarranted. It also displayed the very traits which Eisenhower, prior to the North African invasion, had declared were intolerable. He failed to appreciate that by promising a rapid advance to Berlin, Montgomery was staking his military reputation, something which meant much to him. Had the offensive taken place it would have included one American army, and because of the supply problem, for which Eisenhower cannot be exonerated, it was inevitable that some of the remaining U.S. forces would have to play a static rôle. Such a decision was obviously not suggested on nationalistic grounds by Montgomery, but for sound military reasons. His plan was simply a version of the German blitzkrieg, something Eisenhower should have realized.

After the war, Gen. Wilhelm von Thoma said the most decisive factor in battle is to organize one's resources in order to maintain momentum, a factor not prominent in the Allied advance into Germany. Having failed to keep up the pressure on the enemy, Eisenhower only made matters worse by deluding himself into believing Berlin was nonoperative as a capital; he had gone as far as to assure Marshall that not only was Berlin in ruins, but government offices were being evacuated to safety, thereby giving the American Chief of Staff a completely false impression of life in

Berlin. If he believed Berlin was just another geographical location, the Germans thought otherwise; in this they had the support of such authorities as Clausewitz and Hamley, the former contending that the occupation of the enemy's capital will result in his defeat.

In fact, Berlin was very much alive, with the government still working there, the postal service delivering the mail, newspapers being published, milk being delivered to customers, and about 65% of the factories still in production. Spandau, where the production of ammunition was located, had hardly been hit by the heavy bombing raids. The police were enforcing the law and at least 600,000 people were in employment; water and electricity were being supplied to the public,[5] although the services were a little erratic as the result of the bomber raids. This was hardly the capital portrayed in Eisenhower's message to Marshall.

As well as ignoring the determination of the Germans to hold the city, Eisenhower reversed his own plans, for it had been decided to stage an airborne assault on Berlin. The British First Airborne and the U.S. 82nd Airborne, under the command of U.S. Lt. Gen. James Gavin, were to have attacked the Berlin airfields and Gavin was quite sure the psychological effect of a paratroop landing would have been a significant contribution to the collapse of Berlin's defenses. His optimism was supported by Eisenhower, who in a cable sent to Washington and read by Marshall and Brooke on 25 March, stated he intended to reinforce success with the utmost speed. His euphoria was not long lived; a few days later he announced that based on distance alone it seemed as though the Russians would reach Berlin first, despite their facing the majority of the German army. The airdrop was canceled. To compound his failure to understand the complexities of warfare, he boasted that Bradley had never been held up, nor had he ever paused to regroup when an opportunity to advance was available. In fact, after the fall of Cherbourg, Bradley had halted for several days in order to do just that — regroup. If any commander had advanced successfully without the need to regroup, the element of luck could be discounted. Nonetheless, if a pause to regroup had not been made that does not necessarily show laudable qualities in a general.

Some of Eisenhower's problems in his relationship with Montgomery were of his own creation. On many occasions he was apparently reluctant to divulge fully his intentions because he felt they would be unpalatable to the British commander, and by subsequently indulging in dissimulation he did his own cause little good. Such an instance occurred on 25 March 1945 when Montgomery had a private meeting with Bradley and Eisenhower, at which the Field-Marshal propounded his plan to enter the plains of Germany.

Chapter 21—Eisenhower's Qualifications

This was the meeting at which Eisenhower gave the impression he agreed to the use of the U.S. Ninth Army in Montgomery's narrow front offensive, and at which he failed to mention his intention to remove the U.S. Ninth Army from Montgomery's control, for he had decided not to go on to Berlin. It is indisputable that at the time Eisenhower already knew the Ninth Army was not going to continue under Montgomery's command, for on 28 March, only three days after the meeting, he wrote to Montgomery agreeing with his plans, but informing him that the Ninth Army was to revert to Bradley's command.

The breaking up of a cohesive organization takes time; Eisenhower had to be aware of his intentions on 25 March, but lacked the courage and good sense so to inform Montgomery. His handling of this matter did nothing to enhance his reputation in the opinion of the British commander. Eisenhower was undoubtedly lucky, for in all his dealings with the 21st Army Group's commander he was supported by five British officers on SHAEF staff. It can only be assumed that the existence of this anti-Montgomery clique was unknown to Brooke, who surely would have taken action to break it up had he been aware of it.

In a meeting at 10 Downing Street, Eisenhower was asked if he would be willing to serve under a British officer; his answer was since the British had more experience in the war than the United States it seemed a sensible suggestion. It took only two years for this pragmatism to evaporate. There were elements of Eisenhower's personality and qualifications which were similar to those of the First World War French general Robert Nivelle. He, too, was a man of great charm and persuasion who had been a comparatively junior officer and had experienced unusually rapid promotion. Nivelle had but one plan, his "system," which he was so convinced would succeed that he would entertain no other. There the comparison ends, for following the 1917 Somme offensive, Nivelle was relieved of his command.

Eisenhower's qualifications for the position of Supreme Commander were so minimal that the result was a casualty list which was higher than it needed to have been. He failed to appreciate that by besieging the French Atlantic ports it would have been cheaper than capturing them—cheaper in lives and more advantageous, since the ports were of decreasing importance to the Allies as they advanced eastward. He allowed the port of Brest to be assaulted by Patton's army at a cost of 10,000 dead and wounded, but the reason for its capture was not strategic but for publicity. Later he was responsible for the losses incurred at Aachen, the Huertgen Forest, Metz and the Ardennes, all totally unnecessary.

The main problem which Eisenhower encountered, arose after the

Seine was crossed. He dithered, not knowing what action to take next, apprehensive lest he appear to favor the British, thereby endangering his public reputation in the United States. His wavering was observed by Hodges; he wrote that at one time there had been so many changes in the First Army's instructions there were occasions when it seemed as if nobody in charge had a clear idea of the direction they wished to take to Germany.

The need to ensure a good supply line was forgotten, with the result the Supreme Commander never took into consideration the scarcity of administration when formulating his plans. The poor supply situation was noted in writing by him on 24 August 1944, yet he authorized two offensives, one north and the other south of the Ardennes. Both were halted due to insufficient logistical support. A further example of the existing shortages can be gained from the 12th Army Group's experience; by mid-October it was receiving less than one-tenth of its needs. It made the situation no better when Eisenhower announced he would forgo the capture of a deep-water port in order to mount a determined offensive into Germany. Incredibly, it appeared he was completely unaware of the seriousness of the supply situation, for a deep thrust into Germany would have to have had administrative support. His earlier contention that the logistical problems in the north would be eased with the capture of Marseilles was, not surprisingly, proven wrong. Marseilles, by the end of summer 1944, was capable of supporting only Devers's Army Group.

Had Eisenhower paid more attention to military history he might have known that, in the American Civil War, Gen. George Stoneman's reconnaissance in force along the Orange Alexandria railroad, with the intention of taking the enemy in the rear, failed because of logistics problems. However, Gen. William Sherman's march through Georgia in 1864 succeeded because he had ensured he was well provisioned. In addition, Eisenhower obviously had not read Lt. Gen. Sir E.B. Hamley's exposition of the operation of war in which he wrote: "The most abundant stores will be of no avail if there be a deficiency of transportation."[6] If Hamley, in the 19th century, appreciated the importance of efficient transportation, why not Eisenhower in the 20th century?

For too long, the Supreme Commander remained content with a supply line extending several hundred miles to the beaches and Cherbourg. Prior to D-Day, Eisenhower had indicated he appreciated the value of Antwerp to the Allies; there is therefore no excuse for his subsequent failure to order the capture of this port as part of the termination of the Normandy breakout. By his own admission, its possession by the Allies was essential, and yet he ignored his own conclusions.

By advocating a broad front offensive Eisenhower displayed how inad-

Chapter 21—Eisenhower's Qualifications

equate he was as a strategist. He had under his command highly mechanized armies; opposing him was a German army which, since long before 1939, had used horses to draw much of its wheeled equipment. By 1944, the enemy was experiencing an acute shortage of fuel which hampered the employment of armor and motorized units. The Allies had no such shortage, yet Eisenhower made no attempt to capitalize on the German weakness. He ignored the fact that the German infantry was not mobile, their army having lost an estimated 15,000 vehicles in the first three months of "Overlord," and that this transportation was very much harder for them to replace than it would have been for the Allies, had the loss been theirs.

So concerned was Brooke about Eisenhower's handling of the offensive in the west that the Supreme Commander was invited to London on 12 December to explain his strategy to both Brooke and Churchill. Brooke pointedly accused Eisenhower of violating the principle of concentration by insisting on a broad front assault,[7] and he maintained the Allied armies were not strong enough to continue two thrusts which the Supreme Commander was proposing to mount. Despite Bradley's claim to the contrary, the Germans were suffering from a manpower shortage and reserves were nowhere near abundant. As for the production of war materiel, although some factories had been moved to safer areas outside the range of Allied bombers, the Nazis relied heavily upon the Ruhr for their war materiel, and they had to supply the Russian Front from factories in eastern Germany, Czechoslovakia and Poland. It would have been hard to have transported any surplus supplies from east to west because of the Allied bombing raids. A broad front attack was not essential; the Allies were not forced into it by any enemy action, nor, it must be stressed again, was it practical from the logistical point of view. By contrast, a single front offensive had several advantages. It could create a concentration of men and materiel, and the forces conducting an active defense would have needed less administrative support than they would have done had they been on the offensive. The theory of concentration was not unique to Montgomery; on 8 August 1943, U.S. Army planners had noted the war could be reduced to a stalemate unless, among other things, the Allies succeeded in concentrating their forces.

By mounting a strong attack on just one front, Eisenhower would have compelled the Germans to have countered with a strong defense which would have forced them to try to retain adequate strength to oppose any threat of an attack from another part of the front. Eisenhower failed to exploit the success of the Falaise Pocket (by harassing the enemy and bouncing him across the Rhine before the end of September), repeating many of the errors he had made in North Africa.

Part of the Supreme Commander's problem was his inability to determine the location of the vital center of gravity, the location in the enemy's organization, whether military, social or political, the loss of which leads to his collapse or severe defeat. The Allies had been in northern Europe for three months, but Eisenhower showed he had no notion of how he was to achieve the defeat of the Germans. He was not lost for words on the subject, however, for in a message to his commanders dated 29 August 1944 he stated there were signs of an impending German collapse, and upon the destruction of the enemy forces in the west he intended to strike directly at the enemy heartland. As it transpired, he had difficulty in locating that vital part of the German anatomy.

One week later he made the astonishing diary entry that the Germans were completely defeated. His reluctance to act speedily gave the enemy time to reorganize his defenses; however, had the Supreme Commander made the determination that one vulnerable point was the industrial Ruhr, as Montgomery contended, and had he then concentrated his forces to effect the capture of this area, he would not only have complied with a vital precept of war, he would have succeeded in greatly hampering the Nazi war production. How he could have treated the Ruhr with such patent indifference, when any student of elementary geography knows this area is the industrial center of Germany, is impossible to understand and to have delayed its capture until just two months before the end of the war was inexcusable. His action totally contradicted a letter to his generals, dated 4 September, stating the way to defeat the enemy on the Western Front was to take the Saar and the Ruhr. He even went so far as to say he believed this would entail a simultaneous strike by the 21st Army Group, plus the U.S. First Army and Patton's Third Army. Among other things, the object of the 21st Army Group's offensive would have been the capture of Antwerp.

If Eisenhower was ignorant of the importance of the Ruhr, the Germans were certainly not. Despite its value, and the fact that as far back as 1942 Marshall had advocated the surrounding of the Ruhr, it was not until 17 April 1945 that the Allies had any success, following the collapse of Field-Marshal Walter Model's Army Group B.

The concept of concentrating forces for a strong attack was not something novel to military thinking. There are abundant examples of a commander's success or failure hinging on the essential fact that he concentrated, or failed to concentrate, his forces at the right time. Since West Point based so much of its teachings upon the American Civil War, Eisenhower should have known that the Union Army's march on Richmond was not two disparate assaults, but two columns conducting a concentrated assault. If the Supreme Commander had only expanded his reading he might have found something relevant, such as the article written by Maj. Gen. J.F.C. Fuller in the mid–1920s. In the *Journal of the Royal Artillery* he propounded four principles of warfare. These were surprise, concentration, deep penetration and envelopment, none of which was in Eisenhower's inventory. Fuller specifically criticized the failure to concentrate the tank attack at Cambrai in the First World War. Another article by Fuller, for the *Army Quarterly*, stressed concentration was the essential element in an assault, as opposed to mass which had been used so expensively in the First World War. He also gave supply as a vital condition of war. Fuller was not alone in writing on the subject of modern warfare, and it is deplorable that Eisenhower showed such a lack of evidence that he had read and understood those opinions.

Eisenhower could not appreciate that Montgomery's plan had merit, for to him the finer points of strategy were as the mysteries of the universe are to a child. He found it intolerable to have some American forces go onto the defensive while the 21st Army Group, with American units attached, was advancing. He appeared unaware of the fact the Allies were fighting a war neither for the purpose of gaining prestige for one or other of their armies, nor for their commanders, nor for the Supreme Commander himself, but in order to defeat Nazi Germany. It was not a celebrity contest he had been instructed to conduct, but the destruction of the enemy armed forces.

Eisenhower not did comprehend, before his halt on the Elbe, that he had a clear road to Berlin. There was a huge stockpile of supplies on the banks of the Rhine, more than half the daily tonnage landed at Antwerp was designated for the U.S. armies, and the air forces were capable of ferrying about 2,000 tons daily to landing fields east of the river. The Germans had not a single army capable of opposing an Allied attack from the west; they had no defenses in the rear of the Siegfried Line and the Luftwaffe posed no threat. In addition, there was no natural barrier which could not have been easily overcome. Such was Eisenhower's final strategy that by the time the U.S. armies reached the Elbe, the 12th Army Group was strung out along a 250-mile front, making it incapable of mounting a concentrated attack even had the opportunity arisen.

Eisenhower's method of command differed from Montgomery's; as a consequence of his lack of experience, he tended to operate on the basis of decision by committee, a system abhorrent to Montgomery, and it is difficult to imagine, had Montgomery been ground commander in the final months of 1944, that the German offensive in the Ardennes would have been anywhere near as successful as it was. It is doubtful if Montgomery would have tolerated the area being so thinly held, and for all his self-confidence never did he invite an attack unless he was thoroughly prepared to deal with it, as he was at the battle of Alam Halfa in Libya. Unlike Eisenhower, he had far too much respect for his opponent.

Eisenhower's inability to exercise adequate control over his subordinates was a defect in character. His lack of strategic knowledge was an omission in training and experience. Marshall must be held responsible for encouraging him to take over the command of the ground forces in France, a move which, with any rationality, can only be ascribed to inordinate patriotism. Eisenhower must also be criticized for failing to appreciate his outstanding weakness. He ought to have realized he was a staff officer and the command of not one army, but three army groups, was far beyond his abilities. Nevertheless, having accepted the post, he could easily have limited himself to the responsibilities of Supreme Commander. Since he spurned the use of a ground commander, he could have appointed an assistant, a general who had the essential knowledge which he lacked, someone to have been ground commander in all but name to act as an éminence grise. Despite his modesty, he could not bring himself about to make such an appointment. He had something in common with the commander of the Army of the Potomac in 1862, Gen. Ambrose Burnside. In each case, rarely in the history of the United States army can the appointment to high command have been made upon such a paucity of qualifications.

22
Conclusion

If Eisenhower is to be remembered in military history, it is likely to be first as an officer who was promoted too rapidly and beyond his competence, second as a poor selector of subordinate officers, third as a compromiser and an indecisive character, and fourth as a general with a lamentable lack of imagination when it came to strategy; he learned but one thing from his errors—how to make more. His inability to choose capable officers was evident in his choice of Fredendall to command the U.S. II Corps in North Africa. Maj. Gen. L.T. Gerow, a corps commander in the U.S. First Army, was also selected, not because he had any prior exposure to combat, not because he had established a reputation as an outstanding leader, but purely because he was a close friend of Eisenhower.

While he disliked offending anyone, the result was that he tended to resolve a difference of opinion not by asserting his authority, but by compromise; when that was unlikely to succeed, he resorted to blatant deception. Consequently, there were times when he contradicted an agreement made with Montgomery in order to appease another army group commander. Unfortunately, this only resulted in Montgomery losing confidence in the Supreme Commander.

Hamley gave a portrait of an army commander as one " ... not having a mind capable of comprehensive views, or of deep study, he knows nothing of great combinations. Strategy, in the sense of a flexible science, to be adapted to circumstances, is a sealed book to him; the theatre of war is written as a cipher to which he has not the key—Cautious, from not knowing when he may venture to be bold, and rash from ignorance of what may be attempted against him.—This is no unfair picture of what has often passed muster in the world as a respectable leader to be entrusted with the fate of hosts."[1] Written in the latter half of the 19th century, it is just as apt a hundred years later when applied to Eisenhower.

His defects and flaws may not have been all of his own making. Certainly, he was ill-served by Marshall. Nevertheless, military history is unlikely to deal kindly with him and all the panegyrics by those who, with so little justification, believe he was a near genius cannot alter the conclusion that Eisenhower failed as a military commander.

Notes

Introduction

1. Hanson W. Baldwin, *The Crucial Years 1939–1941* (New York: Harper & Row, 1976), 438.
2. Kent Roberts Greenfield, *American Strategy in World War II — A Reconsideration* (Baltimore: Johns Hopkins University Press, 1963), 86.
3. Mark Clark, *Calculated Risk* (New York: Harper & Bros., 1950), 26.

Chapter 2

1. Robert H. Ferrel, ed., *The Eisenhower Diaries* (New York: Norton, 1981), 43.
2. Joseph Patrick Hobbs, ed., *Dear General: General Eisenhower's Wartime Letters to Marshall* (Baltimore: Johns Hopkins University Press, 1971), 18.
3. Stephen E. Ambrose, *Eisenhower, Vol. 1, Soldier, General of the Army, President Elect 1890–1952*, (New York: Simon and Schuster, 1983), 212.
4. A. Russel Buchanan, *The United States and World War II (Military and Diplomatic Documents)* (New York: Harper & Row, 1964), 120.
5. Martin Blumenson, *Kasserine Pass* (Boston: Houghton Mifflin, 1967), 119.
6. Omar N. Bradley, *A General's Life* (New York: Simon & Schuster, 1983), 126.
7. John S.D. Eisenhower, *Allies—Pearl Harbor to D-Day* (Garden City, NY: Doubleday, 1986), 270.
8. B.L. Montgomery, *El Alamein to the River Sangro* (New York: St. Martin's Press, 1974), 56 et seq.
9. Basil H. Liddell-Hart, *A History of the Second World War* (New York: Putnam, 1970), 346.

Chapter 3

1. *The War Reports of General of the Army George C. Marshall to Secretary of War* (Philadelphia: Lippincott, 1947), 106.
2. Charles MacDonald, *The Mighty Endeavor* (New York: Oxford University Press, 1969), 127–128.

3. Bradley, *A Soldier's Story* (New York: Holt, 1951), 110.
4. Hobbs, *Dear General*, 110.

Chapter 5

1. Philip Warner, *World War II — The Untold Story* (London: Bodley Head, 1988), 180
2. Montgomery, *El Alamein*, 84.
3. Nigel Hamilton, *Master of the Battlefield — Monty's Final War Years 1942–1944* (New York: McGraw-Hill, 1983), 324.
4. Samuel E. Morison, *Sicily-Salerno-Anzio: January 1943–June 1944* (Boston: Little, Brown, 1954), 51.
5. Forrest C. Pogue, *George C. Marshall, Ordeal and Hope* (New York: Viking, 1963), 414–415.
6. H. Essame, *Patton — A Study in Command* (New York: Scribner's, 1974), 109–110.

Chapter 6

1. David Belchem, *All in a Day's March* (London: Collins, 1978), 170.
2. Forrest C. Pogue, *The Supreme Commander* (Washington: Office of the Chief of Military History, Department of the Army, 1954), 228.
3. Mark Arnold-Foster, *The World at War* (New York: Stein & Day, 1973), 105.
4. Liddell-Hart, *History of the Second World War*, 455.
5. Anthony Cave-Brown, *Bodyguard of Lies* (New York: Harper & Row, 1975), 421.
6. John Grigg, *1943: The Victory That Never Was* (New York: Hill & Wang, 1980), 104.

Chapter 7

1. Hastings Ismay, *Memoirs* (New York: Viking, 1960), 361.
2. Robert Betzel, *The Uneasy Alliance* (New York: Knopf, 1972), 312–314.
3. David Eisenhower, *Eisenhower at War, 1943–1945* (New York: Random House, 1986), 139.
4. E.K. Sixsmith, *Eisenhower As Military Commander* (New York: Stein & Day, 1972), 124.
5. Eisenhower, *Eisenhower at War*, 182.
6. J. F. C. Fuller, *The Second World War* (New York: Duell, Sloan and Pierce, 1968), 325.
7. W.S. Churchill, *Triumph and Tragedy* (Boston: Houghton Mifflin, 1953), 65.
8. W.K. Hancock, *Smuts — The Fields of Force* (London: Cambridge University Press, 1988), 417.
9. David Irving, *The War Between the Generals* (New York: Congdon and Lattis, 1981), 265.

Chapter 8

1. Eisenhower, *Eisenhower at War*, 127.
2. Field Marshal Sir Michael Carver, ed., *The War Lords* (Boston: Little, Brown, 1976), 525.
3. Bernard Fergusson, *The Watery Maze* (New York: Holt, Rinehart & Winston, 1961), 337.
4. H. M. Cole, *The European Theater of Operations — The Lorraine Campaign* (Washington: Historical Division, Department of the Army, 1950).
5. Arthur Tedder, *With Prejudice* (Boston: Little, Brown, 1967), 509.
6. David Howorth, *Dawn of D-Day* (London: Collins, 1959), 197.
7. Chester Wilmot, *The Struggle for Europe* (New York: Caroll & Graf, 1952), 264.
8. Andrew A. Rooney, *The Fortunes of War: Four Great Battles of World War II* (Boston: Little, Brown, 1962), 177.
9. David Belchem, *Victory in Normandy* (London: Chatto & Windus, 1981), 93.

Chapter 9

1. Desmond Hawkins, ed., *War Report* (New York: Oxford University Press, 1946), 125.
2. E. Belfield and H. Essame, *The Battle for Normandy* (London: Batsford, 1965), 82, 83.
3. Major General Sir Francis de Guingand, *Generals at War* (London: Hodder & Stoughton, 1964), 200.
4. Pogue, *The Supreme Commander*, 188.
5. Arthur Bryant, *Triumph in the West — (based on the diaries of Field Marshal Alan Brooke)* (Garden City, NY: Doubleday, 1959), 244.

Chapter 10

1. Stephen E. Ambrose, *Ike — Abilene to Berlin* (New York: Harper, 1973), 157.
2. Richard Rohmer, *Patton's Gap* (New York: Beaufort Books, 1981), 154.
3. Henry Maule, *Caen — The Brutal Battle and Breakout from Normandy* (Newton Abbot, England: David & Charles, 1976), 142.
4. Peter Simonds, *Maple Leaf Up↑ Maple Leaf Down↓* (New York: Island Press, 1946), 229–230.
5. Pogue, *The Supreme Commander*, 217.
6. Stephen E. Ambrose, *The Supreme Commander — The War Years of General Dwight D. Eisenhower* (Garden City, NY: Doubleday, 1970), 506–507.
7. Ladislas Farago, *Patton — Ordeal & Triumph* (New York: Astor-Honor, 1964), 529.
8. Richard Lamb, *Montgomery in Europe 1943–1945 — Success or Failure?* (New York: Franklin Watts, 1983), 208.
9. Brian Horrocks, *Corps Commander*, 79.
10. H. Essame, *Patton — A Study in Command*, 197.
11. John S.D. Eisenhower, *Strictly Personal*, (Garden City, NY: Doubleday, 1974), 320, 321.

12. Eric Partridge, *Dictionary of Slang and Unconventional English* (New York: Macmillan, 1970); see relevant definition.
13. H. Essame and E.M.G. Belfield, *The North-West Europe Campaign 1944-1945* (Aldershot: Gale & Polden, 1962), 48.
14. B.H. Liddell-Hart, *The German Generals Talk* (New York: Morrow, 1984), 292.
15. Lt. Gen. Edmund Bruce Hamley, *The Operations of War Explained & Illustrated* (Edinburgh: Blackwood, 1872), 46.
16. Bradley, *A General's Life*, 268.

Chapter 11

1. Nigel Hamilton, *Monty — Final Years of the Field-Marshal 1944-1976* (New York: McGraw-Hill, 1986), 743.
2. Essame and Belfield, *The North-West Europe Campaign*, 48.

Chapter 12

1. Max Hastings, *Overlord* (New York: Simon & Schuster, 1985), 35.
2. Horrocks, *Corps Commander*, 131.
3. John Strawson, *The Battle for the Ardennes* (New York: Scribner's, 1972), 48.

Chapter 13

1. C. Whiting, *Bloody Aachen* (New York: Stein & Day, 1976), 25.

Chapter 14

1. Bryant, *Triumph in the West*, 300 et seq.
2. Churchill, *Triumph & Tragedy*, 68-69.
3. Dorothy Crisp, *The Dominance of England*, 21.
4. Whiting, *Decisions at St. Vith* (New York: Ballantine, 1969), 4.
5. Hamilton, *Monty — Final Years*, 173.

Chapter 15

1. C. Whiting, *Decisions at St. Vith*, 229.
2. Hanson W. Baldwin, *Battles Lost and Won* (New York: Harper & Row, 1966), 354.
3. K.S. Strong, *Intelligence at the Top: The Recollections of an Intelligence Officer* (Garden City, NY: Doubleday, 1969), 81.
4. H.C. Butcher, *My Three Years with Eisenhower* (New York: Simon & Schuster, 1946), 695.
5. Strong, *Intelligence at the Top*, 218.
6. Ambrose, *The Supreme Commander — The War Years of General Dwight D. Eisenhower*, 552-553.

7. Hamilton, *Monty—Final Years*, 186.
8. John S.D. Eisenhower, *The Bitter Woods* (New York: Putnam, 1969), 140.
9. Hamilton, *Monty—Final Years*, 199.
10. Eisenhower, *Eisenhower at War*, 564.
11. Eisenhower, *Eisenhower at War*, 571.

Chapter 16

1. Hamilton, *Monty—Final Years*, 253.
2. Lamb, *Montgomery in Europe*, 371.
3. Lamb, *Montgomery in Europe*, 376.
4. Pogue, *George C. Marshall*, 311.
5. Lamb, *Montgomery in Europe*, 345.
6. Ed Cray, *General of the Army—George C. Marshall Soldier & Statesman* (New York: Norton, 1990), 500.

Chapter 17

1. Bryant, *Triumph in the West*, 436.
2. John Toland, *The Last 100 Days* (New York: Random House, 1968), 328.
3. Essame and Belfield, *The North-West Europe Campaign*, 78.
4. Russell F. Weigley, *Eisenhower's Lieutenants* (Bloomington: Indiana University Press, 1981), 697.
5. Hamilton, *Monty—Final Years*, 480.
6. Nat Frankel and Larry Smith, *Patton's Best* (New York: Hawthorne Books, 1983), 141.
7. John Erickson, *The Road to Berlin* (Boulder, Co.: Westview, 1983), 633.
8. Belcham, *All in a Day's March*, 266.

Chapter 18

1. Bryant, *Triumph in the West*, 189–190.

Chapter 21

1. Roger A. Leonard, ed. *A Short Guide to Clausewitz on War* (New York: Putnam, 1967), 100.
2. Miller, *Ike the Soldier* (New York: Putnam, 1987), 475.
3. Miller, *Ike the Soldier*, 475.
4. Cornelius Ryan, *The Last Battle* (New York: Simon & Schuster, 1966), 16.
5. Hamley, *The Operations of War*, 45.
6. David Fraser, *Alanbrooke* (London: Collins, 1982), 459.

Chapter 22

1. Hamley, *The Operations of War*, 469.

Bibliography

Alexander of Tunis, Field Marshal Earl. *The Alexander Memoirs 1940–1945.* Edited by John North. London: Cassel, 1962.
Ambrose, Stephen E. *Eisenhower. Volume I. Soldier, General of the Army, President Elect 1890–1952.* New York: Simon and Schuster, 1983.
____. *Ike — Abilene to Berlin.* New York: Harper, 1973.
____. *The Supreme Commander — The War Years of General Dwight D. Eisenhower.* Garden City, NY: Doubleday, 1970.
Arnold-Foster, Mark. *The Birth of an Army.* New York: Stein & Day, 1973.
Austin, A.B. *The Birth of an Army.* London: Victor Gollancz Ltd., 1943.
Baldwin, Hanson W. *Battles Lost and Won.* New York: Harper & Row, 1966.
____. *The Crucial Years — 1939–1941.* New York: Harper & Row, 1976.
____. *Great Mistakes of the War.* New York: Harper & Brothers, 1950.
Barnett, Corelli. *The Desert Generals.* London: Kimber, 1960.
Beitzel, Robert. *The Uneasy Alliance.* New York: Knopf, 1972.
Belchem, David. *All in a Day's March.* London: Collins, 1978.
____. *Victory in Normandy.* London: Chatto & Windus, 1981.
Belfield, E., and H. Essame. *The Battle for Normandy.* London: Batsford, 1965.
Biennial Report of the Chief of Staff of the United States Army — General of the Army George C. Marshall, July 1, 1939, to June 30, 1945. Washington, D.C.: Government Publishing Office, 1945.
Blaxland, Gregory. *The Plain Cook and the Great Showman.* London: Kimber, 1977.
Blumenson, Martin. *Duel for France — 1944.* Boston: Houghton Mifflin, 1963.
____. *Kasserine Pass.* Boston: Houghton Mifflin, 1967.
____. *Patton — The Man Behind the Legend.* New York: Morrow, 1984.
____. *Patton Papers.* Boston: Houghton Mifflin, 1974.
____. *U.S. Army in World War II — European Theater of Operations — Breakout and Pursuit.* Washington: Office of the Chief of Military History, Department of the Army, 1961.
____, and James L. Stokesbury. *Masters of the Art of Command.* Boston: Houghton Mifflin, 1975.
Bradley, Omar N. *A General's Life.* With Clay Blair. New York: Simon & Schuster, 1983.
____. *A Soldier's Story.* New York: Holt, 1951.
Bryant, Arthur. *Triumph in the West (based on the diaries of Field-Marshal Alan Brooke).* Garden City, NY: Doubleday, 1959.

____. *Turn of the Tide (based on the diaries of Field-Marshal Alan Brooke).* London: Collins, 1957.
Buchanan, A. Russel. *The United States and World War II (Military and Diplomatic Documents).* New York: Harper & Row, 1964.
Burk, Robert F. *Dwight D. Eisenhower — Hero and Politician.* Boston: Twayne, 1986.
Butcher, H.C. *My Three Years with Eisenhower.* New York: Simon & Schuster, 1946.
Calvocoressi, Peter, and Guy Wint. *Total War.* New York: Pantheon Books, 1972.
Carell, Paul. *The Foxes of the Desert.* New York: Dutton, 1960.
Carver, Field Marshal Sir Michael, (ed.). *The War Lords.* Boston: Little, Brown, 1976.
Catton, Bruce. *Grant Takes Command.* Boston: Little, Brown, 1969.
Cave-Brown, A. *Bodyguard of Lies.* New York: Harper & Row, 1975.
Chalfont, Alun. *Montgomery of Alamein.* London: Weidenfeld and Nicholson, 1976.
Churchill, Winston S. *Triumph and Tragedy.* Boston: Houghton Mifflin, 1953.
Clark, Mark. *Calculated Risk.* New York: Harper & Brothers, 1950.
Cole, H.M. *The Lorraine Campaign. Vol. 1. United States Army in World War II — The European Theater of Operations.* Washington: Historical Division, Department of the Army, 1950.
Colville, John. *The Fringes of Power — 10 Downing Street Diaries 1939–1955.* New York: Norton, 1985.
____. *Winston Churchill & His Inner Circle.* New York: Wyndham Books, 1981.
Cray, Ed. *General of the Army — George C. Marshall, Soldier & Statesman.* New York: Norton, 1990.
Crisp, Dorothy. *The Dominance of England.* London: Holborn Publicity, 1960.
Currey, Cecil B. *Follow Me and Die.* New York: Stein & Day, 1984.
Danchev, Alex. *Very Special Relationship.* London: Brassey's Defence, 1986.
D'Arcy-Dawson, John. *European Victory.* London: MacDonald, 1945.
____. *Tunisian Battle.* London: MacDonald, 1943.
Davis, Burke. *The Billy Mitchell Affair.* New York: Random House, 1967.
Davis, Kenneth S. *Experience of Warfare.* New York: Doubleday, 1965.
____. *Soldier of Democracy.* Garden City, NY: Doubleday, Doran & Co., 1945.
De Guingand, Maj. Gen. Sir Francis. *Generals at War.* London: Hodder & Stoughton, 1964.
____. *Operation Victory.* New York: Scribner's, 1947.
D'Este, Carlo. *Decisions in Normandy.* London: HarperCollins, 1983.
____. *Fatal Decisions — The Battle for Rome.* New York: Harper Perennial, 1991.
Deweerd, H.A. *Great Soldiers of World War II.* New York: Norton, 1944.
Divine, David. *Road to Tunis.* New York: Macmillan, 1944.
Dolan, Edward F. *Victory in Europe — The Fall of Hitler's Germany.* New York: Franklin Watts, 1988.
Editors of the *Army Times. Warrior — The Story of General George S. Patton.* New York: Putnam, 1967.
Eisenhower, Dwight D. *Crusade in Europe.* Garden City, NY: Doubleday, 1948.
____. *Eisenhower at War, 1943–1945.* New York: Random House, 1986.
Eisenhower, John S.D. *Allies — Pearl Harbor to D-Day.* Garden City, NY: Doubleday, 1986.
____. *The Bitter Woods.* New York: Putnam, 1969.
____. *Strictly Personal.* Garden City, NY: Doubleday, 1974.

Bibliography 223

Erickson, John. *The Road to Berlin.* Boulder: Westview, 1983.
Essame, H. *Battle for Germany.* New York: Scribner, 1969.
____. *Patton — A Study in Command.* New York: Scribner, 1974.
____, and E.M.G. Belfield. *The North-West Europe Campaign 1944–1945.* Aldershot: Gale & Polden, 1962.
Falls, Cyril. *The Second World War.* London: Methuen, 1960.
Farago, Ladislas. *Patton — Ordeal and Triumph.* New York: Astor-Honor, 1964.
Fergusson, Bernard. *The Watery Maze.* New York: Holt, Rinehart & Winston, 1961.
Ferrel, Robert H., ed. *The Eisenhower Diaries.* New York: Norton, 1981.
Frankel, Nat, and Larry Smith. *Patton's Best.* New York: Hawthorne Books, 1978.
Fraser, David. *Alanbrooke.* London: Collins, 1982.
Frost, John. *A Drop Too Many.* London: Cassell, 1980.
Fuller, J.F.C. *The Second World War.* New York: Duell, Sloan and Pierce, 1968.
Gavin, J. *On to Berlin.* New York: Viking, 1978.
Gilbert, Martin. *The Second World War.* New York, Holt, 1991.
Greenfield, K.S., ed. *Command Decisions.* New York: Harcourt, Brace, 1959.
Greenfield, Kent Roberts. *American Strategy in World War II.* Baltimore: Johns Hopkins Press, 1963.
Grigg, John. *1943: The Victory That Never Was.* New York: Hill & Wang, 1980.
Grigg, P.J. *Prejudice & Judgment.* London: Jonathon Cape, 1948.
Hamilton, Nigel. *Master of the Battlefield — Monty's War Years 1942–1944.* New York: McGraw-Hill, 1983.
____. *Monty — Final Years of the Field-Marshal 1944–1976.* New York: McGraw-Hill, 1986.
Hamley, Lt. Gen. Edward Bruce. *The Operations of War Explained and Illustrated.* Edinburgh: Blackwood, 1872.
Hancock, W.K. *Smuts — The Fields of Force 1919–1950.* London: Cambridge University Press, 19686.
Harmon, E.N. *Combat Commander.* With M. MacKaye and W.R. MacKaye. Englewood Cliffs, NJ: Prentice-Hall, 1970.
Harrison, Gordon A. *United States Army in World War II — The European Theater of Operations — Cross Channel Attack.* Washington: Office of the Chief of Military History, Department of the Army, 1951.
Hastings, Max. *Overlord.* New York: Simon & Schuster, 1985.
Hatch, Alden. *General Ike.* New York: Holt, 1952.
Hawkins, Desmond, ed. *War Report.* New York: Oxford University Press, 1946.
Historical Division, War Department. *Omaha Beachhead — 6 June–13 June 1944.* Washington, 1945.
Hobbs, Joseph Patrick, ed. *Dear General — Eisenhower's Wartime Letters to Marshall.* Baltimore: Johns Hopkins Press, 1971.
Horne, Alastair. *To Lose a Battle — France 1940.* New York: Little, Brown, 1969.
Horrocks, Brian. *Corps Commander.* New York: Scribner's, 1977.
____. *Escape to Action.* New York: St. Martin's Press, 1961.
____. *A Full Life.* London: Collins, 1959.
Howarth, David. *Dawn of D-Day.* London: Collins, 1959.
Howe, J.J. *Normandy: The British Breakout.* London: Kimber, 1981.
Ingersoll, Ralph. *The Battle Is the Pay-off.* New York: Harcourt, Brace, 1943.

———. *Top Secret*. New York: Harcourt, Brace, 1946.
Irving, David. *The Trail of the Fox*. New York: Dutton, 1977.
———. *The War Between the Generals*. New York: Congdon and Lattès, 1981.
Ismay, Hastings. *Memoirs*. New York: Viking, 1960.
Jablonski, David. *The Desert Warriors: The Battle for North Africa 1940–1943*. New York: Lancer Books, 1972.
Jacobsen, H.A., and J. Rohwer, ed. *Decisive Battles of World War II: the German View*. New York: Putnam's, 1965.
Keegan, John. *The Mask of Command*. New York: Viking Penguin, 1987.
———. *The Second World War*. New York: Viking Penguin, 1989.
———. *Six Armies in Normandy*. New York: Viking, 1982.
———, ed. *Churchill's Generals*. New York: Grove Wedenfeld, 1991.
Kesselring, Albert. *Kesselring: Soldier's Record*. New York: Morrow, 1954.
Kingston-McCloughry, Air Vice-Marshal E.J. *The Direction of War*. New York: Praeger, 1955.
Lamb, Richard. *Montgomery in Europe 1943–1945 — Success or Failure?* New York: Franklin Watts, 1983.
Leonard, Roger H., ed. *A Short Guide to Clausewitz on War*. New York: Putnam, 1967.
Lewin, Ronald. *Life and Death of the Afrika Korps*. London: Corgi Books, 1979.
———. *Montgomery as Military Commander*. New York: Stein & Day, 1971.
Liddell-Hart, Basil H. *The German Generals Talk*. New York: Morrow, 1984.
———. *History of the Second World War*. New York: Putnam, 1970.
———, ed. *The Rommel Papers*. London: Harcourt, Brace, 1953.
Lucas, James, and James Barker. *The Killing Ground*. London: Batsford, 1978.
MacDonald, Charles B. *The Last Offensive*. Washington: Office of the Chief of Military History, U.S. Army, 1973.
———. *The Mighty Endeavor*. New York: Oxford University Press, 1969.
Macksey, Kenneth. *Crucible of Power*. London: Hutchinson, 1969.
MacVane, John. *Journey Into War*. New York: D. Appleton-Century, 1943.
Marshall, Gen. George C. *The War Reports of General of the Army George C. Marshall to the Secretary of War*. Philadelphia: Lippincott, 1947.
Matloff, Maurice. *Strategic Planning for Coalition Warfare — 1943–1944*. Washington: Office of the Chief of Military History, Department of the Army, 1969.
Maule, Henry. *Caen — The Brutal Battle and Breakout from Normandy*. Newton Abbot, England: David & Charles, 1976.
Miller, Merle. *Ike the Soldier*. New York: Putnam, 1987.
Mitcham, Samuel W. *Rommel's Last Battle*. New York: Stein & Day, 1983.
Montgomery, B.L. *El Alamein to the River Sangro*. New York: St. Martin's Press, 1974.
———. *Memoirs of Field-Marshal Montgomery*. Cleveland: World, 1958.
———. *Normandy to the Baltic*. New York: St. Martin's Press, 1974.
Montgomery, Lord. *A History of Warfare*. New York: Morrow, 1983.
Moorehead, Alan. *African Trilogy*. London: Hamish Hamilton, 1945.
———. *Eclipse*. New York: Harper & Row, 1968.
———. *Montgomery*. New York: Coward-McCann, 1946.
Morgan, Lt. Gen. Sir Frederick E. *Overture to Overlord*. Garden City, NY: Doubleday, 1950.
Morison, Samuel E. *The Invasion of France & Germany 1944–1945*. Boston: Little, Brown, 1957.

Bibliography

____. *Operations in North African Waters — October 1942–June 1943.* Boston: Little, Brown, 1950.
____. *Sicily — Salerno — Anzio: January 1943–June 1944.* Boston: Little, Brown, 1954.
Moseley, Leonard. *Marshall — Hero for Our Time.* New York: Hearst Books, 1982.
Nelson, James, ed. *General Eisenhower on the Military Churchill — A Conversation with Alastair Cooke.* New York: Norton, 1970.
Nicholson, Nigel. *Alex — The Life of Field-Marshal Earl Alexander of Tunis.* New York: Atheneum, 1973.
Office of the Chief of Military History, United States Army. *U.S. Army in World War II — European Theater of Operations.* Washington, D.C., 1951.
Partridge, Eric. *Dictionary of Slang and Unconventional English.* New York: Macmillan, 1970.
Patton, George S. *War As I Knew It.* Boston: Houghton Mifflin, 1947.
Pinkley, Virgil, and James F. Scheer. *Eisenhower Declassified.* Old Tappan, NJ: Revell, 1979.
Pogue, Forrest C. *George C. Marshall, Ordeal and Hope.* New York: Viking, 1963.
____. *The Supreme Commander.* Washington: Office of the Chief of Military History, Department of the Army, 1954.
Regan, Geoffrey. *Great Military Disasters.* New York: Evans, 1987.
Ridgway, Matthew R. *Soldier — The Memoirs of Matthew R. Ridgway.* New York: Harper & Brothers, 1956.
Rohmer, Richard. *Patton's Gap.* New York: Beaufort Books, 1981.
Rooney, Andrew A. *The Fortunes of War — Four Great Battles of World War II.* Boston: Little, Brown, 1962.
Ryan, Cornelius. *The Last Battle.* New York: Simon & Schuster, 1966.
Sainsbury, Keith. *The North African Landings — 1942.* London: Davis-Poynter, 1976.
Salisbury-Jones, Guy. *So Full a Glory.* London: Weidenfeld & Nicholson, 1964.
Schmidt, Heinz Werner. *With Rommel in the Desert.* London: Harrap, 1955.
Shirer, W. *Rise and Fall of the Third Reich.* New York: Simon & Schuster, 1960.
Simonds, Peter. *Maple Leaf Up↑ Maple Leaf Down↓.* New York: Island, 1946.
Sixsmith, E.K. *British Generalship in the Twentieth Century.* London: Arms and Armour, 1970.
____. *Eisenhower's Six Great Decisions.* New York: Longman Green, 1956.
Snyder, L. *The War — A Concise History 1939–1946.* New York: Messner, 1960.
Speidel, Hans. *We Defended Normandy.* London: Jenkins, 1951.
Stokesbury, James L. *Short History of World War II.* New York: Morrow, 1980.
Strawson, John. *Battle for the Ardennes.* New York: Scribner, 1972.
Strong, Maj. Gen. Sir Kenneth. *Intelligence at the Top: The Recollections of an Intelligence Officer.* Garden City, NY: Doubleday, 1969.
Tedder, Arthur. *With Prejudice.* Boston: Little, Brown, 1967.
Toland, John. *Battle — The Story of the Bulge.* New York: Random House, 1969.
____. *The Last 100 Days.* New York: Random House, 1968.
Truscott, L.K., Jr. *Command Missions.* Novato, CA: Presidio Press, 1990.
Trythall, Anthony John. *Boney Fuller.* New Brunswick: Rutgers University Press, 1969.
Von Manstein, Erich. *Lost Victories.* Chicago: Regnery, 1958.
Warner, Philip. *Horrocks.* London: Hamish Hamilton, 1984.
____. *World War II — The Untold Story.* London: Bodley Head, 1988.

Weigley, Russell F. *Eisenhower's Lieutenants*. Bloomington: Indiana University Press, 1981.
Whiting, C. *Bloody Aachen*. New York: Stein & Day, 1976.
____. *Decisions at St. Vith*. New York: Ballantine, 1969.
____. *Kasserine: The Battlefield Slaughter of American Troops by Rommel's Afrika Korps*. New York: Stein & Day, 1984.
Willmott, H.P. *June 1944*. Poole, Dorset: Blandford, 1984.
Wilmot, Chester. *The Struggle for Europe*. New York: Caroll & Graf, 1952.
Wilmott, Ned, and John Pimlott. *Strategy and Tactics of War*. London: Marshall Cavendish, 1983.

Index

Aachen 98, 122, 129, 130, 131, 133,138, 139, 146, 157
Adams, Lt.-Col. (U.S.). Creighton *see* Baum Force
Agrigento *see* Patton, General George S.
Alam Halfa 4, 6, 192, 212
Alexander, Field Marshal (U.K.) H.A. 4, 35–40, 45, 46, 47, 48, 50, 51, 52, 54
American Academy of Political Science 19
Anderson, General (U.K.) K. 20, 22, 24, 27, 29, 30, 31, 32, 33, 34, 36
Anzio 57, 58, 62, 64, 70, 179, 204
Ardennes 39, 98, 104, 105, 119, 120, 131, 135, 136, 138; and Bradley's estimate of German strength 98; and Eisenhower's proposed offensive 104; and Montgomery's plan of attack 98; and Montgomery's proposal to divide command 146; and Sibert's warning to Bradley 139

Balkans 48, 55, 61, 62, 66, 67, 70, 113
Baltic 174
Bastogne 150, 151, 155; Allied defense based on 149
Baum, Capt. (U.S. Army) Abraham *see* Baum Force
"Baum Force" 173
Bayeux 110
Bennington, Fort 198
Berlin 2, 111, 113, 114, 126, 127, 128, 135, 136, 164, 168; and Eisenhower's reaction to Montgomery's proposal 106, 108, 109; and "full blooded attack" on 107; and Montgomery's proposed drive for 98
Big Three Conference *see* Teheran Conference
Bizerta 19, 22, 40
"Bladeforce" 22, 24
Bolling, General (U.S.) *see* Berlin
Bologna 59
Bonn 114, 115, 146, 169, 187
Bordeaux 62
Bradley, General (U.S.) O.N. 26, 27, 47, 51, 53, 61, 74, 76, 77, 79, 81
Bratislau Gap 169
Bremen 113, 174
Brest 60, 61, 64, 91, 104, 105, 112, 115, 207
bridges 130, 144, 172; at Arnhem 128; at Eindhoven 128, 129; at Nijmegen 128, 129; over the Rhine 126, 128, 129; over the Seine 79, 133;
bridging: Bailey 112; tank 76
Brigade, Czech 177
Britain: and civilian rations 125, 194; and flying bombs and rockets 153; and industry 9; a maritime nation 11; and U.S. communications to and from North Africa 25
British Broadcasting Corporation (B.B.C.) 4, 156
Brittany 60, 77, 83, 85, 91, 92, 94, 119
Brooke, Field Marshal (U.K.) Alan: dinner with Marshall 7; and Marshall's strategy 10, 12; and 1942 cross-Channel invasion 13; and opposes "Operation Sledgehammer" 9; and visits Fort Jackson 10

227

228   Index

Butcher, Captain (U.S.N.) Harry 100, 102, 141, 199

Caen 77, 79, 82, 84, 85, 86, 87, 88, 89, 90
Calabria 54
Canadians 48, 79, 81, 82, 83, 85, 86, 90, 92, 94, 95
Casablanca 18, 19, 43
casualties 49, 85, 90, 91, 92, 93, 96, 97; at Anzio 57; civilian, British v. U.S. 13; U.S. on "Omaha" beach 81; U.S. v. British and Canadian on D-Day 81
Caucasus 15
Caumont 94
Chalons 162
Chambé, General (Fr.) 70
Chamberlain, Neville 3
Channel, English 43, 47, 62, 75, 79, 80, 81, 88, 110, 115, 183; and ease of crossing 10, 11, 13; and storm 61
Cherbourg 8, 61, 76, 77, 82, 84, 91, 92, 112, 115, 175
Churchill, Winston S. 61, 76, 77, 82, 84, 87, 91, 92, 112, 115, 175; and Marshall's plan re Cherbourg 8; meets Roosevelt in Washington 4, 7
Clark, General (U.S.) Mark 166; and capture of Rome 204; and "Dragoon" 63; and forces available for "Sledgehammer" 11; and French resistance to "TORCH" 20; and man-power shortages 58, 72; and preparedness of U.S. army for war 12; and replaces Lucas 57
Clausewitz, Karl von 134, 135, 171, 182, 184, 193, 199, 206
"Cobra," Operation 86, 88, 89, 93, 94
code books, American and British 56
Coldstream Guards, and Long Stop Hill 25
Colmar Pocket 140, 160, 163
Cologne 98, 114, 132, 133, 146, 157, 159, 160
Combined Chiefs of Staff 54, 64, 75, 83, 112, 120, 147, 161, 186, 199; created 6; and Eisenhower's message re North Africa 37; and Eisenhower's telegram re Sicily 48
commandos 56, 71, 80
committee, Eisenhower's planning see Eisenhower, General Dwight D.

Commonwealth forces (British) 3, 5, 166
Condé 100, 101
Congress, U.S. 6, 121
Coningham, Air Vice Marshal (R.A.F.) Sir Arthur 42
Connors, General (U.S.) Fox, and his library see Eisenhower, General Dwight D.
Cotentin 8, 84, 92, 94, 108
Cunningham, Admiral (R.N.) Andrew 69
Cunningham, Admiral (R.N.) Sir John 48, 49
Czechs 177

Darlan, Admiral (Fr.) J.F. 21, 22, 23
De Gaulle, General (Fr.) Charles 22
De Guingand, General (U.K.) F. 101, 156, 175; and attends Versailles conference 115; and importance of airfields 84; and "Market-Garden" 130; and meeting with Eisenhower 100
Dempsey, General (U.K.) Miles 90, 128, 161
Denaia Pass 37
Denmark 113, 170, 174, 175
Devers, General (U.S.) L. 57, 60, 61, 69, 71, 73
Dickson, Colonel (U.S.) B.A. 142, 143
Dieppe 15, 127, 201
Dill, Field Marshal (U.K.) Sir John 6, 10
Dinant 150
discipline: and Eisenhower 57, 96, 121, 129, 196, 200; and U.S. 1st Division 37; see also Patton, General George S.
Doenitz, Admiral (Ger.) 174
Dorsal, Eastern 29, 30
Downing Street, No. 10 3, 207
Downs, Bill (C.B.C. correspondent) 87
Dresden 113, 164, 171
Dunkirk 3, 13, 145, 191
Düren 159

Eastern Task Force 20, 22, 45
Egypt 4, 15, 47
Eifel 138, 139, 140, 143, 149
Eighth Army (U.K.) 9, 19, 20, 55, 59, 88, 116, 189, 192, 193; and commanding officers 4, 192; and El Alamein 5,

193; and Medinine 38; and Messina 49; and part of 15th Army Group 48; and Sicily landing 49, 51; *see also* Montgomery, Field Marshal Bernard L.
Eisenhower, General (U.S.) Dwight D. 9, 13, 16, 17, 18, 19, 20, 21, 22, 23, 24; and Afrika Corps 5; and appointed Supreme Commander 15; and discipline 53; and Far East and Iceland 7; and high ideals 19; and lack of experience 8, 21; and lack of qualifications 16, 17; and need to be balanced 6; and planning committee 45, 155; and prestige 121, 155, 211; and "Sledgehammer" 12
Eisenhower, John D. 13
El Guettar 38, 39, 40 42
Emanuel III, King Victor (Italy) 55
Embassy *see* code books
Enna 51
Etna, Mount 51

Faid 29, 30, 31, 34
Faid Pass 37
Falaise 86, 92, 94, 95, 96, 98, 203, 205; and Gap 96, 98, 104; and Pocket 88, 92, 209
Far East 7, 16, 54, 141, 187
Fedala 23
ferries, train 51, 52
field hospitals *see* Patton, General George S.
Fifth Army (Anglo-American) 58, 59, 72, 73
Fifth Army (Ger.) 123, 139
fighter-bombers 39, 94, 95
fighters (planes) 49, 95, 139
Fondouk 29, 30, 34, 39, 40
food ration 44, 124
Foord, Brigadier (U.K.) E.J. *see* G-2
Forest, Black 174
France 43, 52, 55, 58, 59, 60, 61, 62, 63, 64, 65
Frankfurt 112, 113, 114, 125, 134, 137, 163, 165, 168, 169, 173
Fredendall, Gen. (U.S.) Lloyd 27, 28, 29, 30, 31, 32, 33, 34, 35, 37, 38
Free French 21, 24, 68, 103, 106
Freyburg, Gen (N.Z.) Sir Bernard 39
Fuller, Maj.-General (U.K.) J.F.C. 211

G.I.s: and Eisenhower's opinion of 200; and impressed by Montgomery 116; overweight 12; and at Sbeitla and Kasserine 33; *see also* food ration
Gale, Maj. General (U.K.) H 116
Garian, The Lady of 5
Gela, Gulf of *see* Seventh Army (U.S.)
Germans, American speaking 144
Germany 3, 6, 7, 9, 43, 49, 53, 60, 61, 63, 67
Giraud, General (Fr.) Henri 27
Gott, Lt.-General (U.K.) G.H. 4
Grand Council, Fascist 55
Grant, General (U.S.) Ulysses S. 120, 172, 201
Grant tanks 5
Granville 108, 130
Grigg, Sir John 77, 181
ground commander 118, 120, 121, 126, 134, 154, 156, 163, 165, 166, 167; *see also* Alexander, Field Marshal H.A.; Anderson, General K.; Eisenhower, General Dwight D.; Montgomery, Field Marshal Bernard L.
G-2 (Intelligence Officer) 28. 31, 34, 77, 83, 103, 110, 138, 139, 140, 141
Guards Armoured Division (U.K.) 95, 150
guns: British 17 pounder 86; British 25 pounder 36, 119; German 88mm. 6, 31, 87
Gurkhas (Indian Army) 38, 39, 40, 166

Hallouf *see* Gurkhas
Hamley, Lt.-General (U.K.) Sir E.B.: and communications 116; and enemy's capital 206; and portrait of army commander 213; and transportation 208
Handy, Brig.-General (U.S.) Tom 27
Hanover 113, 145
Harmon, General (U.S.) Ernest J. and Tebessa 33, 34, 38, 151
Hasselt 154
Hewitt, Admiral (U.S.N.) 49
Hill, Long Stop 25, 26, 35
Hitler, Adolf 3, 13, 19, 22, 55, 56, 60, 62, 65, 66, 70
Hobart, General (U.K.) Percy 76
Hodges, Lt.-General (U.S.) Courtney 106, 122, 130, 133, 136, 140, 141, 142, 144, 148

230   Index

Hodgson, P.A. 200
Hoge, General (U.S.) William 173
Holland 98, 128, 174
Hopkins, Harry 70
Houffalize 148, 149, 150
Hull, General (.S.) John 12
Hull, Colonel (U.K.) Richard see "Bladeforce"
Hungary 63, 68

Il Duce see Mussolini, Benito
Intelligence, SHAEF see G-2
Iran 16
Iraq 16
Irwin, Brig.-General (U.S.) S. Leroy 34
Ismay, General (U.K.) Hastings 9, 10, 170
Italy see Calabria; Salerno; Sicily

Jebel el Ahmera see Hill, Long Stop
Jebel Ksaira see Fredendall, General Lloyd
Jebel Lesouda see Fredendall, General Lloyd
Joint Chiefs of Staff (U.S.) 18, 65
Juin, Marshal (Fr.) Alphonse 68, 70

Karlsruhe 163, 174
Kassel 134, 174
Kasserine Pass 2, 28, 31, 32, 33, 34, 35, 36, 37, 70, 150
Kesselring, Field Marshal (Ger.) Albert: and Alam Halfa 4; and Po Valley 71; and political concerns 23; and reinforces Sicily 48; and Rome 56, 61; and Sbeitla 31 and toe of Italy 55
King, Admiral (U.S.) Ernest J. 9, 12, 17, 54, 62
Koch, Colonel (U.S.) 103, 138, 139

landing craft 9, 10, 12, 15, 23, 43, 49, 62, 64, 81
landing zones 75
Leclerc, General (Fr.) 38
Leese, General (U.K.) Oliver 51
Le Havre 12, 109, 112, 202
Leipzig 113
Le Kef 29, 33, 34, 35, 36
Liaison officers see Montgomery, Field Marshal Bernard L.
Libya 4, 15, 16, 26, 42, 192, 205, 212
Liège 141, 145, 146

Ljubljana 55, 59, 62, 64, 66
Loire, River 77, 98, 162
Long Range Desert Group see Peniakoff, Vladimir
Lucas, General (U.S.) 57
Ludendorf Bridge 168
Lüebeck 113, 175
Luftwaffe 84, 96, 105, 198, 211; and effectiveness of bombing 48; and Normandy 79; and North Africa 31; and Sicily and Italy 52, 57; and spare parts 83
Luxembourg: and Bradley's H.Q. 145, 148; and German preparations for Ardennes offensive 139; and ground commander 166

Maastricht 134, 137
Magdeburg 164
Malta 9, 46, 47, 49, 54, 165
Manteuffel, Hasso 114, 143, 145, 150, 154
Maquis 68, 83, 201
Mare Nostrum 98; see also Mediterranean Sea
Mareth Line 26, 27, 38, 39; see also Bradley, General O.N.; Eisenhower, John D.
"Market-Garden," Operation 111, 128, 130, 131
Marseilles 60, 61, 62, 68, 115, 208
Marshall, General (U.S.) George C. 6, 9, 10, 11, 12, 13, 15, 16, 17, 18, 19; and Cotentin invasion 8; and discussion with Brooke 7; and Europe first policy 7; and German strength in France 8; replaces British tank losses 4
Matmata Hills see Mareth Line
Medinine 38
Mediterranean Sea 24, 26, 46, 47, 48, 52, 54, 61, 62, 63, 64; and supplies for Operation "Torch" 23; and U.S. restrictions re Operation "Torch" 17, 18
Medjez el Bab 25
Messina 49, 51, 56
Metz: 125, 130; and Ardennes offensive 138, 177; and Berlin 107; and Bradley 125; and Eisenhower 60; and Gap 130; and Operation "Dragoon" 100; and Patton 106, 130; and U.S. casualties 207

Index

Middleton, General (U.S.) Troy: and the Battle of the Ardennes 144; and Brest 105; and Brittany 94; and commands VIII Corps 94; and Operation "Cobra" 93
Montgomery, Field Marshal (U.K.) Bernard L. 5, 6, 17, 19, 20, 46, 47, 48, 51, 54, 55; and Berlin 164; and commands Eighth Army 4; and liaison officers 191, 126, 148; and North Africa 27, 36, 38, 39, 40
Morgan, General (U.K.) Sir Frederick: and "Dragoon" 60; and single front offensive 119; Supreme Commander Designate 44
Morocco (French) 18, 21, 23, 183; (Spanish) 17, 21
Mortain 94, 95, 104
Moselle 106, 125, 132, 151, 163, 164
Mulberry harbor 15, 88, 89. 104, 115
Munich 113, 114, 174
Mussolini, Benito (Il Duce) 19, 55

Namur 145, 146, 158
The New York Times 21, 156
New Zealand, troops 38, 39, 192
Nijmegen 128, 129, 132, 141, 146, 158, 161
Nivelle, General (Fr.) 207
Norway 113, 162, 175

Oder River 153, 169, 172
Odon River 86
offensive, broad front 37, 68, 102, 104, 109, 114, 141, 160, 162, 163, 179
On War see Clausewitz, Karl von
Oran 18, 19, 52
Orne River 777, 86, 88
Ostend 127

Pacific First policy 7, 9
Palermo 49, 50, 53
Panzer 5, 32, 33, 36, 38, 39, 40, 48, 55, 69, 85
Paris 122, 142, 177, 201; and Bradley 92, 93; and Caen 82; and Eisenhower's strategy 103; and Seine bridge 96; and uprising in 103; and used as a pivot 98
partisans (Czech) 177; (Italian) 55
Pas de Calais 83, 85, 98, 106
Patton, General (U.S.) George S. 18, 20, 23, 21, 25, 38, 39, 40, 42, 45, 47; and addresses 45th Division 52; and hospital visits 52
Pearl Harbor 6, 136, 199
Peniakoff, Vladimir 27
pens, submarine 68
Pentagon 183
Pershing, General (U.S.): and A.E.F. (1917–1918) 118, 184
Peyrouton, Marcel 29
phase lines 77, 78, 79
Pichon 30
Pilsen 176
plains, German 160, 163, 205, 206
"Plunder," Operation 161
Po Valley: and importance of 61; and Kesselring's opinion of 71; and Marshall's opinion of 70; and reached by Allies 73; and Westphal's opinion of 71
Poles 95, 98
political disturbances in Germany, forecast by SHAEF 103
Pretelat, General (Fr.) André-Gaston 141, 142
Prime Minister, British *see* Chamberlain, Neville; Churchill, Winston S.
Public Relations Dept.: and Ardennes 144; and Montgomery's Caen strategy 89; and SHAEF's 157, 158; SHAEF's and "Goodwood" 88

Quebec Conference 48, 67, 72, 74, 119, 125, 185

Ramsey, Admiral (R.N.) Bertram 106, 112
Redoubt, Southern 177, 178, 179
Regensburg 113
Remagen 168, 173
replacements 42, 58, 59, 71, 72, 85, 93, 135, 136, 158, 185
Rheims 122, 149, 162
Rhine, River 99, 100, 102, 106, 108, 111, 112, 114, 115, 123, 126
Rhone Valley 72
Ridgway, General (U.S.) Matthew 150, 175
Roberts, Brig.-General (U.S.) Frank N. 63
Roberts, Maj.-General (U.K.) G.P.B. 123

"rock soup" *see* Patton, General George S.
Roer, River 133, 139, 140, 158, 159, 161
Romania 16
Rome 33, 55, 56, 60, 61, 64, 65, 71, 85, 186, 204,
Rommel, Field Marshal (Ger.) Erwin 23, 51, 52, 53, 54, 55, 56, 58, 94, 97, 103; and Alam Halfa attack 4; and commands Afrika Corps 4; and links up with Tunisian forces 5; and opinion of Battle of El Alamein 24; and plans to enter Algeria 49; and transfer tanks to Italians 50
Roosevelt, Franklin D. (U.S. President) 47, 55, 60, 61, 62, 65, 66, 67, 70, 71, 119, 133; and agrees to "Europe First" policy 7; and Casablanca conference 43; Commander Italy 45; and exchanges cables with Churchill re North Africa 18, 19; and North African invasion 17; and Peyrouton's appointment 23; and selects Eisenhower Supreme; and Washington conference 4, 7
Rotterdam 48, 106, 112
Royal Artillery, Journal of see Fuller, Maj.-General J.F.C.; guns
Royal Navy 40, 54, 71, 80, 81, 100
Royal Palace, Palermo *see* Patton, General George S.
Russia 9, 11, 12, 15, 16, 47, 62, 63, 65, 67, 68
Ryan, Cornelius 205
Ryder, Maj.-General (U.S.) Charles W. 22

Saar 96, 100, 102, 103, 107, 108, 109, 111, 112, 122, 126
St. Lô 84, 85, 86, 93, 95
St. Malo 92
St. Paul's School 77, 84
St. Vith 149, 150, 151
Salerno 54, 57, 58, 70
Sant' Agata *see* Patton, General George S.
Sbeitla 29, 30, 31, 32, 33, 34, 38
Sbiba 33, 35, 36
Scheldt 91, 115, 123, 126, 129, 183, 187
Schleswig Peninsula 170
Schmidt 133
Scoglitti 52

Scorpion *see* Sherman tanks
Scotland 19
Seine, River 80, 83, 85, 91, 92, 96, 98, 103, 104, 109, 126
Selective Service 58
Seventh Army (Ger.) 89, 138
Seventh Army (U.S.) *see* Patton, General George
Sfax 5, 35
SHAEF 69, 72, 77, 79, 86, 88, 93, 100, 102, 103, 104
Sherman, General (U.S. Civil War) 208
Sherman tanks 4, 5, 6, 31, 32, 76
's Hertogenbosch 141
Shott el Faraj 26
Sibert, Brig.-General (U.S.) E.L. 139
Sicily 43, 45–49, 52, 54, 55, 58, 70, 74, 75, 81, 116
Sidi bou Zid 29, 32, 37
Siegfried Line 106, 107, 108, 122, 125, 126, 128, 130, 133, 158, 160
Silesia, and coal fields 168
Simonds, General (Can.) Guy 109
Simpson, General (U.S.) W.H. 150, 155, 159, 160, 161, 171, 172, 185
Siracusa *see* Eighth Army
Sixth Army Group (U.S.) 83
"Sledgehammer" 9, 10, 12, 13, 17, 48, 109
Smith, General (U.S.) Bedell 43, 47, 62, 70, 77, 111, 112, 116, 126, 129, 142, 146
Smuts, Field-Marshal (S.A.) Jan: and Adriatic invasion 64; and opinion of post-war Russia 169; and opinion of "Sledgehammer" 9; and opposes "Dragoon" 67; and St. Paul's School meeting 79
Souk el Arba 29, 43
Spa 144, 147, 148
Spandau 206
Stalin, Joseph 62, 66, 67, 71, 72, 153, 169, 170, 171
Stavelot 144, 145
Stettinius Edward 19
Strasbourg 160
Strong, Maj.-General (U.K.) K.W.D. 110, 140, 141, 142, 146, 147, 155, 159, 170
Stuttgart 174
submarine: midget, on "Omaha" Beach 80; pens 68
Suez Canal *see* Eastern Task Force

Summary, Intelligence *see* G-2
Supreme Commander *see* Eisenhower, General Dwight D.
"Sword" Beach 83

tanks, Scorpion 76; *see also* Grant tanks; Sherman tanks
Tebessa 23, 27, 29, 31, 33, 35, 58
Tedder, Air Marshal, R.A.F. (U.K.) Sir Arthur 42, 48, 49, 51, 79, 87, 93, 134, 137, 152, 153, 170
Teheran Conference 59, 62, 67, 196
Tenth Army (Ger.) 55
Thala 29, 33, 34
Tobruk 4, 9
"Torch," Operation *see* Mediterranean
Torgau 174
Trianon Palace Hotel 159
Triers 122
Trieste 67, 179
Tripoli 5, 19, 46; *see also* Eastern Task Force
Troina *see* Patton, General George S.
Troyes 98, 162
Truman, U.S. President Harry S 170, 172, 176
Truscott, Gen. (U.S.) Lucien K. 10, 17, 27, 31
Tulergma 34
Tunis 18, 22, 23, 24, 25, 26, 34, 37, 40, 45, 49, 179
Typhoons (planes) 95

ULTRA signals 34, 60, 65, 86, 95, 123, 129
unconditional surrender 56
Union Army (U.S.) 210
United Kingdom 7. 9, 12
United States 6, 7, 8, 11, 13, 45, 46, 58, 59, 61, 64; and Dill's opinion of 6; and "Europe First" 7; and size of pre-war army 6; and unified command with U.K. 7
U.S. Army Engineers 25
U.S. Consul in Tunis 27
U.S. Navy 18, 57, 81, 100; and English Channel 11; and landing craft 10; and "Pacific first" 7
U.S. War Department 7, 121, 141, 180
U.S.A.A.F. 40, 80
U.S.S. *Augusta see* Patton, General George S.

"Veritable," Operation 158–161
Versailles 114, 150, 155
Vichy 22, 23, 71
Vienna 72, 169, 170, 175, 177, 179, 205
Vire 90, 91, 93
von Arnim, Gen (Ger.) Hans Jurgen 26, 29, 30, 31, 32, 33, 36, 39, 40
von Blumentritt, Field Marshal (Ger.) Guenther 109, 114, 122
von Kluge, Gen. (Ger.) 92, 94, 95
von Rundstedt, Field Marshal (Ger.) Gerd 109, 114, 138, 139, 148, 172, 179, 190, 193
von Thoma, General (Ger.) 205
Vosges 151
Vielsalm 149, 150

Wadi Akarit 39, 40
Wadi Zigzaou 26, 39, 40
Walcheren 123
Ward, Maj.-General (U.S.) Orlando 27, 28, 29, 30, 31, 33
warehouses, (U.K.) 21
Warsaw 48, 73
Washington 4, 6, 7, 17, 18, 20, 27, 37, 38, 42, 47,
Waters, Capt. (U.S. Army), John 173
Wellington, Duke of *see* Montgomery, Field Marshal Bernard L.
Wesel 163, 173, 174
West Point 68, 116, 136, 181, 188, 195, 198, 200, 210
Western Task Force, H.Q. 45
Westphal, General (Ger.) 71, 109, 139
Westphalia 139
Weygand, Gen (Fr.) 26
Wheeler, Senator (U.S.) 136
Whiteley, Gen. (U.K.) Sir John 108, 146, 147, 149, 155, 175
Williams, Brigadier (U.K.) E. 77
Wilson, Field-Marshal (U.K.) Sir Henry M. 64, 65, 67, 69
Wolfe 70

Yalta Conference 163, 170, 173

zones, occupation 170
Zonhoven 138, 166

www.ingramcontent.com/pod-product-compliance
Ingram Content Group UK Ltd.
Pitfield, Milton Keynes, MK11 3LW, UK
UKHW041945140426
5217IPUK00014B/660